HISTORY OF ART

THE SPIRIT OF
THE FORMS

Fig. 167

THE CAGE

Elie Faure
HISTORY OF ART

THE SPIRIT OF
THE FORMS

v. 5

TRANSLATED FROM THE FRENCH BY WALTER PACH

De Luxe Edition

Garden City Publishing Co., Inc.
GARDEN CITY   NEW YORK

1937
Garden City Publishing Co., Inc.

THE SPIRIT OF
THE FORMS

I offer to my brother
JEAN LOUIS FAURE
this summary of thought which
owes to him the larger part
of its independence

TABLE OF CONTENTS

vii

Fig. 1

Olympia

INTRODUCTION

MUST one rejoice in it? Must one regret it? We have reached a critical point in history when it becomes impossible for us to think profoundly—or to create, I imagine—if we isolate ourselves in the adventure of our race, if we refuse to demand a confirmation of our own presentiments from the expressions in words or in the arts that other races have given of themselves. I say "a confirmation," although at first it may be the contradictions, or at least the differences that strike us. In appearance an abyss lies between the Negro or Polynesian idol, for instance, and Greek sculpture at its apogee. Or between that idol and the great European painting of which the Venetian School has revealed to us the means and the possibilities. And yet, one of the miracles of this time is that an increasing number of spirits should become capable not only of tasting the delicate or violent savor of these reputedly contradictory works and finding them equally intoxicating; even more than that, they can grasp, in the seemingly opposed characters, the inner accords that lead us back to man and show him to us everywhere animated by analogous passions, as witnessed by all the idols, for all of them are marked by the accent of these passions.

I am not unaware of the danger of these statements. At certain epochs—the classical Greek or French epoch, for instance—it was good for the poet to be unaware that he represented only one aspect of the divine soul, and to direct all the diffused powers deposited in him by culture, his intuitions, and his needs toward a single, narrow, and very definite perfection; he could thus attain the expression of the pathetic moment in which his race was to enclose these powers within the frames of reason. But we are no longer at this point. Such an attitude to-day runs the risk of rendering impotent those who adopt it. For the present, at least, to limit one's effort to the historic ideal of a race, or of a people—an ideal that has been transposed, moreover, or displaced—to refuse to perceive the unique face of man under the masks that cover it, is no longer a sign of force but rather of senility.

Many times in history, toward the end of the Old World, for instance, or after the Christian efflorescence of the Occidental Middle Ages, the critical spirit has found itself in the presence of such an accumulation of the unknown, after having catalogued its prodigious attainments, that it has had to appeal to all the groups of men affected by the same problems, in order to seek the solution with them. In our days, however, it is no longer merely about the basin of the Eastern Mediterranean or in Western Europe that we must assemble the elements of a mysticism that is alone capable of putting an end, at least for the present, to the kind of enervating disorder that transports us. The critical spirit has become a universal poet. It is necessary to enlarge inordinately, and unceasingly, the circle of its horizon.

I do not say that we are approaching the spiritual unification of the world. We are still far from that, if indeed we shall ever realize it, or if it is even desirable that we should realize it. But if industrial architecture, for instance, which pursues its own end rather than seeks to please—perhaps, after all, the way not to displease—is roughly outlining before us a universal language, I do not believe it can ever imprint upon this language a uniform accent, nor do I hope that it will do so. The mobility of the spirit, favored by the exigencies of environments and the mixture of the species, should, in my opinion, continue to accept all the living varieties of its expressions in the arts, tending, for that matter, through a growing appreciation of the universal conditions of its own conservation, to be understood by a more and more extended number of men.

It is not necessary that the desire for spiritual unity which is growing in the bosom of the élite, should become, in the multitudes, a need of uniformity. Those who are not capable of grasping the stammerings of this unity in the innumerable idols by which all the races of the earth have staked out their path, are also the least capable of bringing to their own race a contribution powerful enough to permit it to leave its mark on the future.

When you have understood the profound causes of a tendency opposed to your own—or seemingly opposed to your own—you are seized with a strange tenderness for it, which arises because you have found in it your own doubts and struggles. You choose thenceforth the road that was instinctively and became logically your own, with all the more decision and lightheartedness the less you know yourself understood by the men who have gone through the same battles as you. On the day when those who love peace understand the grandeur that can clothe war, perhaps they will be closer to the universal peace they wish to bestow upon us. On the day when this religion appreciates the esoteric symbols of this other, it will not be far from admitting the rites that are the furthest removed from its own. The academician who is revolted by a Hindu idol will be closer to Raphael on the day when he feels the spiritual power which the Hindu idol represents.

Whether one feels it or not, whether one wishes it or not, a universal solidarity unites all the acts and all the images of men, not only in space but also and especially in time. The intuitive, intimate notion of time, always living and present, is moreover the best means at our disposal for seizing the inner meaning of all the figures of dimensional space, which it has deposited upon its road as a river deposits its alluvions. One understands everything the moment one goes back to the sources. A Negro wooden image and a Greek marble are not so far apart as one thinks. Let one look at a pure work of the Egyptian Middle Empire if one wishes to grasp, in the rhythmic equilibrium of its undulating surfaces, the passage of the rough and ingenuous planes of the first into the free but concentric movements of the second.

In fact, the affirmation of this solidarity is by no means the fruit of a mystical intuition. This solidarity really exists. It belongs to the development of universal history of which it was one of the driving forces, perhaps the strongest and most supple of all. The art of all time, the art of every place, grow closer and closer together. No doubt it is the immemorial Negro art which, through the valley of the Nile, spread over the two worlds when Polynesian art, one of its branches perhaps, arrived and blossomed in America, or, in the Malay isles, met the currents that carried up the Ganges and the Irrawaddy the spirit of Greece and

Egypt transformed by its passage through Assyria, Persia, India, and Indo-China, the latter impregnated with the Chinese soul which had, moreover, been fecundated by India and Persia, by way of the gorges of the Brahmaputra and the Tarim.

The circle of universal art is completed when Persia, on the other hand, spreads in Asia the Arab art that emerged from Roman art and Byzantine art, themselves branches of Greek art, when the progress of Islam encountered in Italy, in Spain, in France, the degenerate forms of this Greek art cast up by the navigators on the shores of the Mediterranean and ascending the Danube and the Rhone to confront there, in the cathedral, the musical spirit descended through the valley of the Oise from the plains of the North. Especially when its great expressions are unaware of each other and their common sources are lost in the night does the evolution of the intelligence seem to pass everywhere through almost similar phases of organic integration, harmonic equilibrium, and critical dissolution which give to its appearances surprising analogies of structure, rhythm, and accent.

Let one follow, if one doubts this, the parallel march of the Greek and French statues; in the one case from the *Orantes* of the Acropolis to the athletes of Lysippus and the mausoleum of Scopas; in the other case from the virgins and the saints of the porches of Chartres to those of the porches of Bourges, passing, there, through the pediments of the Parthenon and Olympia, here, through the kings of Amiens and the prophets of Rheims. Or, if one prefers to draw at haphazard from the repertory of forms, without troubling about schools and techniques, dates, mythical pretexts, or local character, one has only to compare this Greek terra cotta found in the tombs of Tanagra with this Chinese terra cotta found in the tombs of the Tangs,

this bas-relief from Moissac or Arles with this bas-relief
from Angkor-Vat, this foliage of a church of Ile-de-
France with this foliage of an Indian stupa, this Japanese painting of the fifteenth century with this Sienese
painting, and the frescoes of reindeer hunters with the
frescoes of Bushmen. In such a comparison one will
find moving relationships that suggest identity of origins and cause one to understand that flint axes
or human bones can hardly be distinguished from
one another whether one discovers them under the
alluvial deposits of the Missouri or the Niger or rolling
among the pebbles of a river of France or a torrent
of Alaska.

It is natural henceforth that the intelligence, after
having, through the studies of the archæologists, rigorously classified the forms of art that express it in all
places and at all times, tends to find under their diver-
gences a sort of unity of plan, following a labor similar
to that which Lamarck accomplished in connection with
the natural forms differentiated by his predecessors.
The spirit of the forms is one. It circulates within them
like the central fire that revolves at the heart of the
planets and determines the height and the profile of
their mountains according to the degree of resistance
and the constitution of the soil.

The images of the gods are as unstable as possible,
even if it is a question only of the gods of a single people,
precisely because they represent, in the world of appearances, the invisible circulation of a permanent force,
determined on breaking or transforming all obstacles,
which has run through its arteries, animated its nerves,
united and salted down its bones ever since the origin
of man. It is the permanence of this force that we must
find and demonstrate under the diversity and the variability of the symbols that conceal it. I ask nothing
better than that it should be called God, on condition

that its essence remain intangible and only allow one to perceive, from time to time, a more or less essential, more or less profound aspect of its being, which it is the unique task of the poet to reveal before it vanishes for ever. A very moving myth of the Polynesian cosmogony teaches us that a god only becomes a god at the moment when he assumes form. This is true. But it is also true that at the moment when he assumes form he begins to die.

Thus, the work expressing the unanimous plastic drama is for us all the more poignant because it strives to give more stability and to impose more durable static laws on an image of life which it feels to be continually more unstable and more involved in the future through a more imperious dynamism.

The whole history of an artist, the whole history of a school, the whole history of art is dominated and conditioned by this drama—through the imperishable desire to hold fast the universal life that escapes us at every instant, in the image that is capable of defining it for all time. If one does not comprehend this, no form of art is intelligible outside the narrowest naturalism. If one does comprehend it, the forms most remote from the appearances of life—Aztec art, for instance, which is almost illegible at the first glance and unites, in the equilibriums of its masses, the most anomalous and often the least definite objects and organs—become immediately and plainly intelligible. They obtain that quality of supernatural viability in which the highest expressions of lyricism, the rising intoxication of life becoming conscious of its ascent, come into communication. The modeler of gods, at bottom, is the spiritual universe hastening unceasingly in pursuit of its center of gravity which, by turns, invites and then shuns its embrace. Art is only the humble and marvelous image of the cosmic order itself, that state of provisional equilibrium between chaos on this side and chaos on that. Those who deny that it is of use should consider what would happen to man if the force that maintains the planets in their orbit suddenly ceased to exist.

These are big words, perhaps, if one thinks of this fable of La Fontaine, this Bœotian figurine, this Persian colored print, this playful young woman of Fragonard offering between two fingers the strawberry of her breast. Nevertheless, could we seize the most furtive grace, taste the discreet accord of the most delicate tones, penetrate the anguish or the sweetness of those eyes that meet ours, if subtle antennæ, starting from the secret centers of our sensibility, did not unite it infallibly to the mysterious, even if imponderable attraction of these arts? The connection is established through lines of force that assure the absolute solidarity, both biological and spiritual, of their structure and our own, and affirm the presence, in them as in ourselves, of two similar needs for harmony which their unexpected accord intoxicates with security.

There is nothing incompatible between this mathematical certitude that we seek confusedly in a work of art and its always fugitive and always alluring life which we can only surprise there in flashes. Quite on the contrary, we find an obscure consolation in this perpetual flight, as soon, at least, as we know that it turns unwearyingly about a center that exists in us as in it, although we are incapable of placing and fixing it for all time.

Thus there is no end to the drama or to the indefinite anguish of man that offers him, until the universe has ceased to exist, first for him, afterwards for his species, a limitless visible field of emotion and activity. I think this is the character, at once logical and fluctuating, tragic and consoling, of art, which desires that all definitions one has given and will give of it shall remain

and should remain incomplete. Art, which is our reason
for being, will only perish with us. It is art that nourishes and maintains our spiritual energy. It is art that
delivers to us the secret of the hopeless but necessary
effort of Sisyphus. Man emerges from the ashes of
man and sees again the divine face the moment he
surprises the new shoots among the ashes of the altar
he has overthrown.

I am afraid I have not succeeded in maintaining, in
the pages of this book, that grand circulation of energy
which renders the most insignificant image of a bird
found in the sands of Egypt as inevitably consistent
with an aeroplane of to-day as is the most worn of the
silhouettes of the mammoth engraved on the walls of
the Fond de Gaume with the Pagoda of Srirangam or
the Parthenon of Pericles. What I should also like to
have shown is how a statue taken from any temple
whatsoever reproduces the very profiles of this temple
through its planes, whose moving waves will seize in
space, in order to incorporate them with themselves,
the passages and the reflections that determine painting and cause to be born from painting, through their
mingled rhythms, the invisible harmonies from which
music will spring.

I would have wished, finally, to reduce to a few
evident relations the infinite complexity of the relations
revealed by the infinite variety of the images, and the
depth of the abysses which their study opens in us.
In fact, it seems to me probable that the relations expressed by Phidias, for example, simple as they appear
to us, nevertheless remain essential, and that if the
impression made on our sensibilities by a cathedral or
by a symphony of Beethoven is more harmonious or
more intense, it is because the analytic elements expressed by them are not yet as intimately a part of
us as the ideas in which the spirit of Phidias once recog-

nized its sources. What we call "depth" is perhaps at the beginning of each of our inquiries. One finds, in the thinkers of the time before Phidias, intuitions as complex as those of the philosophers of India or Germany, intuitions that all contribute to form the intellectual harmony of Plato, as highly refined as it may seem. A single curve expresses one day what a hundred entangled curves before that time evoked confusedly. Simplicity is an achievement incessantly ambushed at every turn of the road and which poets alone can wrest from the immense and always renewed sum of the unknown.

I have therefore not been able, I have not known how to be simpler. And perhaps, after all, that is not my function. I watch dancing, but alas, I am not a dancer. The most candid being can *feel*, or even *express* the most admirable poem which the most complicated being will always show himself incapable of *understanding* and *explaining*.

So many create or act with direct force while I suffer and hesitate to seize a solution that unceasingly escapes me. One can find in the slightest sketch of a master— or perhaps even of a little boy drawing something in a spirit of sheer impudence—matter enough to ruin the edifice that I have tried to build and that represents thirty years of meditation. God is a child who amuses himself, passes from laughter to tears without reason, and every day invents the world for the torment of the abstractors of its quintessence, the pedants and the preachers who pretend to teach him his trade of creator.

ELIE FAURE

Paris, Spring 1930

THE SPIRIT OF THE FORMS

I do not paint the being,
I paint the passage.

—MONTAIGNE

Fig. 2

DAUMIER

Fig. 3

ROMAN TEMPLE, FRANCE (Brittany)

Chapter I. THE GREAT RHYTHM

I

THE older I grow, the more I observe, the more I notice how I live, the less can I conceive it possible to consider the history of peoples and the history of the mind otherwise than as a series of alternations, now rapid and now precipitous, of disintegrations through knowledge and integrations through love.

It is the rhythm that Laplace, Lamarck, Spencer catch in the evolution of the universal drama itself, beginning with the original phase in which the nebula was formed, to end in the final phase in which shattered suns and dead planets return to the dust of the skies, passing through the successive stages that lead from matter to life, from life to mind, from mind to matter— into which mind is absorbed, acquiring from it renewed strength, after having conceived it and directed it for

1

a time. It is the rhythm of the chemical drama in which synthesis and analysis are alternately engendered. It is the rhythm of the physiological drama in which the systole and the diastole by turn fling life to the

Fig. 4
GREECE (VII Century)

periphery and take it up again, poisoned and benumbed, to remake it. It is the rhythm of the biological drama whence, from the sexual cell, surges the adventure of the superior organism which hunger and love cause to

recreate the sexual cell in order to precipitate themselves, through it, into a new organism.

What we know of history is still and will probably
always be trifling. Perhaps,
indeed no doubt, it is only
beginning. But it is necessary
to resign oneself to learning
nothing of it if one does not
decide to seek in its unfolding
an influence, confused beyond
question, of which one can seize
the aspect when one regards it
from afar and where, instead of
considering it according to its
so-called advances, its so-called
recoils, its avowed intentions or
our avowed interests, one resolutely seeks this rhythm in
which the spirit, now determined by its events, now reacting in order to organize them,
only plays the role of regulator,
but of a unique regulator.

Already, in what remains of
it, that residue of intelligence
which persists on the surface
of its inner movements and
persists there alone when everything else of these same movements has disappeared—the
verbal poem that inscribes itself

FIG. 5

FRANCE (XI Century)

in the book, the plastic poem that inscribes itself in the
monument, the scientific poem that inscribes itself in the
formula—it seems that a sufficiently clear curve
appears, of which the ascensions represent periods of
association, and the descents represent periods of moral

dissociation between men, with a maximum of cohesion at the summits of the curve, a maximum of anarchy at its lowest points. The Saint-Simonians described as "organic" and "critical" these alternating periods.

G<small>REECE</small> (Beginning of the VI Century)

But they did not seek to understand the corroborating testimony, to my sense irrefutable, in idols, temples, dwellings, tombs.

If one succeeds in discovering this character in these forms, I believe one is authorized to extend it to the whole of history of which they constitute so to speak the spiritual crystallization, the highest life of the soul arrested in letters of stone at the moment when it contradicts itself and is torn apart in the drama of events.

Without question, in facts that are studied from too close by, this rhythm does not appear so simple. There are breaks, seams, infringements. In the bronze there is a flaw. A fissure stripes the architrave. A new sentiment awakens that makes the pyramid tremble or the dancer trip. It happens, for instance, that in the case of a people in full and regular evolution, a pacific or warlike invasion breaks, dislocates, or simply turns aside the curve of this evolution. In the essential themes of the symphony of history, which are now the accord of all the spiritual elements introduced by the multitude into the monument, now the definition, in individual works, of those elements dispersed in the search for a new communion, other themes enter confusedly—provisional syntheses, researches for an embryonic equilibrium shattered as soon as they are achieved, attempts that are only sketches—or miscarry, or do not endure.

In the heart of the intellectual analysis that characterizes the Hellenic spirit, decidedly in dissolution from the time of Socrates, the moral synthesis that will define Christianity already speaks in stammering accents, even in the plastic form, the gesticulating groups, the deep sunken eyes, the equivocal play of light on the surface of statues. In the heart of the Occidental

Fig. 7

FRANCE (First half of xii Century)

analysis, on the other hand, when the art of cathedral-building is breaking down in France, when the Florentine or Sienese palace itself loses the purity of its outlines and encumbers itself with ornaments, the moral organism of Protestantism attempts to build a new monument over the débris of the æsthetic organism of Catholicism.   Nevertheless, despite these accidents, these advances, these regressions, these apparent contradictions, the grandiose alternation of the religious illusion that erects the temples in a fury of love and the critical knowledge that overthrows them, in order to open, by a minute enquiry, other roads to the spirit, remains a permanent, and to my mind decisive, reality.

Here is the Doric affirmation, the architectural unity coinciding everywhere with an incontestable mythical unity, the austere monument on which the unanimous piety of the crowds inscribes, on the pediments and the metopes, the motionless dance of forms, the harsh and wholesome certitude displayed by the purity of the outline.   Here are the ornate capitals, the fragile, fluted column, the isolated and more and more mobile statue, the artist outside the common workshop, in the private studio and in the world, the drama torn away from the collective conventions of the theater in order to enter the individual meanderings of the sophistical and the romantic, religion corroded by analysis, sensuality turning to eroticism, and corrupting sentiment, the intelligence inaugurating experience and substituting a fragmentary truth for a universal truth.

Here, after Æschylus, is Aristotle.   Here is the Christian affirmation, the Catholic dogma blocked out in the Roman temple the thickness and unbroken mass of which express its coherence; the rigorous rhythm of the elongated figures that people its capitals and its tympanums, later the flight of the pillars, the soaring of the vaults express the transport of the whole people toward the invincible hope that the universe is only the sensible symbol of a marvelous world promised to the unanimity, the candor of the faith.

Fig. 8

Greece (Second half of the vi Century)

Fig. 9

France (Second half of the xii Century)

Here, in the very arrises of these vaults, in these figures that become gradually slender and complicated, a curiosity is born, grows, affirms itself as conquering and tyrannical: here are the vanished symbol and the object scrutinized for itself, the flower born from the seed, the woman in love studied in the virgin mother, the man springing from the god. Here the printed character replaces the wrought stone, the spirit rushes to the conquest of terrestrial happiness, becoming cruel in order to attain it and discovering behind the paradisiac threshold of knowledge, where it entered dazzled, the hell of doubt and remorse.

Here is Montaigne, then Pascal, after Dante and Saint Thomas. Yesterday, here as well as there, man went to meet the world, seeking to incorporate himself with it in a vast religious unity in which his intuitive pantheism affirmed itself in his instinct to conceive the monument according to the universal plan. To-day, here as there, he draws the world into himself, seeking to incorporate it in his being in a strict personal unity in which his reasoned anthropocentrism shows in the care with which he expresses his sentiments. Socrates dreaming, toward the end of his days, of learning music again is the conscious symbol of this gigantic oscillation that ceaselessly swings our spiritual history between the peaks of mystical intoxication and the peaks of reason. When one has scoured in all directions the clear but limited territory of the intelligence, one finds oneself one day or another on the edge of the abyss of the unknowable where the intoxicating need for a new illusion reappears.

II

If this outline seems to you a little too schematic, imagine the evolution of the Greek statue born toward the middle of the seventh century, B.C. and arriving at the limit of its growth toward the middle of the third, or after four hundred years. And follow with the same glance the march of the political body which will show you, if there is any logic in the form, the significance of the rhythm it must obey.

In Hellenic society as we know it, toward the eighth century of the ancient era, for instance, the myth prevails uncontested. It even attains its phase of full crystallization. It is, for the men of the tribe, the unique reason for being born, loving, suffering, dying. Held in common, universally admitted at least in the same tribe, the belief leaves no room for doubt. Certainly, God is not a single being. He is, on the contrary, multiple. But belief is single. And it is this that is divine. It is upon this belief alone that the moral unitary principle rests without which neither the city nor the family would be. Marriage is holy, therefore indissoluble. Celibacy is forbidden. Morally, the child exists only as a function of the father, who exists himself only as a function of dead ancestors whose sepulchers sanctify—and even legitimize—his essential quality. Not only the individual does not exist, but his existence would be contrary to the very conception of the home which is perhaps the nucleus, perhaps the contraction of the city[1], in any case forming with it an indissoluble organism from which nothing can be taken away without ruining one or the other.

The liberty of the human being is neither conceived nor conceivable outside the family group which no longer conceives its own liberty outside of its setting and its gods, the neighboring family groups bounding

[1] From the point of view I assume, it matters little whether the family, as Fustel de Coulanges would have it, is the embryo of the State, or whether the State, as the sociologists of to-day believe, is anterior to the organization of the family. When the great collective art appears, State and family are profoundly solidary and constitute the apparently indestructible social frame where this art develops.

FIG. 10

GREECE (First half of the v Century)

it on all sides. The whole of human society is immersed in the diffused divinity of nature, personified by the gods that connect man with her by a thousand bonds of rites on which the laws are based. The sanctity of the soil is a reality the more inexorable the more it represents a spiritual style menaced by the rival tribe, and the more difficult it is to maintain. The moral universe is a single block.

Now at this moment the *Xoana*, the primitive idol cut in olive-wood, is nothing but an almost formless embryo, a roughly shaped doll in which the forms are indicated after the symbolic manner of a child who draws heedlessly

and makes a great rectangle
for the body, a smaller rectangle for the head, two
narrower and longer rectangles for the arms.[1] In comparison with the statues of
the following century, it is
like those peasant houses
one still sees in our days
in certain Greek country-
sides beside the oldest
marble sanctuaries: four
vertical posts that will become the peristyle, four
horizontal posts that will
become the architrave.[2] It
satisfies the simplest of
spiritual needs, as this cabin
satisfies the simplest of
our material needs. As yet
almost no differentiation
exists, in the minds of those
who have made them, be-
tween the natural elements
which they utilize both for
belief and for shelter and
the sense of this belief and
the comfort of this shelter.
The matrix that binds them
is the common belief.   The
members are prisoners of it,
as the individual is a prisoner of the social principle
from which he does not dare

[1] Fig. 4.
[2] Fig. 130.

Fig. 11
FRANCE
(First half of the XIII Century)

and cannot and will not enfranchise himself, from which he does not even dream of enfranchising himself, because this premature enfranchisement would immediately involve his downfall. He is ignorant of the relations that rivet him to this principle, the régime of castes imposing them upon him for his own good. Society, like the idol, is impersonal, congealed, symmetrical, so to speak. The writers of the time are the legists whom the spirit of the gods inspires when in rhythmic prose, they chant the verses of the sacred law.

A half century. Due to the frictions of families among themselves, the family, while still as firmly rooted, has nevertheless become less rigid than the city. It infuses into the city a life that is more and more organic. The multiplication of the social cells enlarges their horizon, while an aristocracy supported upon a morality that is intact, and believing in the interest of its own conservation, recalls the chisel that cuts in the marble the simplest planes and the most rigid profiles. The idol has become denser. It tends vaguely to the circular form, as if to gratify a primitive need for mass and unity. An architectonic instinct as confused as it is essential appears in the hanging arms, the parallel legs, the horizontal shoulders, the almost conic torso in which the bony heads and the muscular masses already undulate feebly, a whole stiff and hard ensemble, the symmetrical elements of which express the feeling of an elementary rhythm like two feet striking the ground in cadence or two hands clapping at regular intervals.[1] No individuality. Although this statue may be called an athlete, it is an impersonal monument that represents almost any athlete, almost any naked man. It offers only one difference of ethnic quality from the Ionic statue, which appears about the same time in the Ægean Isles, the spirit remaining the

[1] Fig. 6.

Fig. 12

Greece (First half of the v Century)

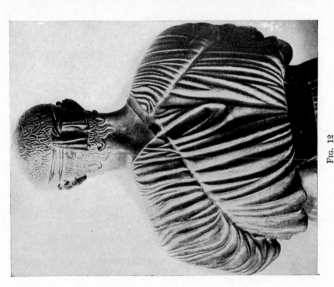

Fig. 13

France (First half of the xiii Century)

same and evolving the same relationships out of the same interrogated elements. The Doric statues are men, the Ionic statues are women, the former hard, all of a piece, the latter sensual, equivocal, subjected to more furtive planes, with a tendency to a more insinuating sphericity, the limbs more imprisoned.[1] But, here as there, it is always architectural: nothing emerges, nothing can emerge from this vertical cylinder in which all the movements and all the prominences are lost, like the knots of the tree, before the birth of the branches, in the mass of the rugged trunk. Cramped, strained, swollen in this sheath, the deep life assumes there a benumbed character, still somnolent, but of an impressive and irreducible unity.

Another half century. The increasing antagonism of interests and the abuses of the aristocracy create in the masses of the people secret currents that shake the edifice, feebly at first, but enough to awaken there new needs, new ideas. If the solidity of the castes seems still unmoved and can appear even increased, since they feel their original integrity to be menaced, they are less completely shut up within themselves. See the heroes, the horses of Delphi, the *Caryatides* of Cnidos, the *Orantes* of the old Parthenon. In these touching statues in which the Doric male and the Ionic female eye one another but refuse to unite, the plane appears for the first time as a more definite idea, a little less lost in the ensemble, traversed by a great shudder. It strives to emerge from an anonymous architectonic formula in order to build, in the clay which it carves, an autonomous idol stirring a little, a strange smile on the lips, a foot or an arm thrust forward. Its difficult passage animates the profiles a little, makes the surfaces undulate indistinctly. The equilibrium of the masses delineates itself, succeeding their symmetry, and it is

[1] Figs. 134, 135.

to the movement of profound forces traveling over the
form within that the planes owe their vigor.[1] The
cylinder is living, the knots and the shoots bursting
into bloom, the branches are growing out of the trunk.
The writers of the time are philosophical poets who
create a system of the world, a monumental display
that is roughly sketched, but grandiose and moving,
emerging painfully from the myth without the will or
the power to separate itself from it. In thought, in
politics, as in the idol itself, the individual dimly appears in a few monstrous brains.

Another half century. Through tribes, through parties, through classes, ardent groups are organized, still
stiff, almost mechanical, in which, although the instinct
of the antagonistic interests and needs already appears
strongly, the individual consciousness of each of their
elements, cannot yet express itself. Drama is born in
the theater because it is born in the social body. If
Æschylus makes the pitiless laws of custom and destiny
weigh upon man, a light grows in him, the animating
spark of which Prometheus has taken from God. It
is this, henceforth, that constitutes the unique center
about which, in the idol of this time, the masses gravitate, as if it were necessary that man, who is trying to
define himself, should still remain within the circle so
deeply grooved around his activity by his ancestors, so
that he may deepen and unify this activity. Still rude,
but less strained, the plane gathers up the light that
unites it with the neighboring planes through irregular
but continuous passages, so placed as to construct or
rather to suggest the same turning surface, from whatever side it is seen. One sees the *Charioteer* of Delphi
and the warriors of Ægina emerging from the uniform
mold, whose almost absolute roundness had been imprisoning their movements.[2] Disengaged from archi-

[1] Fig. 8.   [2] Figs. 6, 12.

tecture, a monument complete in itself, full, defined, circular, the statue finds its relation to universal life and recognizes its place in the midst of everything that exists. The myth is still almost intact, but its symbolic meaning rises to the level of the peaks of the spirit.

A half-century, and we touch the supreme point of the oscillation. The pediments of Olympia have told of the antithetical struggle of the powers of the soul against the powers of instinct; halfway between these sculptures

Fig. 14
Greece (Middle of the v Century)

and the already less poignant pediments of Phidias, there was an imperceptible and perhaps unrealized moment when Hellenism defined the essential moral drama that justifies the existence of man. The choice, a decisive choice, imposes itself on him. Two forces are at work in his heart: on the one hand the intoxication of belonging to a coherent social body that directs all its acts to a common belief designating surely the things that please the gods and those that do not please them, the intoxication of arousing, through all his acts, the unanimous approbation of the dead, and, on the other hand, the desire to explore the new moral regions that curiosity, interest, and a vague but ardent desire lights and develops in his soul, his own soul—the personal

and no doubt single being with its increasing demands.
Between the political parties that are of almost equal
strength, an uncertain and furious struggle begins,
marked by alternating victories and defeats, with sometimes an hour's truce imposed by some powerful spirit.
The family, still solid, has become the scene of another,
more secret struggle in which the egotism of children,
of women, who grow in consciousness, in appetites, in
dignity, will become unbounded unless the dignity, the

Fig. 15
FRANCE (Middle of the XIII Century)

consciousness, and the appetites of its chief remain
within the frame of his duties and his rights. The
pursuit of wealth and of the pleasures and public honors
connected with it, develop strength of character, audacity, skill, knavery in the man who desires it. The
power to resolve these universal conflicts that belongs
in the family to the father, and, in the city to the master,
finds its expression in the heroic firmness that permits
Sophocles, faced with the confused intoxication of the
old moral unity represented by the chorus, to present
the will of the noble man in whom intelligence awakens
and combats the whole of the fateful universe that is
leagued against him, just as it permits the sculptor of

FIG. 16
GREECE (End of the
v Century)

the same epoch to establish, between contrasted masses and antagonistic gestures, an equilibrium that triumphs over disorder and chaos, that forces them to return to the same ensemble and flings them with the same enthusiasm into a continuous movement. The Doric male and the Ionic female penetrate each other in an embrace which the suppleness of Myron and the vigor of Polycletus by turns knot and unknot, and the statue thus evolved acts, marches, fights, rests in an august liberty. It is no longer merely architecture by itself. It enters, with its neighbors, into a more complex organism, united in monumental undulations in which the forms, however separate, realize, through their succession, a plastic melody of balanced curves.[1] It is like branches spread by the same tree—the *Charioteer* of yesterday—which twist and become entangled, while the sap runs to their very extremity. One finds, in the statue, the whole harmony

[1] Fig. 14.

of the ensemble which itself borrows from the statue the law of its autonomy. Here are the large, bare planes with which the whole surface vibrates, the long silent passages that unite them and animate them in an endless cradling movement. The continuous flow of the great expressive billows takes place with the same energy that drives the blood into the veins and tightens the aponeuroses and the muscles under the skin. The spiritual flame drops into the intervals of silence, to solidify the forms from one end of the pediment to the other.

At this moment, looked at from above and from a distance, if one refuses to see the accidents of the road, a powerful harmony prevails. The parts are so animated by life that the necessity for one engenders itself in the others. Man is face to face with man. He belongs with him to a society of which the principle is accepted by all even if his antagonisms and his contradictions still live on. The plane, in the sculptural technique, is only the necessary persistence of the religious and social laws which the decisive

Fig. 17

FRANCE

(End of the XIII Century)

FIG. 18
GREECE (First half of the
IV Century)

awakening of the individual conscience unites with the neighboring plane through the undulation of the passage and the line of the profile. Tragedy and sculpture live in the harmonious form of their contrasted elements because, if man affirms himself, the god has not quitted him but confronts him through instinct and conscience, through sensuality and reason, through the idea and the reality in the very heart of the hero.

Another half-century. And here we have the free man, at least free to define himself. He has willed it. He has not the right to complain if progressively doubt, anxiety, anguish invade him in the measure that the family falls apart, the law yields or changes, the city be-

comes now more indul-
gent, now more exact-
ing in regard to him; if
the myths are disputed
and the need to play
grows with leisure, celibacy, fortune, the intro-
duction of outside
women into the house-
hold, the introduction
of freed slaves, of nat-
uralized foreigners into
the agora, the introduc-
tion into the spirit
which grows effeminate
and complicated, of un-
known ideas and images
invented by the philos-
ophers, or imported by
travelers. The great
cosmic syntheses are
forgotten or neglected,
man having returned
into himself, and drawn
in with him the diffused
god that yesterday peo-
pled the world and
lived under all these
aspects where the prim-
itive poet ingenuously
sought the syntheses.
The moralist succeeds
the legist, the psychol-
ogist the theologian,
the sophist the philos-
opher. Euripides, in
the theater, forgets or

Fig. 19

FRANCE

(First half of the xiv Century)

provokes the gods, and delves in the depths of the man's mind in order to ravish his secret. Socrates claims to teach man to know himself and perceives nothing in the world to interest him outside of that knowledge. In vain Aristophanes delivers Socrates and Euripides over to the laughter of the crowd; he keeps step with them, since social criticism mounts the stage with him. The dialectic of Plato leads the principle of unity back to the interior of the being. It is not by chance that democracy triumphs because the increasing need of political equality in the emancipated citizen demands satisfaction. Here the weapon that he has demanded becomes tyrannical—penetration of the projects and interests of others, a stratagem to baffle them, an attention always on the watch to profit by circumstances, to give birth to the drama or take part in it, the critical spirit increasing at the expense of the constructive intelligence—and it isolates from the ensemble the object pursued and surrounded with a too meticulous attention and the too paltry care for detail. The inquiry of Aristotle disperses to infinity the observation, the knowledge, the character of this object. Neither is it by chance that he is the contemporary of Lysippus, and that anatomical science, which he founds, appears at the very hour when the muscular model gradually substitutes itself for the architectural plane.

Not only has the statue at this time come forth from the original matrix, but it forgets what that matrix was. Obstinate restlessness, sensuality surround it. Considered, then caressed with an insistent love, it lets fall the veils that once caused the transparencies and the meanderings of the streams to flow over it.[1] The form gains in sensibility what it loses in energy. Besides, the statue which, a century earlier, having gathered together its strength, aspired to appear in

[1] Fig. 16.

decorative groups, now aspires to isolate itself anew
and only reluctantly remains in groups. Individualized,
it tries its strength with new gestures, with pensive
attitudes. At the risk of dismembering it, its constitutive elements study their own structure. It will
soon meet Praxiteles who will tenderly awaken in it
the centers of pleasure. After him the psychological
passage will profit by the hesitation of the plane and the
floating of the profile to encroach upon their domain,
to blend, in an increasing confusion, the essential and
simple relations which they reveal in the object, and in
that way remove itself from the vivifying contacts of
this object with the world. The individual is no longer
a function of the world. It is the world that becomes
a function of the individual. And as the individual
is not necessarily a demiurge, he will no longer re-invent
the world except by chance impulses.

A half-century later, one will easily grasp the profound social causes of the last stage of the spirit. The
myths, broken down, no longer arouse, except in very
humble people, anything but revolt or laughter. The
stoics and the cynics logically push the moral tendencies
of man in the opposite direction, toward the spiritual
impasses from which he cannot escape save by renewing
his mysticism. Now sensual, now abstract, the cults
of the East creep in and replace everywhere the local
religion, destroying every day a little more the ancient
unity of the spirit. The belief in equality is proclaimed
by all, whether overtly or not, since man is the equal
of man when he considers himself as gravitating exclusively about one of his two poles—either his instincts
in their most intransigent bestiality, or his spirit in its
ideal purity disengaged from every carnal tie; and this
belief is intensified, in direct ratio to the increasing
inequality of conditions. The individual wants to be
right against the city, against the family, presently

against the individual. His own individuality gradually rends him asunder. The idol is now a fantastic image which the genius of a solitary artist frequently can render living, but which the spread of the craft and the vulgarization of culture condemn most often to express only the mediocre anxieties of the anecdote and of vogue loved by "free" souls seeking to delude their restlessness, satisfy their folly, tickle their self-sufficiency, cure their ennui.

The statue enjoys henceforth an egotistical independence that only increases its torment. Too isolated, now, it calls to its aid the elements of the picturesque. Its action begins to break the ideal circle in which it but lately inscribed itself almost mechanically. The passage inundates the plane, which weakens, hesitates, barely contains the inner life that is frittered away in details. Stuffs, draped in all directions, mask its insufficiency.[1] The brush of shadow plays upon it, effaces it, renders it equivocal or deceitful. An indefinite undulation envelops, like a fog, the inner structure which is covered over and then melts away. The too narrow parallelisms, or rather the too eccentric movements stiffen the monumental ensemble or move it from its orbit. The unity becomes incoherent or breaks. Too heavily laden, the branches crack. The relations float and begin to intertwine at random.

When Rhodes and Pergamos were in the ascendant, a half-century later, the organism was decomposed. In the increasing social and political anarchy, the constant mingling over all the shores of the Orient, of opposing mysticisms, worn-out Sophistries, mutually destructive private interests, in the appeals to a beneficent tyranny and a purifying barbarism, the plastic frontiers were forced on every side. The architecture of the idol was no longer even a memory. The modeling having lost

[1] Fig. 18.

Fig. 21
FRANCE

Fig. 20
GREECE

(Second half of the XIV Century)

the plane, tried to follow step by step the anatomical incidents that broke the profiles and peopled the but lately expressive silence of the surfaces for the benefit of the picturesque little story and the most banal sentiment. The wild gesticulation, completely disoriented, expresses a moral disorder from which all continuity of reasoning and action, all logical structure, all equilibrium have disappeared. The spirit which, dislocating the plane, then playing with the passage, had quitted for a century the inner regions of the statue now appears in the twisting hands, the hanging legs, the locked muscles, the convulsed faces, the invading attributes and the disordered hair.[1] It is not only that the center of attraction of the masses is lost. The sculptor no longer knows that this center once existed and that it determined the entire form, whose movements and surfaces gravitated about it. Spread over all the incidents, all the prominences of the statue, weak sensibility and mediocre sensation attempt to substitute their clamor and their emphasis for the powerful global consciousness that united, in the monumental form, the knowledge and the love of the object with the belief that the object made part of a sacred ensemble of which religion, the city, the family, war, peace, food, birth, and death are solidary manifestations. One would say that the gesticulations and the grimaces of the idol cry out for its lost unity. Besides, it is no longer an idol. It is an article of merchandise.

III

If now one follows from close-by the evolution of sculpture in France, in which Christian art attains its most complete and also its most moving development, one realizes that it is identical, aside from its motives,

[1] Figs. 20, 22, 24.

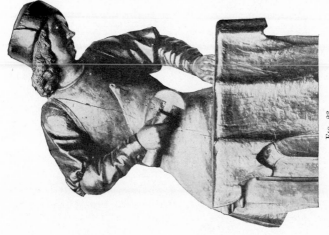

Fig. 22

Greece (III Century)

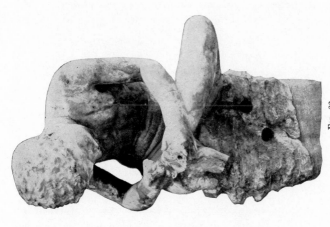

Fig. 23

France (xv Century)

with that of Greek sculpture.[1] And this in the course of a period of almost equal duration, from the end of the eleventh to the end of the fifteenth century, or also four hundred years. One could take, here and there, a statue or a decorative group, place them both face to face and follow their parallel march from half-century to half-century, to establish here as well as there the progress of the undifferentiated and global organism to the organism whose functions gradually differentiate, then balance their antagonism and their solidarity, then separate too much from one another, then lose sight of their relations and return to chaos.[2]

[1] The choice of the illustrations for this text has been very difficult. Since the proof clearly springs from the demonstration, it is necessary that the examples should be chosen as much as possible, in the one case and the other, from the same school. But if it is relatively easy to do this for Greece up to the fourth century, and if the Doric and Ionic schools and the Attic school that rose from them can be invoked alone, or almost alone, it is otherwise with France. The sculpture of Chartres, for example, from which I have chosen my best examples, was developed only from the middle of the twelfth century to the end of the thirteenth, or during about one hundred and fifty years, scarcely more than a third of the period embraced. There were, besides, in France as elsewhere, from one region to another, intercrossing influences that were able here and there to cause the image-makers to take a different direction from the natural evolution to which the local tradition would certainly have led them. Sometimes, one or several stone-cutters, coming from a neighboring or faraway province, became the inspiration of the milieu where they found themselves.

On the other hand, we should avoid so yielding to the attraction of the subject as to consider exclusively the technique. It is only too easy to take two statues clothed in a similar manner and expressing a similar moral attitude, to show a relationship that, in this case, is only due to chance. Another pitfall had to be avoided. Certain statues of Rheims, for instance have an evident Mediterranean air that could have supported all too easily our exposition by demonstrating, not the spiritual relationship of Greek sculpture to French sculpture, but the influence that Greek sculpture, through the intermediation of the Roman models, was able to exercise on French art at a given moment and in circumstances that were otherwise exceptional. What we have attempted to show, at least to those who possess some notion of the language of sculpture and the history of the Greek and French societies in the course of the periods of their most original development, is the parallelism of the rhythms of the technical evolution of sculpture and the social and psychological evolution of sentiments and customs.

[2] Figs. 4 and 5 to 24 and 25.

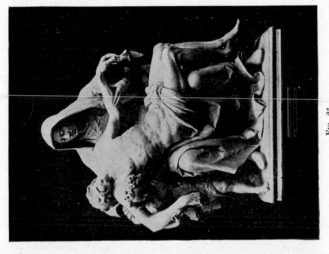

Fig. 24

Greece (ii Century)

Fig. 25

France (xvi Century)

I am not following in detail the process of the radical dissolution, then the progressive integration, through which the ancient world disappeared in order that from its ruins might rise the Christian world. This happened, as it will happen in the future no doubt, in the same way that the constitution of a new chemical body borrows its elements from other chemical bodies in solution which happen to be in the region where its movement of synthesis establishes a center of attraction. The patient and fanatical activity of the Jewish apostles and the hundred, then the thousand, then the hundred thousand ingenuous disciples, sailors, peddlers, soldiers, loose women who went about affirming, through ports, markets, barracks, wretched dens, that nobility belonged, in this debased, skeptical, self-indulgent world to the poor, the sick, the slave—all this activity, prepared a new communion in the heart of individualistic anarchy, the despair of which stoic heroism had alone the power to support. It scarcely matters, at bottom, that the origins of each new communion differ from the origins of that which it comes to replace. The essential thing is that it should be. The prime movers concerned have always used the pretext of ideals to reclothe the mask, but it is in the illusion of these pretexts that these movers fructify. At almost the other extremity of Europe, in order to satisfy analogous needs perhaps, or in any case, other beliefs, Christianity took ten centuries to reconstitute society and the family which their own vigor and their own abuses appeared to have ruined forever. One communion that succeeds another in the diffused instinct of the species, resembles a love that succeeds another love in the heart of the individual. The critical phase that separates one love from another is abolished. The constructive phase opens. And as the first leads to the second because it is weary of reasoning, analyzing, amassing the materials of knowledge that are of no use to it, the second leads back to the first by gradually destroying its strength through the passionate and distracted use it has made of it. If the individual, or the species, is not capable of maintaining the state of love in his heart during his life, it suffices at least that he has known it once for him to desire to know it again, and History, like man, does not seem to have any reason for being save the search, the possession, the loss, and then the new search for this state.

When the first sculptors began to appear toward the end of the eleventh century, on the tympanums and capitals of the old Roman sanctuaries, a formidable society, all the elements of which were consolidated, was constituted anew. The liturgy is the symbol of this perfect organism. Theology shuts up in a doctrine as compact as stone the constitution of a family and a hierarchy from which not one piece could be subtracted without causing it to fall. An aristocracy that is brutal but completely cemented into the same block, props up the high walls with a solidity that comes from the obscure consciousness of the redoubtable risks it agrees to run. The universe has become an immense symbol of the moral world built up through ten centuries of meditation at the heart of the continuous drama. As ancient man summed up the poetic teachings in his faith, the new man unceasingly brings to it, in order to incorporate them in the strictest fashion, the poetic teachings of his faith.

If one goes from the rigid figures of Autun[1] or Moissac which express, like monotonous music, the symmetrical and precise rhythm of the social Catholic construction, to the ornamental profusion, the increasing individualism of the flamboyant agony in which the ogival church gradually disintegrates, one passes, toward the middle of the thirteenth century, through a point of equilibrium

[1] Fig. 190.

in which the statue, animated by another expression
no doubt, observes, toward the entire theocratic order,
relations similar to those that characterize its Greek
sister, between the pediments of Olympia and the pediments of the Parthenon, in its relation to the city.

See the human statues of Rheims, Amiens, Notre
Dame, the lateral portals of Chartres. There we have
the same measured expression, the same harmony of

FIG. 26
THE PROFILE (The Parthenon)

proportions in the form, of disposition in the group,
the same accord between the plane, the passage, and
the outline, the same spontaneous and perfect fusion
of the symbolic significance and the naturalistic per-
ception of the object, the same grandiose sentiment in
which sculpture is suspended between the intoxication
of unbroken beliefs which have not yet entered the era
of discussion, and the curiosity to live which tends to
take possession of it. It is also the epoch in which the

Fig. 27

THE PLANE (Egypt)

commune attains its maximum of creative virtue, thanks to the organic equilibrium of the corporative groups, in which Saint Thomas Aquinas seals the keystone of the vault of Catholic rationalism, in which the Crusade spreads, like an irresistible alluvion, the radiant security of the French genius. Enveloping with its unity, conquered and preserved through struggle, the necessary antagonism of the corporations and the clergy, of feudal right and popular stirrings, the architectural edifice of Christian conceptualism attains its point of consummation.

It was necessary to progress in order to construct it, through the pure, elongated statues of the central porches of Chartres, the cadenced rhythms of Saint-Trophime of Arles, the budding of the capitals from which the flower and the fruit do not yet emerge, all that folding together of the chrysalis, still wrapped in its sheath, through which we can glimpse the members that are to unfold, the wings that are to spread, the unnameable thrill that runs over the exquisite surfaces of the form in preparation, as if it were on the point of bursting forth. It was necessary for the military orders to bring about a respect for theological unity throughout all Europe in order that the continent should burst into flower, even if this very process was to destroy theological unity itself. It was necessary that the naissant commune should affirm, through insurrection, the right of the people and the crafts to introduce, into this growing unity, the living and poetic sentiment without which the chrysalis would have remained the formless larva imprisoned in the cocoon. It was necessary that in the bosom of the Church itself should be born, between Abelard and Saint Bernard, those first controversies that give to a hermetic society, along with life, movement, and flame, the illusion that it is strong enough to realize liberty without changing its form.

Fig. 28

The Passage (Rubens)

On the other slope of the evolution, we find the portraits, the tombs, the rapid and picturesque individualization of the setting. They constitute the intermediary stage between the hour when an anonymous chief architect built up—in the musical curves and the uninterrupted winding of the nerves and the rose-windows of Soissons—the Parthenon of the Middle Ages and the hour of the disintegration of the ogival nave that was to mark the decisive passage from a form of collective civilization to a form of individual civilization. The destruction of the Templars and the coming of the Jacquerie marked it in the social and political body, while in the bosom of the communes, at this same moment, the enriching of some at the expense of others, the corrosive action of luxury, the victorious reconquest of feudal tyranny or the organization of the monarchic unity caused the disintegration of the elements of the plastic edifice and broke the backbone and the skeleton of the vessel, the ruins of which the sculptors will strive to ornament, ransack, and torment.

IV

If the evolution of this organism of the image that sculpture represents, from the embryonic period to its decomposition, did not sink all its roots into the very history of the souls of men, it would have no meaning. The craft transmits itself, to be sure, perfects itself, affirms itself, complicates itself, becomes corrupt, and is lost. But the craft expresses man, and it is man, in the last analysis, who perfects, affirms, complicates himself, becomes corrupt, and is lost. The statue does nothing but imprint upon the soil the trace of man, as if it walked in his steps. It is man, the inner man, in his greatest candor but also in his most essential aspect. It is not, indeed, each man taken separately. It is a sublimation of man in general, of his secret life in its higher forms, the average spiritual residue which he leaves, so to speak, where he has passed.

If I have taken the statue as an example in Greece and France it is because, by keeping it in sight, we can better understand the bonds that attach us all, through it, to the forms of expression from which it emerges, which emerge from it, and at the center of which it remains, like a mute testimony of our diverse adventures. Those which precede it are those, precisely, which survive in it up to the instant when its appearance delineates those that will succeed it. If I may permit myself a definition that is no doubt a little schematic but made thus to enter the heart of the problem at a single stroke, I would say that sculpture being the plane,[1] architecture is the outline,[2] and painting the passage.[3] That the outline—architecture—corresponds to a social edifice very precisely defined. The passage—painting—to a wavering, progressive, regressive, subtle individual, penetrating into all social accidents with the shadow and the light. The plane—sculpture—has a point of equilibrium in which the individual attaches himself again strongly to the social body that nevertheless allows him to assume all independence compatible with their common security. That sculpture, the transitory plastic expression between an organic state and a critical state of society, participates less and less, in the measure that it approaches the point of equilibrium, architecture expressing this organic state, and painting, more and more, in the measure that it withdraws from the point of equilibrium, expressing this critical state.

If, in fact, after having envisaged the evolution of the

[1] Fig. 27.
[2] Fig. 26.
[3] Fig. 28.

statue in its relation to the evolution of customs, politics, ideas, I seek to understand what it expresses relative to the forms that precede and the forces that follow the instant when it attains its equilibrium, the signification of the temple and the painted canvas relative to man appears to me at the first glance. The Doric or Roman temple is embedded in all its parts in the rigidity of the

Fig. 29

Animation of Surfaces (Greece, The Erectheum)

social myth which it expresses. At its beginning, not a single piece of sculpture adorns it. It is as naked as the law.[1] It is the crowd to which the legist or the priest dictates the discipline necessary to the maintenance of the spirit in the frontiers outside of which the family and the city—or the family and the Church—run the risk of finding before them the intricacies of curiosity, inquiry, adventure in which they would lose themselves. When men believe in common, they build in common.

[1] Fig. 3.

Fig. 30

ANIMATION OF SURFACES (France, Chartres)

If sculpture is born, it is because the individual is beginning to exist. It is the individual himself, but
profoundly religious, rugged, obedient with a sort of
intoxication, still entirely involved in the original organism. Men *believe* in common when sculpture appears.
But already a few have begun to *think* no longer in
common.

The statue emerges from the temple in almost the
exact measure in which man emerges from the crowd,
and at the same moment. It does not appear so long as
man obeys blindly the theocratic powers charged with
organizing the bases of his essential functions. It will
not leave him so long as man cultivates his energy, his
character and his audacity to the profit of the cohesion
of the social group that but lately utilized him with the
intransigence which this organization demanded. Man,
disengaging himself from God, is in his heroic phase.
Here it is the Crusade, there the national wars. At the
very moment when the plane realizes for an hour the
accord of the profile and the passage, we are present at
the stammerings of primitive painting; architecture,
meanwhile, showing an increased tendency to over-
animate its surfaces and to associate itself with light
by enlarging its bays and lightening its supports. This
is dazzlingly clear in the revolution that substitutes for
the massive Romanesque church the aerial ogival
church that is gradually peopled with reliefs over which
play shadow and light filling its interior, thanks to the
multicolored stained glass windows, with flowery meadows, setting stars, illumined seas, and twilit woods—
woods, where the mobile glimmering of the seasons
casts moving shadows of blue vapor, green and red
leaves, coral snow, and that are filled with the soughing
of the wind, the warbling of birds, and imagined murmurs.[1] The Greek temple remains more uniform in the

[1] Fig. 30.

course of the rapid effort that leads sculpture from the roughest of archaisms to the melody of Phidias: it is because Christianity has not yet come to fill the soul of the multitudes with more confused, more complex sentiments, vaguer and more sensual mystic aspirations, a vaster accumulation of suffering and hope. Nevertheless, the columns of the peristyle grow more elongated and more frail, letting more daylight enter between them, the flow of the fluting is cut deeper and closer together, the curving grace of the Ionic[1]—soon to be followed by Corinthian profusion—substitutes itself more frequently for the trenchant austerity of the Doric, the metopes become peopled, the walls are covered with paintings, the gold of the suspended shields sparkles among the blues, the greens, the ochres and the vermilions, whose relations become more complex, an opening is contrived in the roof of the edifice so that the polychrome confusion of the idols and ex-votos may have full play in the interior.

If the myth and the law, at this critical hour, no longer had the strength to hold the individual, architecture would no longer have the strength to hold sculpture. After having invaded with its increasing multitudes, in Greece, the friezes, the cella and all the unoccupied space on the rock of the fortress, in France, through the trades, the saints, flowers, animals, the entire façade, and the lateral porches of the ogival edifice, the statue descends into the streets, apartments, gardens. It is like the individual who puts his trust in quantity, in the measure that he acquires equal rights to mask the inequality of his abilities, but whose social quality gradually drops. We have seen its irresistible modifications. The portrait appears. The type is effaced. The passage tries to insinuate into the plane

[1] Fig. 29.

which it invades, as against the profile which it destroys, sensations, sentiments, and ideas which the stone or the marble, even when fondled and caressed by the light, are not capable of expressing. As the statue-maker, at the price of ruin, appeals to the processes of painting—values, contrasts, half-tones—so painting develops and flings itself ahead of man, attempting, like a loving siren, to snatch him from the social ship that is going to perdition. It is in the fourth century that the great painters of Athens—Parrhasios, Zeuxis, Apelles—appear. It is in the fifteenth century, in the Occident, that painting, through the artists of Avignon, the Flemings, the Burgundians, the Italians, begins to escape from its primitive processes in order to attempt to realize an expression that is complete and self-sufficient from the deepest, the most complex, the subtlest nuances of the spirit. At this hour, in the Occident as in Greece, the great religious architecture is no longer anything but a memory.

When painting appears, there is no longer room for sculpture, except perhaps for the decoration of fountains and gardens. And the greatest architecture is dead beyond call. What architecture and sculpture try to say at this moment painting alone is able to say. And this because it is—in plastics, be it understood—the only language that suits the emancipated individual. It is the emancipated, or, to express it better, the expanded individual.[1] One makes the tour of the edifice. One makes the tour of the statue. If the great syntheses that all are able, if not to comprehend, at least to experience, the great continuous contours of the masses, tending to geometrical expression, cease to be the language of the sculptor and the architect, it is because they no longer represent the common beliefs that can

[1] Fig. 31.

Fig. 31

INDIVIDUALIZATION OF THE OCCIDENTAL (Veronese)

be expressed only under their own unbroken, global, compact form, which is seized at a glance.

Painting is an entirely different thing. It is free. Its space is not real. It belongs to the spirit alone. Only the spirit can move in it, in every direction, in order to survey as it likes the masses and the arabesques on its surface and in its depth, to plunge the forms into the shadow, bring them out into the daylight, insinuate

Fig. 32
SYMPHONIC PAINTING (Rubens)

the daylight and the shadow into their most secret intervals, mask, proclaim, suggest as it likes the most complex and the simplest sentiments, the subtlest and the most energetic sensations, unchain together all the resources of its chromatic keyboard, extracting there a chord, touching here a note, creating the sea, creating the sky, veiling them in mist or clouds, making forests open or dense, speaking only of man or ignoring him completely. The painter is the religious or non-religious individual, cruel or tender, sensual or chaste, lyrical, story-telling, or dramatic, by turns or simultaneously;

he is free to be nothing but himself, to recreate for his own use a universe assured of being viable, however fantastic it may be, if only it is coherent and logical, even and more often especially, in spite of the decayed prejudices and superstitions of the crowd that emerge from the temple, as he does.

The decomposition of the organism, of which the crowd and he are elements that have been rendered independent, makes of the crowd merely an amorphous mass of elements without cohesion, lacking the cement of society and the myth. The individual alone can dispense with this cement since in his own heart he bears a myth and a society. In these redoubtable critical periods, in which almost all disoriented individuals wander in the arid solitudes of their spirit and no longer act save by their chance impulses or their habits, a few, and the painter in particular, carry on the heroism of the world. They have no other function than to recreate in their soul, in their own manner, the primitive unity, so as to transmit it intact to the organism that is to be. When the columns of the temple collapse the function of the painter-hero is to present his two shoulders for the burden of the architrave, until another approaches and permits him to die.

v

Let us examine more closely this powerful hold that painting exercises over strongly individualized times. Let us place ourselves immediately in the heart of the sixteenth century, when the masters of Venice seem to give the formula by which European painters will live for three hundred years. There, if one compares it with contemporary manifestations in the Orient or with those of the preceding century in Italy as well as in France, Flanders, or Germany, it already shows an evident symphonic character—to use, for the sake of a better understanding, the language of music.

Giorgione, Titian, Tintoretto, Veronese, preceding the musicians by two centuries, unite, in the painted work, all the elements that make it a world of complete expression. They do so for the first time in the modern world—for this, no doubt, was the less complicated task of Parrhasios among the ancients.[1] Space is conquered. Its laughter, and its peace, and its dramas, all its aspects enter into the moving form, in order to mold it by the play of reflections that mingle it with the light. No longer does anything stand separate from other things. An immense visual orchestra, through a permanent exchange of calls, echoes, values, entangled passages, attunes the storm that rises against the horizon to the nipple of a breast caressed by the shadow of a tree, adds to the death-scene of the day an amber necklace warmed by the skin that is inundated with blood, and makes the silhouette of a flower tremble in a rivulet, with the silver fringe of a cloud.

When this has come to pass, the series of forms gives to this universal, dancing movement of colored atoms that speak to each other and recognize each other, the profound reality of a lasting world, by means of the arabesque undulating about an invisible center, through all the dimensions of the imaginary space in which the spirit of the painter moves. Up to Giorgione and Titian, in spite of the effort of Masaccio,[2] painting remained melodic. As the singer unrolls his sonorous curve in a succession of sounds throughout time, the painter arranges in space his juxtaposed colors. The individual, in whom the elements of the social style in dissolution were placed beside one another before be-

[1] "He carries off the palm," says Pliny, "for those last touches that terminate and complete objects." This is perhaps the definition of value and the half-tone.

[2] Fig. 138.

coming a function of one another, advanced step by
step toward his proper unity, which he was not bound to
formulate save on the day when he had the audacity
and the genius to organize these scattered elements in
himself. When the social organism is complete, every
man carries his part. When it is broken down, a few
sing for all.

The glory of Italy, in the modern world, is to have
given birth to the first beings sufficiently strong to play
this rôle. This explains also why as a country it was
the first and the most quickly extinguished. Overwhelmed by his passions, the individual develops himself but wears himself out more rapidly than elsewhere.

The great individual symphony naturally appeared
in the country that was already affirming itself, in
Europe, as the most individualized since the epoch when
the French cathedrals expressed the Christian equilibrium at its most moving hour. Before the middle of
the twelfth century, Arnaldo da Brescia proclaimed the
Republic in the city of the papacy. When the first
university—that of Paris—appeared outside Italy, that
of Bologna had existed some fifty years. And it was
law that was taught there, and not theology. In the
thirteenth century, the Italian church had already lost
its primitive purity. While the Commune of the North
of France drew the best advantage it could from the
invention of the ogive, inviting the masses which were
already escaping from the Roman theocracy to build
its social poem, the Italian cities were substituting more
or less everywhere the municipal palace for the religious
edifice. The fierce crenelated walls rose upon the naked
flagstones, testifying to a particularism that accentuated itself from day to day. The individual grew up in
the midst of street quarrels, nourished on envy and
fury. Since that time when the image-maker and the
painter labored in France, rubbing elbows in the same

workshop, when no personal poem of lyricism or thought
dreamed of assembling in itself the multitudinous unity
of the cathedral, Francis of Assisi and Thomas Aquinas,
and presently Dante, Giotto,[1] Duccio, Simone Martini,
the brothers Lorenzetti[2] summed up in words, formulas,
or paintings of an admirable synthetic force, the most
conscious and the noblest things to which the Christian
idea was able to give birth in heads and in hearts. The
symphonists of Venice could be born when da Vinci,
Michael Angelo, Raphael, completing the effort of the
Tuscan melodists Angelico, Ghirlandajo, Lippi, Signorelli, Piero della Francesca[3] had cast into the mold
of their spiritual energy the Italian form that had
reached its most implacable reality: Italian individualism held so advanced a position that it preceded by an
entire century all the Occidentals who tried to express
the highest sentiments and the vastest sensations that
symphonic painting has ever tried to grasp. From the
middle of the sixteenth century, in fact, the social
body died in Italy, while in the Occident, thanks to the
religious wars, the moral energy maintained in the struggling creeds a spiritual cohesion which the social force
had not yet deserted. When this moral energy gives
way, when the individual thinks of the interests of his
purse more than of the interests of his faith, the harmonies of Velasquez assemble, about the face of a child,
the most secret things that wander in Spanish space, a
space which the silver of the mirages and the roses of
the twilights fill with the stir of flowers. Elsewhere,
the gigantic orchestra of Rubens organizes into its
tumultuous harmonies, the blood and the fatness of
Flanders, together with the trees and the waters con-
torted by its illumined mist. Elsewhere again one sees

[1] Figs. 81, 158.
[2] Fig. 94.
[3] Figs. 92, 142.

Fig. 33

HARMONY (Velasquez)

Rembrandt loading his canvas with the gold of glowing stuffs and the fire of the tropics in order to caress the brow of a poor man or illuminate a cradle.[1]

It is then neither in the Renaissance, nor in the Reformation, nor in the Revolution, no doubt destined to rend mediæval society asunder finally and deliver to all men the means to separate themselves from one another in order to liberate the elements of the re-modeled social body that, to my mind, resides the great event of the modern European world. It appears in this apparition of a new symphonic spirit sketched by the Venetians, introduced by Rubens, by Rembrandt, by Velasquez into the sensuality of Europe, by Spinoza and Leibnitz into its thought, by Newton and Lamarck into its science and by German music into its sentiment. The individual realized by the great painters of the seventeenth century was, upon his encounter with pessimism, to seek beyond it that pantheistic annihilation which is only a first step toward a new fusion of the elements scattered in the great common mold. The plastic symphony finally touches the limits of space everywhere; it can no longer emerge from it and move in its own sphere—an immense one but limited by the eyes. The intercrossed echoes of this sphere end by assuming a hollow and monotonous accent, and the plastic symphony will reach out toward music, which can construct an imaginary world liberated from every object and capable of carrying all hearts, beyond the visible world, to the infinite domain of the organizing illusion, where appears the spectacle of a will victorious over the abyss. When great painting tends to suggest the symphony of sound, it must give way to that symphony if it does not wish to die. It is very moving to realize that Keiser, Handel, Sebastian Bach were born

[1] Figs. 32, 33, 58.

a few years after the death of Velasquez and Rembrandt.

The poem of sound fills houses, gardens, streets, woods, villages, the ships on the waters, the places of worship and pleasure. It is endowed with a power of sensual solicitation which painting does not know. One must take some trouble to see painting, consent to open one's eyes and, especially, to reflect. The ear, on the contrary, even when one's attention wanders, is captivated by rhythm, the more so as this rhythm prolongs in time the relations, the accords, the passages that painting establishes in space alone. The poem of sound exercises over instinct a more insistent, more durable, more profound activity which, even if one resists, tears one away from one's thoughts. It is the fourth voice of man, which comes when men are separated to such a point from one another that, even when they ignore—even when they deny the fact, they tend to draw nearer to one another. It no longer expresses man at the summit of himself, but man allowing that summit to be assailed by murmurs, cries, complaints of other men, and the forgotten universe. Social pantheism does not possess any means of action more powerful than music. When music arises, architecture is not far away.

In the modern world, it is not difficult to see that it appears as the supreme instrument of integration, at the hour when painting, still too intellectual—although no doubt the very peak of the constructive intelligence —proves powerless to express the vague rebirth of the most intimate, the most diffuse and the most irresistible among all the social instincts. When Italian music arrives, great painting dies. And here once more it is under the form of the melodic arabesque that music offers a remedy for the almost complete general anarchy, so true it is that its hour has not come, since the plastic symphony is at this moment unfolding all its resources in the non-Italian Occident. The great melodist Monteverde is the contemporary of the great symphonist Rubens, and he is the first modern musician, for Palestrina prolonged the Gothic world at the very hour when Tintoretto was advancing with great strides into the era of the individual.

It is to the Germany of the eighteenth century where, after two hundred years of revolutions and wars, the social body is most divided, the individual most dispersed, least defined, most unhappy, that it is reserved to throw into confusion the plastic relations by plucking the sentimental relations from their disorder and orienting the world toward a new organism discarding the symphonies of the objective intelligence in order to unite the sole forces of hope and will. This was its function at the moment. This was also its historic mission. The master-singers were already building a sonorous, diffused, gregarious, organic cathedral at the hour when the master-masons in France were finishing the same labor, with stone, plumb-line, and glass. It is the rôle of music itself, which from remotest antiquity, has brought the nomad and the savage together to intone the chant of law. It is the rôle of the Orphic or Homeric *Ædes*, restoring the moral ruins of primitive Hellenism, that were scattered through the isles by the invasion of the Dorians. It is the rôle of plain-song which in primitive Catholicism where the individual still remained completely invisible, preceded by several centuries the architectural synthesis of the Occident. Whereas the painter-hero bears the multitude in himself, the musician-hero gathers it around him.

VI

However, I know exceptions—in the Helleno-Latin world and even in France—to the phenomenon of the rhythmic alternation that masks the evolution of art, and consequently of the spirit, and consequently of history. Among such exceptions are the utilitarian architecture of the Romans, the French civil architecture of the seventeenth and eighteenth centuries, both appearing on an unsettled social terrain at the moment when the myth had left men's hearts and the individual was trying to find himself amid the desert of his powers.

Fig. 34

Utilitarian Architecture (Rome)

When the great architecture of Rome appeared, the primitive religion had involved the aristocracy in its downfall, and in order to hold in check the common people, at every moment increased in number, stirred up, refreshed through the flowing back into Rome of antagonistic races, cults, systems and interests, a convulsive tyranny had replaced the granite mold in which the republican constitution had shut up the individual. Now, in the entire history of building, nothing is purer, nothing is harder, nothing is more categorical than these naked walls that suspend in space tiers, arches, and vaults, and spread, to the confines of the known world, the legalistic and order-bestowing spirit of the Romans. But there, precisely, is the key of the mystery. With the Roman myth dead and all the ancient civilizations entering the Latin city at the very hour when their own myths were also dying or confusedly outlining themselves in the bosom of an immense moral anarchy, a powerful political organism sprang up as best it could, alone knowing its object in the universal chaos, and alone dowered with an organizing science capable of remedying the absence of the social bond. Everywhere administration replaced religion. The moral law, in giving way, left the field free for the civil law. An era of expectation opened, in which the artificial armature imposed by the conqueror came to weld the spiritual fragments of a great amorphous body and, by revealing the common needs, prepared for the unfolding of a common confession.

It is under the Antonines that the statute of the Roman provinces attains its most robust organization and the Law assumes the character of the most solid civil monument of antiquity. But it is also under the Antonines that the most finished and the most imposing constructions of Rome rise up more or less everywhere, august masses, continuous curves, gigantic ramparts, dense matter, vertical weights, permitting the lightness and the audacities of structure which iron alone has since been able to attain, an order imposed by the intransigent formula of the legist and the engineer.[1] Utilitarian constructions responding to vulgar needs, as the written law imposed by force, in default of faith, responds to vulgar needs. But because they respond closely, without an error, without an oversight, without

[1] Figs. 34, 127, ?13.

an omission, they satisfy at the same time the spiritual needs that unite, through the intermediation of number, the most moving harmonies which the myth has inspired.

This was an expectant system, an arch thrown between two worlds, firm and bold as only an arch can be, because having a river to cross, it has no choice between several solutions. And perhaps we ourselves are present

Fig. 35

UTILITARIAN ARCHITECTURE (France, Saint-Pierre-du-Vauvray)

at an analogous phenomenon—in our epoch which recalls this other epoch in so many respects—in the dissolution, the interpenetration of myths, the flowing of races and peoples into one another, the universal ascent of the poor, and the vague outlines of a new mysticism. Perhaps, in the universal anarchy, when religious architecture has disappeared and civil architecture has gone astray, industrial architecture[1] is also the arch thrown between two worlds, substituting the activity of the scientific mentor for the activity of the decayed social myth, as the administrative and juridical

[1] Figs. 35, 71, 215, 218.

mentor formerly built, upon the ruins of this myth, his pitiless armature. Perhaps this modern mentor has been imagined not only to supply the place of the social myth in the measure in which he assures the material needs of man, but also to satisfy, as the Roman mentor once did, those common needs and interests susceptible of leading man on into common beliefs.

Fig. 36
RATIONALIST ARCHITECTURE (France, XVII Century)

We ourselves scarcely suspect what the Catholic edifice owes to the order-bestowing and regulating spirit of the Romans. Do we know what the spiritual organism, whose approach we anticipate, will owe to the continuous teachings of the factory and the machine, of the airplane, the ship, the automobile, the only modern monuments that resemble the constructions of the Roman engineers through their strict adaptation

to the exact ends expected of them, through their
trenchant precision, the beauty of their proportions,
their powerful lightness, and their aspect as of living
monsters? Like the Roman constructions, utilitarian
and only utilitarian, do they not offer us like them the
geometrical shelter in which we can taste the intoxication of a reality—and perhaps of a belief—in process
of becoming?

It is not altogether to the same causes that classic
French architecture has owed its appearance. If the
social myth, shaken by the Renaissance, had lost the
ardent ingenuity from which sprang the ogival art once
the monarchy was realized it maintained, through the
political and religious institutions, an equilibrium sufficient to prevent the individual from escaping from
their grasp. The genius of France is, first of all, architectural. But it tends to express its genius quite as
well in its painting, its philosophy, its literature, as in
its buildings and its gardens. It introduces it into
politics through its constant anxiety to realize the
State. It has attempted, through its resistance to
Protestantism, to maintain it in religion.

At the same time as Descartes, and at the hour when
the Venetian plastic polyphony was assuming its "freedom of the city" in Europe through Rubens, through
Rembrandt, and through Velasquez, Poussin[1] was somewhat neglecting the full range of his abilities in order
to express monumental rhythms in painting. For one
hundred and fifty years, France, bewildered by the
sudden rise of Italy, was searching for the powerful
faculty that had once permitted it to write, during
almost four centuries, the loftiest poem in stone of the
Occident. It had attempted a hybrid architecture in
which the profuse anemia of the Gothic decoration
destroyed the Italian profile, itself already considerably

[1] Fig. 147.

compromised by the press of individualism that at the same epoch substituted, in the peninsula, the great symphonic painting for the trenchant simplicity of the building. It had not yet assimilated, or even truly considered this great painting, preserving as it did in its corporations and its religious struggles, enough enthusiasm and social passion to conserve the anguished desire for architecture, but possessing already individuals sufficiently well defined to prevent it from coming to a head.

The double influence of the monarchy and of Cartesianism came in time to prevent this growth of individuality through centralization in the field of politics and method in the field of theory. It retarded the final dissociation by substituting for the abolished collective mysticism an intellectual construction, ingenious but hardly durable for reason was to end only too quickly in rationalism, as faith, in other days, ended in dogmatism. In spite of all, the check functioned with a power unique in the history of the spirit. After the Romanesque, after the Gothic, came a third complete order.[1] Bare pilasters, alternating regularly with the rectangular, vertical, and horizontal windows, restoring, through their rhythmic and measured play, the civil edifice to the scale of the intelligence, were to substitute for nearly two centuries, to the delight of practical reason, the rectilinear deductions of the highest culture for the symmetrical axioms of the highest theology and for the radiant intuitions of the highest equilibrium that ever existed between the popular fervor and the social system. Gardens, roads, bridges, tragedy, comedy, music, morality, sculpture, painting, all obey at the same time this need for the subordination of the sensibilities and the passions to the cadences of the will.

A kind of semi-anonymity prevails, giving to this

[1] Fig. 36.

time a little of the character of those in which the individual is completely effaced. The statues in the alleys,
the basins of the fountains of Versailles, the colonnades,
the trees, the architecture of the fountains appear, at
first sight, to be from
the same hand. A
cold but severe and
magnanimous unity,
whose elements lack
prominence and ac-
cent, prevents us from
distinguishing these
elements of the en-
semble, or from imag-
ining that they can
express the aspira-
tions, the anxieties,
the torments of a
single spirit. In the
Alexandrine, one finds
the three unities, the
entire bureaucratic
organization, the
academies, the school
of Rome, the same
impersonality. If ec-
clesiastical architec-
ture repels Calvinism,
Jansenism represents,
in the bosom of the

Fig. 37

INDIVIDUALIZATION OF EGYPT
(Greek Period)

Church, a constructive moral reaction against the psychological dissociation which the Jesuit pursues. No
one at this time takes La Fontaine seriously. Pascal
is shocking. The Le Nains are ignored. This whole
order leads France, and the world behind it,—staggering
a little, attenuating from day to day the walls, the

supports, the theme, the idea, the word, and by the natural bent of a pitiless logic,—to the Revolution. But when the sentimentalism of Rousseau has broken Cartesianism, when the individualism of Voltaire has broken the corporation, there is no longer a single force, either social or spiritual, capable of constraining and containing the individual. He throws himself into the integral discovery of himself, with a fury the less dissimulated because, in spite of the half-Flemish Watteau,[1] he is almost three hundred years behind the painters of Venice, almost two hundred years behind the painters of the Low Countries or Spain, almost one hundred years behind the German musicians. With a splendid intoxication and at a single stroke, Romantic painting in France realizes the individual symphony[2] and new elements of drama, of the picturesque, of emotion. But it is to the detriment of architecture, the glory and sustenance of this country for eight centuries, which also gives way at a single stroke. A double and grandiose catastrophe leading the social body in an inverse march to the bottom of the abyss and leading the chosen individual to the summit of the spirit. In fact, we perceive here the disorganization which the emancipation of man inflicted on society by breaking the organism that architecture expresses, and also the oppression this organism inflicted upon man by forbidding him access to the miraculous unity which polyphony alone could win for him. . . . I know no more striking testimony to the power and the cruelty of the myth, and at the same time to the solitary grandeur and the powerlessness of the hero.

VII

Now, outside the ancient European world, outside Christian civilization, were things happening the same

[1] Fig. 57.   [2] Fig. 157.

way? Does one see everywhere, as one has seen it in
Greece, in France, in Italy, in Occidental Europe in
general, the man-statue emerging from the society-
architecture in order to define itself through painting
and tending, through the intoxication of music, to recreate the social spirit and the edifice destined to shelter
this spirit?

The Oriental civilizations are not easily penetrable
by us. The block, at first, is closed. When we insinuate
ourselves into it, the immense network of popular
polytheism and philosophic pantheism forbids us to
advance there. A troubled atmosphere surrounds it,
enervates it, like the breath of flowery marshes from
which fever rises, almost unbreathable by us, who love
distinct contours, light air, clear waters. The rapid
evolution of the civilizations of Europe, born, ripening,
declining in the course of a period that does not exceed
four or five centuries—sometimes one or two, as in
Spain or in Holland—has ill prepared us to comprehend
these motionless metaphysical monuments to which
legend accords sometimes ten thousand years of existence, for which History has not been able to fix a
beginning.

At first, for example, if one places oneself at a little
distance in order to embrace the ensemble, neither religion, nor philosophy, nor the social organization of
Egypt, China, India, appear to have changed sensibly
since time immemorial. During five thousand years we
know only one religion, which is moreover esoteric, in
Egypt. India returns to Brahmanism after having
created Buddhism, then absorbed it in the mystical
flood that ascends unceasingly from the sensual depths
of its imagination. China, which at first welcomes
Buddhism, employs its long, somnolent, and grim patience in recovering gradually the thousand little practices of its utilitarian fetishism. Islam suppresses almost

suddenly the manifestations of its spiritual activity rather than change one fragment of its social system. It is necessary to accept or reject these gigantesque constructions *en bloc.*

It is their massive character that first introduces us into the intimate reality of their creative genius. The spirit of architecture dominates it. Or rather, form is scarcely conceived outside the building. Even if the structure is devoid of a major plastic value, as in India, sculpture and painting appear in it only as detached debris.[1] But if the building is bare, as in China, sculpture, although isolated, shows its relation with it by preserving its architectonic appearance even in the most bristling heraldic monsters. Even if, as in Islam, there is neither sculpture nor painting apart from architecture, one sees ornament ending in a geometrical formula that does not permit to the decorator any excursion into life.[2] If the great alternative rhythm exists in these amorphous organisms, it will only be in a rudimentary way, rising and descending from century to century or even from millenniun to millennium, like a tide that does not sensibly change the general aspect of the sea and in no respect alters the mass. Even when one cannot trace it there distinctly, a fact subsists: since religion, morality, and the social bond remain intact, nothing emerges completely from the architectonic sphere in the interior of which the spirit consents to move.

We know too little about the history of Egypt to work out from it these alternating periods. Sometimes we think we grasp them. But the chronology deceives us. This statue which we imagine to be later than this other which is more archaic in aspect, is on the contrary earlier by a thousand or two thousand years. The uniformity of Egyptian statuary is only apparent. A

[1] Fig. 131.   [2] Fig. 114.

series of fluxes and refluxes gullies the surface. But their depth escapes us, and their significance. For we are almost completely ignorant of the variations of the doctrine, and of the social movements to which these variations respond, their echoes in literature, morality,

FIG. 38

MUSICAL SCULPTURE (Egypt)

customs. Nevertheless, a few phenomena identical with those that mask everywhere the decomposition of the social body appeared toward the decline of the culture of Egypt. And they are significant. Thus, from the Saïte epoch, when the individual portrait became common—the statue still preserving its architectonic air[1]— no more temples were built. Thus, the Greco-Roman

[1] Fig. 173.

epoch saw the spirit of mass and cohesion crumble in the statue and even in the portrait—the spirit in which Egypt had defined itself during fifty centuries—to a point where the sphinx and the gods contemporaneous with the Ptolemys had completely forgotten their religious or symbolic character and constituted an industry of household goods of the poorest quality.

Thus the Christian epoch coincided with the appearance of these painted portraits[1] in which the inner life blazes out, hallucinating, musical, radiant, and at the same time concentrated, an immense afflux of simple souls invaded by faith. The passage of the Egyptian organism into the Christian organism experienced the poignant crises undergone by all Hellenism at the same epoch, in the course of which it seemed that the social world was ruined forever and the individual was set aimlessly adrift, the great architecture and the great sculpture no longer being even a memory.

As long as the Egyptian social edifice endures, in any case, that is to say up to Rameses III, Egyptian art did not even conceive the individual as independent of this edifice, and if we ourselves attempt to conceive its statuary as independent of its architecture, we do not comprehend it. Not that it pretends to associate it with construction. On the contrary, it separates from it more distinctly than in Greece. It leaves naked its hermetic temples, shutting up in their closest shadow some mummy of a crocodile, some statuette of a hawk. But during four or five thousand years, the statue does not emerge from the geometrical principle that presides at the arrangement of hydraulic works, at the building of the pyramids, the temple porches, the gigantesque colonnades imposing the genius of man on the monotonous universe.

This is still more impressive, more significant, than

[1] Fig. 37.

the progressive emergence of the statue out of the sanctuary that marks the plastic epopee of Europe. Egyptian society is so hierarchized, so strictly imbricated in the political organism, massive as those blocks of basalt supported for eternity by their weight alone in the hypostyle halls, that it leaves the individual free to dream as he likes within the absolute limits which it traces for him on all sides. Thus the engineer of the country digs the reservoirs and the canals outside which the water of the Nile cannot spread, thus nature herself sets, by the line of the alluvion, an implacable separation between the nourishing earth which the dampness penetrates and the unfertile earth which the sun sterilizes. The Egyptian statue[1] moves in the interior of its own frontiers outside of which begins the reign of fiery space. It is a form in itself, a microcosm. It has no reason for being, if it is not conceived geometrically, according to the plan of the visible universe that begins where it ends.

The age-old immutability of the laws that cause wheat to grow explains here in the most certain fashion the immutability of the soul. The individual depends upon it to such a point that his profound instinct forbids him to go beyond the geometrical form which the regularity of natural phenomena imposes on his relations with the political order and which cadences, in its grandiose monotony, the rhythm of his spirit. If his energy and his curiosity give way, the academic formula will intervene in order to maintain them notwithstanding in the frame fixed by nature and law. If they abandon him altogether he will give way to men bringing from outside into this absolute immobility of the banks of life, the revolutionary mobility of their passions. And, remaining the same at bottom, the individual will let his temples crumble while he con-

[1] Figs. 27, 38, 173, 175, 197.

tinues to sow, watch things grow, and gather the wheat at the same periods, from the beginning to the end of time.

There is the Egyptian mystery. The individual appears there furtively, is indicated with an exquisite and sometimes cunning finesse in the painting of the tombs in which all the regular, busy, humble, and healthy life of the boatman, the shepherd, the farmer, the miller stands out on the high walls in features as subtle as the poetry of dawn in the country, the trembling of the waters, the beating of wings, the uninterrupted warbling of birds, as the calyxes of flowers opening to the dew, as the singing of oarsmen, the quivering of grasses, or as precious stones clear and trembling on all sides.[1] But he never emerges from it, any more than the astronomical universe itself, any more than the caste that maintains him, in law and myth, discipline and instruction. Its slow, limited evolution is accomplished exclusively within the great architectonic rhythm.

One sees, in the very mass of the cube of basalt, diorite or granite, the limbs of the statue unloosening a little, becoming rounded, tapering off, the features of the face allowing the imprisoned flame to filter through, and its spirit requiring the undulating planes that limit it to insist only a little here, to escape furtively there, to prolong, through a miracle of the associated plastic and poetic sentiments, their uninterrupted modulations up to the secret limits of an interior space which the light from without embraces on all the surfaces in order to unite solidly with it.[2]

Since the sculptor cannot emerge from the necessary myth and the visible world, the invisible world belongs to him. Within the impassable limits of the image, he can subtilize, caress, modulate its mass to infinity in order to prolong it everywhere over the continuous wave

[1] Fig. 90.   [2] Fig. 38.

of a mute harmony. A unique miracle. The intentions
of painting take the directions of music by means of
sculpture which, on all sides, is blocked out in the impeccable profiles of construction. The individual symphony is accomplished silently in the statue itself while
the painting of the tombs nowhere oversteps the bounds
of the melody. One would say that Egypt wishes to
signify in this way to future times that everything can
be expressed between the rigid frontiers of the most
intransigent myth, on condition that it does not substitute the individualistic principle for the individual
reality, but also that it does not sacrifice this same
reality to the social principle. Individualism, it is true,
momentarily takes its revenge in teaching Egypt that
an organism, however logical and formidable it may be,
perishes within its own frontiers if it does not appeal
some day to the individual passions in order thus to
surprise the constitutive elements and prepare their
future combination in a different order.

In India, the spectacle, at first very remote from the
former, offers, if one considers it closely, singular analogies to it. There is no geometry here. It is all a
confused organism, budding with succulent plants un-
equal in height, form, distribution upon some poisoned
marsh. And yet, nothing escapes any longer from a
tyrannical social conception that invokes, in order to
subsist, the spiritual delight of a sinister and grandiose
myth represented on the earth by the implacable regime
of castes and maintaining itself for thirty centuries
without sensibly stirring. Or rather, in that case stirring inwardly without admitting anything from without, or assimilating in a moment what comes from
without, like a sombre flood, swarming with monsters
and covered with brilliant flowers, which undulates
slowly between the choked banks of a religion as fertile,

in the renewing of its symbols, as birth and death. As
the mild and regular milieu of the one place engendered
optimism and induced the individual to establish himself in an immobile social system, the chaotic, inclement,
feverish milieu of the other engenders pessimism and
forbids the individual, even if he wishes to escape from
a pitiless mystical system, to overstep an expanse that
is too constantly in motion for him to be able to determine its boundaries.

Here the individual unceasingly lifts above the flood
a brow, a hand, a knee. But the flood always draws him
in again. Hindu sculpture makes one think of a man
engulfed in the mud and struggling in vain to emerge
from it. Lyricism and despair rub shoulders in people's
souls. The religious and sensual spirit emerges from
an eternally moving matter that creates it every moment and swallows it up the moment after.

Hindu sculpture[1] is the image of this universal movement which does not emerge from its indefinite frontiers
and whose very lack of definiteness forbids it to emerge.
As in Egypt the pictorial spirit undulating with subtlety in the mass of the statue refused to quit the social
edifice, here the pictorial spirit tries at every instant to
overflow the sculpture, in order to enter it again at
once with a kind of sadness. Here, no more than the
gods, no more than individuals, no more than architecture itself, is sculpture arrested. A disorderly and tragic
movement animates it. Through great shafts of light
and shadow, through powerful contrasts incessantly
provoked and broken, it overwhelms the delicately
shaded rock in the manner of a painting, by throwing
into relief or effacing such prominences as the undulations of reptiles, the sudden leaps of wild animals, or
the spasms of love. The sculpture remains drowned in
its atmosphere of stone. The fevered spirit rushes into

[1] Figs. 39, 131, 132, 177, 178, 207, 216.

eccentric experiments condemned unceasingly to defeat, but imposing on the sculptured material the spirit of great painting. This is the opposite of Egypt where the sculptured material is constantly subdued to the spirit of architecture in order to live concentrically.

But, here as there, the whole problem turns about the individual emerging from the social mold and resolves itself in sculpture which there refuses to emerge from the temple and here cannot emerge from it. And as it took the Greco-Roman invasion to make Egypt leave its hermetic block, it was only at the beginning of the tenth century, when the Musselman appeared in India, then the Christian, that a little foreign air entered this intoxicating atmosphere, while architecture, entirely spiritualized at the outset, became attenuated very quickly, grew exhausted, and vulgarized, and sculpture, which changed in former days the shape of the mountains, began to lose itself in anecdote, the picturesque, and ornament.

It was, moreover, at the moment of the great Buddhist epoch that Hindu sculpture changed the form of the mountains, as it changed it in China and had the strength to raise, in Cambodia and in Java,[1] the monumental enchantments of which the universe common to man, to forests, to animals formed a part in order to whirl there, dance there, disappear like an *apsara* declaimed by the thousand united voices of violins, brass instruments, tambourines, human voices, indistinct murmurs, and mingled perfumes. Buddhism was to penetrate Hindu pessimism and Chinese positivism by means of sculpture, because it developed about a need for social idealism that conditioned the discovery and the culture of the individual. But, in China as in India, the unity of the ideal edifice was such that it took four or five centuries, as in Egypt it took four or five millenniums, to complete this formidable event:

[1] Figs. 91, 97, 136, 188.

a hundred men, a thousand men perhaps, cut into the same rock the image of the same god, without having the image of this god emerge from a unity so strictly united to their spiritual structure that it seemed to spring from the same heart, to be conceived by the same head, realized by the same hand.[1]   An analogous phenomenon took place a few centuries later in the Christian Occident and more especially in France, if we compare the cathedral with a thousand voices to the colossus or the carved grotto.   And it was an inverse phenomenon that brought, like the Greek decadence, the Renaissance of the Occident: often a thousand anarchic individuals seemed to have carved the most fragile statuette, composed the smallest picture. The symphonic unity has left the multitude and its dispersed elements to take refuge entirely in the heart, the head, the hand of the hero.

In China, in India, as in Mexico, or in Islam, as in Egypt, as in Dorian Greece and mediæval Europe, the hero is almost unknown.   The legend of Rama appeared with Buddhism, and it is indeed his history that blossoms on the palace of Angkor.   But it is the only instance and the only place in the Orient that one can compare with the Parthenon and the cathedral for the equilibrium which they seek between the adventure of man and the immobility of the god.   In the Orient the hero is the multitude.   One sees marching, across the Chinese desert, colossal statues, warriors, elephants, dromedaries, and horses, united like the buildings with the plain and suggesting, in the solitude, those natural accidents that mark its character like the geological skeleton that crops out of the soil here and there.   The earth rises in them, it accompanies them, as it accompanies everywhere the Chinese cultivator, who is entirely impregnated with it, and to whom his familiar divinities reveal

[1] Fig. 40.

Fig. 39

PICTORIAL SCULPTURE (India)

the consistency of soil, the direction of the wind, the phase of the moon, or the weather propitious for his work.

If the individual appears faintly, and very timidly, it is, as in India, from the time when European armies arrive and rend asunder the common edifice where the individual took shelter. The multiplicity of cults, torn to pieces by fetishism, is only moss on the surface of the motionless moral rock which the ancestors have erected. And if a style of painting,[1] as moving as the mingled voices of flutes, hautboys, and harps, a style profound, discreet, emanating from abstract space like a molecular condensation, appears in the Buddhist convents precisely at the hour when Buddhism, between the eighth and the twelfth centuries, tends to return little by little into the social monument that changes only in appearance, it does not quit the harmonic themes in which the great individual symphony does not even dream of appearing.

It is like a vague attempt to disengage from the social body a few rare melodies. It only interprets the universe supported by its neighbors, talking with them in undertones, murmuring beside them, embroidering like a silken tissue the subtle veil which the anchorite places gently on his soul in order that the innumerable multitude of disciplined souls may not know by what insensible detours he sometimes deserts his roads. Taken *en bloc*, China, its sculpture, its pottery, and its bronzes veined like viscera, is shut up in a hermetic and circular form from which it cannot emerge. One must go to Japan, its pupil, to find a rhythm analogous to those that have characterized the Occident.

When sculpture, here, has broken the Buddhist profiles in order to gesticulate in the age far from the religious organism, painting rapidly appears, then the

[1] Fig. 41.

Fig. 40

COLLECTIVE UNITY (China)

nicknack, the article of trade, the carving of furniture, anticipations of a growing individualism which ends by bursting the armor of the mediæval period but which thereby destroys itself also.

Japan stands out in Asia as an exception.

We know the names of all her painters, the names of all her engravers, almost all those of her sculptors after the Buddhist epoch, even those of her potters, her blacksmiths, her carpenters, and her gardeners. A profound phenomenon, which always denotes a social analysis, effectuated or in process of becoming. If one finds it in China only in connection with painting, that is to say the faint attempt made by the individual to differentiate himself a little, if not to emerge from the social body, it is entirely unknown in India where not a single one of the confused waves of the ocean of forms bears a name.

It is entirely unknown in Egypt, where the geometrical rigor of the mass to be built demands an impersonality equal to that of science. Almost unknown among the Arabs, almost among the Persians, save in the sixteenth century, when the individual tends to appear in painting. It is the significant sign that appears in Italy after the Middle Ages and repeats itself and multiplies with incredible profusion, whereas in France it appears only in the fifteenth century,[1] when the worker quits the workshop of the Church for the antechamber of the château, and from that time on is stressed from century to century to the point of insanity, as happens throughout the Occident. It marks equally the passage of the Hellenic social organism at the very first symptoms of its dissociation, for the names of the Greek sculptors only appeared between Solon

---

[1] We have only known the names of the master-builders since the records of the municipalities have been opened up; but before the fifteenth century, not a single name of a sculptor.

and Pisistratus, when its architectonic sheath begins to incommode the statue. And its absence is the more striking in Byzantium since one observes there, during

FIG. 41
THE INNER MELODY (China)

four or five centuries, the annihilation of Greek individualism, its confused absorption by the pantheism of Asia in which sculpture and painting sink back into the basilica, just as the individual returns to the

Church to form for himself there a pretext and a center of communion.

Nothing demonstrates better than these periodic silences the living reality of the great alternating rhythm that runs through the very center of the arts. When architecture dominates, the anonymous is the rule. When sculpture appears, a few names emerge, at first legendary. From the moment when painting arises, one knows all the names of the painters, as well as all of the sculptors, and often even the builders. Music, through the processions which it regulates, through the dance which it quickens, tends to make the individual enter the crowd again and the name return to obscurity. All this is deeply impressive. If the community spirit prevails, humility is the law, since man believes like man and an inner bond identifies them profoundly. If the critical spirit disrupts this bond, the mystical communion takes refuge in the isolated man who has, hopes to have, or believes he has the strength to maintain it among us and whose sword is called, according to the quality of this force, vanity, self-sufficiency, pride or consciousness of a superior destiny and mission.

The name on one hand, and anonymity on the other, are signs of epochs. According as one or the other prevails, we know how the relations of each man with the social body or with the individual will be determined: with the name, romance, psychology, painting, with anonymity, architecture, metaphysics, law.

VIII

Henceforth, the words that one is accustomed to use in order to designate the different aspects of the styles— primitive, archaic, classic, academic, decadent, etc.— seem to me to assume a meaning much more human than that with which they are generally endowed.

Stone and dust, they become thought and blood. They
are the songs of the epopee. One thinks, in connection
with them, of the adventurous and at the same time
necessary course of the organisms into life.

Emerging from the original confusion, one sees them
appear in formless masses, without differentiated
organs, then attempt an embryonic order in which the
organs shape a rough, inexact form, the members of
which seem to be still engaged in the obscure matrix,
then, through the more and more complex and harmonious blending of the great instincts rising toward consciousness, the forms acquire, thanks to the solidarity
of the energies that travel over them, ease and sureness,
then an inner wastage attacks the tissues, the organs
pass into deliquescence, or, on the contrary, ossify,
the mutual relations hesitate and presently are lost.
. . . A grandiose fatality thus assures eternal birth,
eternal growth, eternal old age, eternal death. A
fatality that determines, no doubt, by maintaining it
in the same pitiless orbit, the unity of thought and the
moving variety of the appearances it assumes. The
human spirit turns unceasingly in a circle, but it perceives, from each of the points of this circle, in proportion as this circle turns with it, continually, different
landscapes.

There is nothing in common, for example, between
archaism,[1] engaged entirely in a global conception of
form whose roots plunge into the social myth and whose
methods are borrowed from the architecture that expresses it, and the primitivism that gropingly seeks,
on the contrary, to free the form from its archaic bonds
in order to make it express the sensations and ideas
that are personal to the painter. No doubt, whatever
may be the rhythm of an epoch, there are, in all epochs,
in order to maintain the need of changing the rhythm.

[1] Fig. 42.

spirits in advance of it, spirits behind it: furtively, here, in the center of architecture, a primitive appears, and there, in the full current of individualism, a classic monument rises, recalling the greatest hours of the myth at its apogee. But, in taking a wide view of the movements of the spirit, one cannot but discover in it a constant pulsation.

FIG. 42

ARCHAIC SCULPTURE

(France, XI Century)

When there are only individuals, there is no archaism, or then it is an artifice, as one sees it appear in those periods of extreme social decomposition in which the too intelligent man sets himself to search for his primitive purity and, in despair, demands of the past the lost architectonic rhythms. Where there are no individuals, there is no primitivism, or then it is something that has come from a faraway race or religion that attempts to stammer a language which it does not hear. Archaism is at the threshold of organisms that are growing: it is the nubility of space. Primitivism is at the threshold of analyses that are opening: it is the nubility of man. And although there can exist archaic painters contemporaneous with still complete organisms —such as the miracle of Italian individualism expressing to itself alone, through Giotto, the immense social complexity—although there can exist primitive sculptures contemporaneous with beginning analyses, it is necessary to consider both these cases as exceptions.

The sculptured form is attached to the idea of archaism, the painted form to the idea of (primitivism). The sculptor, who has scarcely emerged from the archaic matrix, attains already a great harmonic equilibrium while the painter feels his way among unknown materials. Della Quercia, Ghiberti, Donatello, full-blown, complete sculptors, possessing all the resources of form in movement are older or of the same age as Fra Angelico[1], who would suffice to define primitive art in its most touching aspect, but also the one in which it most humbly seeks to discover the privileges and the means of painting. Giovanni Pisano himself, born more than a century before Angelico, seems younger than he. In France, Jean Goujon, in whose undulating elegance already appears the disquieting note of the social world that will make the sculpture of the eighteenth century one of the most delicious of things, but one of the most fragile because it is as far removed as possible from the conditions of that art, is the contemporary of François Clouet who did not yet suspect the harmonic inter-crossings through which the great painting was to determine the musicians to demand of the orchestra resources it did not yet possess.

There is something profoundly dramatic in these contemporary voices, rising from the same desires, victims of the same disappointments, aiming at the same hopes, that seek each other and are concealed from each other because they do not use the same language or, if they do speak it, falsify it, and unwittingly express, on one hand that which gives way and is lost, on the other that which is fortified and concentrated in the spirit of a race unanimously bound for the same ends.

[1] Figs. 43, 44.

Fig. 43

PRIMITIVE PAINTING
(Fra Angelico, xv Century)

The elements of the fugue call, reply, advance, pursue, pass each other, retrace their steps in a vast, captivating ensemble that reconciles its contradictions and its antagonisms in order to force the unity of man to achieve its poem in spite of the difficulties and the snares of the road.

Thus the drama pursues its way to the end. Academism, which invokes classicism, has a contrary purpose, since academism, in those epochs when the fermentation is most acute, when all laws, all systems, all dogmas are under discussion, when the family is dismembered, when the leprosy of interests and the flame of intelligence consume the ruined social body, maintains a miserable fiction of order and unity in chaos, while round about it a

Fig. 44

MATURE SCULPTURE (Della Quercia, XV Century)

thousand new expressions are born or developed, and a few men concentrate the chaos in the order and unity of their spirit.

Academism is made for poverty-stricken souls, for the herd without a master wandering with the random guidance of its most vulgar sentiments in search of the most facile—since they are the most habitual—expressions which other poor souls suggest to it. It is the only tendency in which there is no sense of the drama which, when it appears, resolves the symphony of color or sound in the heart of the solitary and which classicism, in all epochs, has resolved in the unanimity of consciences or hearts.

For if antiquity knows at least one classic point of equilibrium that responds to the fugitive instant when man, appearing in the bosom of the myth, succeeds, through a powerful effort, in maintaining its intoxication in his rising intelligence, France has twice known this strange hour. Once, at the moment when the Romanesque and the Gothic confronted each other with their antagonistic conceptions, theocratic architecture arriving at the very height of its task, saw sculpture invading its porches and capitals just when the nerves and the long shafts of stone spring forth from all sides in order to raise, aerate, rock the immense vessel. The other occasion, more restricted but more evident, at the moment when the Occidental soul, in decomposition, was bringing from Italy the elements of an individual style and thus threatening to overwhelm France and that country worked out an intellectual construction capable of enclosing this style in an expression of the ensemble and of reascending the flood.

These moments are perhaps the summits of the plastic drama, and note clearly—the Greece of Phidias and Sophocles is not an exception—it is just when they supervene that tragedy appears: however awkward and

stiff it may be in the twelfth century, at the hour when
the crisis of collective consciousness bursts forth and
shines, making of Chartres the most profound drama
in stone that men have erected, it is in the twelfth
century that tragedy introduces the pathetic element
into the Miracle play, wrested from the clergy at the
same time as architecture and sculpture, and written
in the vulgar tongue to be heard by all.

Fig. 45
CREATIVE DECADENCE (Bonnard)

Just half way between Corneille and Racine, Versailles subordinates the anguish of lofty consciences to
victorious reason, an anguish not stilled in the heart of
the tragic poet whose name is Pascal. And as to the
Prometheus of Æschylus, whose lamentations fill the
interval that separates the drama of Olympia from the
drama of the Parthenon, it is the central point of a
greater symbolic drama that stretches between the

myth of Adam expelled through knowledge from the terrestrial paradise and Jesus, discovering, through knowledge, in his intimate paradise, a new intoxication from which the cathedral will spring. It is perhaps by chance that Hindu tragedy seems to be contemporaneous with those sculptured caverns to which Buddhism, threatened with being swallowed up anew in Brahmanism, summoned the forests, the rivers, the beasts, fornication and death to the aid of the inner man whom universal matter was engulfing. But in any case, in the Northern races, drowned in the rain and consequently ignorant of the plastic drama, did not Shakespeare appear at the very moment when, standing on the threshold of the social edifice which the fall of Catholicism had shaken, the individual comes to affirm that he alone can raise it up again?

Tragedy is the meeting point, in the consciousness of the poet, of the ancient values that have reached their maximum of spiritual maturity and the new values that spring up on every side.

Tragedy, in all cases, contents itself with affirming. It has never held back a race on the edge of the abyss. On the contrary, that course is quickened when drama becomes more widespread, when the poet has known how to assemble it, opening up, in the spectator, unsuspected avenues, awakening passions and terrible curiosities, arousing the need to try its heroic strength, or to submit its weakness to the ordeal of hell.

Launched into the future with the individual, painting, then music, accompanied by the novel and later by the resurrection of lyricism, cause to appear in certain spirits, either for blame or praise, possibilities of a communion whence new forms will spring up. The word "decadence" has no meaning unless one envisages a civilization as a closed circle outside of which everything is darkness and will remain darkness. But the world has other resources in its need to live, and therefore its need to create unceasingly, and in the superb indifference with which it takes from the chosen race the flame which will illumine the race yet to be chosen for the realizations of which neither the one nor the other knows the meaning or the aspect. What one calls "decadence"[1] is precisely the epoch in which the greatest number of differentiated elements ferment, decay, die, spring up or grow, and in which, consequently, new relations appear, in which unsuspected groups are organized, in which virgin forces are united for the sake of a future they will not see. If everything dies of the principle that causes it to be born, if, for instance, Greece is killed by its limited research for truth in the object, Islam, through its exclusive spiritualism which pursues the arabesque in a too abstract circle, India through the sensuality that engulfs its spirit, everything is born again of the same principle that has caused it to die elsewhere.

Greece built its house with materials gathered amid the Assyrian, Egyptian, Phœnician ruins. It is thanks to the already degenerate Greek statues brought by Alexander to the Indus in his military chariots that the immense flood of Hindu sculpture, through the mediation of Buddhism, inundates Asia. And who knows if the first Egyptian statue was not born and will not be reborn of some immemorial form, already in a period of decline, which black Africa introduced, by its caravans, into the upper valley of the Nile?[2] The Byzantine decomposition endows Italy with the idol the adoration of which gives life to it. France beholds three centuries of the agony of the Italian spirit. Moreover, these beneficent invasions are anticipated and desired in people's hearts. With the historic drama, the plastic

[1] Fig. 45.
[2] Figs. 47, 49, 93 bis, 198–199.

drama continues. Negation, hazard, despair, paradox can feed the fire as much as faith. The continuity of an effort never lies in imitating the external appearances of the effort that preceded. It can go forward much more truly in forms that appear to contradict it than in forms that pretend to continue it. When, for instance, some civilization, reaching the extremity of analysis, breaks and throws into confusion its idols and, rather than copy itself indefinitely, attempts, with their débris, to outline some barbaric form that seems the antithesis of the mission it has fulfilled, does it not thus give the noblest proof of the courage of man, who, even at the cost of disavowing his past, keeps on imagining in order not to die?

FIG. 45 A

FIG. 46

NEGRO SLAVES (Egypt)

Chapter II. THE IMPRINTS

I

TAKE any tribe of negroes or Polynesians. From the first hours of your contact with it, an astonishing fact transports you with enthusiasm or indignation.

It is spontaneously artistic.

The black man practices without relaxation, without effort, and with an ardor that borders on violence, all the primitive forms of art. They are his very existence. He lives them, so to speak, in the activity of every day. He is, in truth, drunk with sound and color. Feverish cadences, burning visual orgies veil his eyes, hum in his head, mingled with wild odors and too heavy perfumes.

He scans his work and his walk with rhythmic chants
and songs. The rows of silver circles about his arms,
his neck, his legs, gleam and ring at every step. Everything for him is a pretext for music and the dance,
nubility, betrothal, marriage, funerals, the departure
for the hunt or war, ritual feasts, meals, music, the
dance in which all the women, all the men, all the children of the tribe take part.

The industries of the household, of costume, war, the
chase, are inseparable, in their origins, from the first
and the most essential manifestations of art. There is
no trade that is not the continuous exercise of a lyricism
that is rudimentary but impossible to restrain. The
currier, the potter, the jeweler, the smith, the carver,
the armorer, the embroiderer, the dyer reveal themselves as born artists through the sureness of decoration,
of ornament, of the association, a hundred times varied
and always infallible, of tones. Everything is carved—
utensils, arms, furniture, masks for the dance, for the
hunt, for war. Everything painted or dyed—cotton
drawers, thongs, belts, boxes, seats, mats, shields.

The idols, cut in rugged and simple planes, in a candid
care for the most intense expression, and besmeared
with blue, ochre or red to sharpen the accent, burn with
a life that is abstract and furious at the same time.[1]
Whether the African stains his earthen walls that are
like coagulated blood, or the Polynesian chisels his
wooden cabins with scrolled volutes of which one finds
the multicolored repetitions on the skin of his body and
his face, a permanent attraction to the sensual side of
everything that has life form obliges the black man
to pursue it and emphasize it everywhere. If others—
the white, for instance—seem to possess before all the
moral and social sense of life, the negro has the rhythmic
sense to such a degree that he cannot conceive or express

[1] Fig. 47.

it otherwise than according to sonorous rhythms, formal or elementarily colored, but as irrepressible as the beating of his heart.

FIG. 47

RHYTHM (Negro Art)

Once, says Gobineau, when there existed three primitive races—the black, sensual, impulsive, drunk with rhythm and color; the yellow, close to the earth, charmed with well-being and somnolent reverie; the white, energetic, war-loving, made to create order and dominate—one day a drop of fire was poured by the black woman into the torpid marsh of yellow blood, into the cold torrent of white blood. On that day, that day alone, the lyrical sense was born in the man of extreme Asia and in the Indo-European. There, in the troubled depths of an interested positivism, here, in the vigorous assizes of a discipline of combat hitherto immovable, this drop of fire, bringing with it the furious love of form, rhythm, and color, started the conflict that lyricism alone can solve. As far as one looks, into the origins of history, at least since history has been expressed by means of the image, one discovers the burning trace of this great event.

Ancient Egypt would no doubt have rested on the broken flints of its most ancient necropolises if the black migrations had not impregnated it gradually through the upper valley of the Nile. Still earlier, if one evokes the presence, in Spain and Southern Gaul, of images sculptured on tools or carved on rocks, we

Fig. 48
PREHISTORIC ROCK FRESCO (Spain)

learn that the negroid skeletons are found in the lower sediments of the shores of all those countries, oriented toward the black continent where similar forms decorate the caves and the weapons of the hunters. The most ancient monuments of India are later in time than the encounter of the whites who came from the West and the North by way of the rivers, with the blacks coming up from the South. In all living white peoples in whom the black impregnation is lacking or is too light or too remote—Scandinavia, North Germany, England, Russia, Poland—the plastic manifestation is indirect: it reveals imitation, the school, acquired virtuosity, strain. And the exclusion is still more striking if one turns toward the yellow man in whom the virtue of the black ancestor shows itself as actively as in the man of the Occident.

His trace is easy to follow in the Indo-Chinese or the Malay, both constantly impregnated, on whatever side they turn, with the blood of the Polynesians or of the Dravidians of Hindustan. Less evident, perhaps, in the Chinese, in whom the infiltration is more ancient and

Fig. 49
AFRICAN ROCK FRESCO

the mass of whom, for fifteen hundred years, have hardly allowed themselves to be encroached upon except on their borders. It is, nevertheless, after the Macedonian armies had reached the Indus that the first Chinese sculptors appear, two centuries before Christ, so close to the Greek form in their nervous, dry, drawn appearance, less preoccupied with the mass than with the contour and the detail, and it is after the inundation of China by Buddhism through Hindu immigrants— whole tribes, I imagine, whose successive waves broke into foam for four hundred years—that the efflorescence of the Chinese monumental sculpture took place, peopling the deserts and the mountains, filling them with carved grottoes and avenues of colossi resembling an army of invaders.[1] The art of the Hans, the art of the Tangs rose upon a propitious terrain.

Through Tibet, through Indo-China, if one believes in the accumulation of negroid types along the valleys of penetration of the southern rivers, profound ethnic migrations occurred continually, pouring into the blood of the yellow races the tributary streams of black blood that have twice embraced it. Even if one admits that Chinese pottery,[2] the most anciently known after the Lacustrine potteries, had appeared in the yellow lands before any mixture of blood, it is not possible to conclude from this that the Chinese had been able, alone among all peoples, to escape the black ferment, the art of the turner being common to all the primitive races because of its utility. All the more that perhaps here it serves as one of the solutions of the problem of the origin and haunting persistence of rhythm.

Think of the love of the Chinese for the clay of his fields, the baking of which he watches over, the cracks of which enchant him, which he sometimes buries in order to impose upon it the long and intimate caress of the dampness of the under-soil. Think of the care with which he vitrifies his porcelain-clay, hammers his bell or his bronze vat, everything that is gently and melodiously sonorous, everything that seems to be born only from the whirling movement of the lathes. His somnolent reverie, which opium makes still heavier, seems to follow for centuries the musical humming of the paste as it begins to settle, through its mechanical rotation, into a minute planet, while the heedless hand imprints upon it furrows like those made by the wind.

[1] Fig. 40.
[2] Fig. 50.

Did not the invincible tendency of the great Chinese sculpture to pursue the spherical model that hums endlessly about a central invisible nucleus come from remote atavisms transmitted by the primitive coppersmiths and potters who must have been lulled to sleep amid their activities by one of the most ancient musics known? This slightly sullen contemplation, this floating and restrained meditation may have aroused in the Chinese soul, in default of the visual imagination, the inner rhythms that resulted later, after the yellow migrations into Eastern and Northern Europe, in preparing the Slavs and the Germans for the blossoming of the poem of sound, the Slavs and the Anglo-Celts for the blossoming of the verbal poem.

FIG. 50

THE MUSIC OF THE LATHE (China)

It is especially in the white peoples of Finnish blood—Russians, Germans—that one meets this invincible aspiration to music, into which they have been driven by the plastic imagination deprived of the aptitude for expression in form by the absence or the rarity of the black blood.

Wherever, therefore, the pure white or the pure yellow live, plastic art only appears as an imported article or an amusement of the learned. Only where the black has touched them do we find the higher forms of the imagination organized in visual images, among the former by means of the order-bestowing reason, among the latter by means of patient, slow, subtle meditation.

It then resumes its exclusive rights, the burning drop of blood is lost in the memory of the species, which seems to happen in present-day China, deprived for fifteen or twenty centuries of all contact with the black peoples.

I am thinking of the Hindu drama in which the too large and too continuous affluence of black blood gives birth to a constant rupture of equilibrium, man wallowing in the mire with the flame in his heart. I am thinking of the equilibrium won, on the other hand, on the architectural plane of the Egyptians and the Europeans. Almost everywhere there are white tribes better organized for war, driven by their need for order and seeking a place in the sun, who precipitate a flood of fresh blood into the feverish morass where it spreads its iron control over the ferments of the mire. And almost everywhere flowers spring up on the surface of the waters when the first anarchy begun by the drama gives place to the temporary stabilization of the social body.

It may be that this tragic genesis lasts four or five centuries, as among the Greeks, or seven or eight as among the Italians or the French, or ten or twelve as in Spain; but these are only historical incidents, shortened when the races that meet on the same territory settle down there, or prolonged in new migrations, which a more or less favorable milieu alternately hastens or retards. But the fact remains constant. Thus one sees the pale Iranians overflow the plain of the Ganges to lose themselves among the Dravidian masses till the rise of Hindu art.

Thus one sees Greek art springing up on the shores of Attica to testify to the encounter of the Dorians who have come down from the North and the Ionians and Mycenians impregnated, through Syria, with the blood of the black slaves who people the harems of the Orient.

Thus one sees the Teutons covering with their successive alluvions the plain of the Po and the Apennine valleys where dwell the Italians previously brought into relation with the black peoples by the politics of Rome, so that a new Italy may begin the strong flight that will transform Europe; leaving to its less virile Venice the privilege of a richer expansion, thanks to the continued

Fig. 51
Roofless Theater of the South (Taormina)

mixture, in the veins of the Italianized Nordic and Celt, of Semitic blood and black blood.

Thus one sees Christian art emerging from French soil because tribes of Franks have come into relation with Celtic peoples who have long been in contact with the southern races.

Thus one sees the Visigoths disputing with the Suevians over a Spain impregnated with black blood up to the day when, delayed by terrible convulsions of war, by the arrival of the Arabs, by the fragmentation of territory, an ephemeral and lofty flower rises from the field of carnage. Even in the case of the Germanic Low Countries which were in continual relations with the Mediterranean and the Orient through Bruges, Antwerp, Amsterdam, and moreover occupied for nearly a century by Spanish armies, we witness the birth of a plastic art as warm as that of the South: tropical gold in the mist, wings of purple in the waters.

This ethnic drama is so universal that it seems to us necessary. All its vicissitudes are repeated in the New World where first the Toltecs, then the Aztecs from the North come into contact with the primitive populations of Yucatan and Mexico and cause the aboriginal art to spring up which the black Polynesians, after having peopled Easter Island with colossi, awakened along the ridge of the Andes when they skirted the American continent in their canoes. . . . Everywhere the white conquerors appear before a splendid but fissured edifice which they destroy; opposing their simplicity, their health, their abstract order to a culture superior to theirs but worn out, rotten, through centuries of a domination that has become too easy and is foundering in the moral anarchy of individualism and security. Swallowed up at first in the mass, their spirit emerges from it one day, mingled with that of the mass, under the form of unknown images in which blend and push forward, in a shining equilibrium, the qualities of the new species created through a few centuries of the mingling of elements hitherto hostile and in any case separate. It is a chemical operation in which the will counts for nothing.

On the contrary, it is born of it and guides the newcomers through a thousand tragedies toward the anticipated forms destined in their turn to decompose in order to experience other contacts and undergo other recastings. There is in these penetrations, these fermentations, these perpetual fluxes and refluxes a guarantee of renewal, and consequently of the love of images, susceptible of consoling man; man who is so avidly attached to the form that torments him but who is forever incapable of seizing it.

II

Suppose now that the primitive black tribe gradually spreads through some European group by emigration toward the less torrid climates, by conquest, by slavery, by the entrance of its women into the harems of the white chiefs. Suppose the lyric *élan* has been imprinted thus upon this revivified group in which the white blood still dominates. Will the poem about to burst forth preserve the accent of the plastic art of the blacks or, modified in its customary inspirations and expressions by the inner landscapes which the black atavism retains and by the exterior landscapes which the new species experiences, will it assume a special accent in which the traces of its origin will not be found? The element that Taine invoked and Gobineau misunderstood has just appeared. It tirelessly exercises its obsessing function. A metamorphosis is produced; no doubt the inverse metamorphosis will be produced when the black blood dominates, as in the Hindu, for example.

Not only the ethnic material but the plastic material has changed. A fruitful marriage takes place between them which will resolve the biological drama begun by the mixture of bloods and the change of setting according to the proportion of this mixture and the character of this setting.

It is in fact because it rains that these roofs slope, that these theaters are covered, when elsewhere the

Fig. 52

ROOFS OF THE NORTH (Dürer)

tiers are exposed to the broad daylight.[1] On the burning sands, people have neither roofs nor tiles, but flat terraces so as to enjoy the coolness of the evening. There, as here, the earth, the air, exercise over the builder an admirable tyranny. The former furnished him the materials, which, if the edifice is made from the trees of the country, of the limestone that crops out everywhere, of the marble or granite of the neighboring mountain, imprint upon it a sort of evident sensual kinship with the flesh, the muscles, the skeleton of the same soil. The latter, saturating it with warm rays, gives to its walls the tone of the unhewn rocks, the parched leaves, the fruits that are ripening round about, the dust that mingles with its débris.

Moreover, by drenching the edifice with rains and mists, by clothing it gradually with mosses and lichens, the climate unites it with the forests, with the fields which, like it, are bathed in this air. The night dew, the weight of the dead leaves or the snow, the fissures made by the sun or the frosts, the birds' nests that hang there, the seeds that fall and spring up there, the pollen of the flowers or the spray which the wind flings there— everything connects the edifice with the solids and liquids of its country by a thousand invisible bonds. The rivers clasp it like arms, or cause man to place it at the bend which they make, where their waters slacken their speed. The roads attract it and press it upon the bosom of the little hills. The toughness, the friability, the humidity of the subsoil, the dimension of the openings necessitated by the quality of the air and light for the building, determine its proportions, its situation, and the thickness of its walls.

One need not go far to find moving examples of these irresistible differentiations that give to the constructions of neighboring provinces the decided accent of these

[1] Figs. 51, 52.

Fig. 53

Misty Surroundings (Chartres)

provinces, even when these constructions serve the same use, tend to the same end.

The same rigorous principle determines, for instance, the whole ogival architecture of France in the Middle Ages. But look at this land of the Ile-de-France where the brooks quiver, where the verdure quivers, where the mud of the roads is saturated with dead leaves, where the haze over water, shimmering in sunshine, gives the atmosphere a mauve color, and then these towers that rise from it, mauve also in the evening, murmuring with looms, covered with wild plants, animated, greenish, trembling like a watery meadow: if their walls offer wart-like surfaces to the diffused light, it is that it may play easily over their curves.[1]

Observe, on the other hand, this soil of Languedoc or Provence where the rock pierces the surface and these fierce fortresses, naked as a stony waste, where the flame of the ogives ascends between the red buttresses: the light of the South cannot corrode them where they rise in a single block, well aware that ornamentation and the play of the surfaces would be concealed by the brightness.[2]

Now cross some ancient country where the spirit of the age has hardly penetrated, where the towns and villages have remained what they were three or four hundred years ago, three or four thousand years perhaps, where even man has scarcely changed in his aspect, his customs, his costume, his ideas. Everything there seems an emanation and even a function of the earth. See, on the banks of the Nile, how the temples with their regularity of shape and the straight lines of their silhouettes repeat the aspect of the cliffs that border the Valley of Kings, how their hypostyle halls with the upright shafts topped with leaves recall

[1] Figs. 30, 53, 63, 88, 129.
[2] Figs. 124, 125, 195, 206.

open palm-groves under which the light shines.[1] See
how the little Greek temples crown the promontories
that seem their natural pedestals, with their triangular
pediments like the form of little hills, where not a
single tree rises, everything on the scale of a compact,
measured, restrained landscape. Look at these Italian
towns that blend in the distance with the geological
formations running toward the crest where they sprawl
out, twisting their stone roots amid the stone heaps
there, like them brown or red, arid like them; and the
bare towers that rise above them with the stiff *élan*—
different from others and egotistical—of the cypresses
that rise on every side.[2]

These Roman edifices provided with thickset limbs
to dominate the stony plains, long limbs to stride over
the rivers as they carry water from the springs to distant
places, to the height which the extent of the desert or
the depth of the ravine demands. These cupolas of
Islam seem to revolve, like slow, pale whirlpools in the
warm, quivering air. These pagodas of India reproduce, from top to bottom, all the plants, all the beasts
of the jungle; and now all the beasts of the jungle
swarm through them and the plants have made them
a part of the jungle.[3] These walls of Japanese temples
with their congealed and frozen motifs in the lacquer
have a monotonous and systematic variety, which repeats all the aspects of the bouquets of cryptomerias
and cedars crackling and whirring with insects and
birds.[4]

Stop. Enter the houses or the churches.

See those little savory pictures, full of health and

[1] Fig. 80 bis.
[2] Fig. 54.
[3] Fig. 131.
[4] Will reinforced concrete end by dominating in all regions of the world,
as many architects think, especially Le Corbusier-Jeanneret? Will it
everywhere manage to substitute the geometrical anthropocentrist ab-

balance, where you meet again the same servant you have just passed, washing the door-sill or the windows, this same young woman sewing under the curtain of her window, this sick child in its mother's arms, these vagabonds near whom you were sitting a few hours ago in a tavern on the quai. Try to divine, in the shadow of this chapel, what rises tier upon tier behind these tormented forms and these haggard faces marked by the passions, the bristling palaces, the parched, burned landscapes where the parasol-pine and the cypress alternate, clear-cut little hills against a sky that is streaked with hard white clouds. Enter these narrow hypogees, surprise, in the gleam of the torches, these busy laborers amid the reeds by the river, these ducks, these paddling geese, these slender ibises, these palm-trees, these date-trees which you have left behind you in the broad daylight.

Consider these fluid canvases on which you find the tall, undulating women, the beautiful children, chubby

---

straction for the climatic and ethnic empiricism which has prevailed hitherto? Yes, to be sure, at least for a time, if the function of the edifice, from the pole to the equator, is and can be exactly the same. No, if the architect attempts, for the sake of expressing a single and systematic idea, to resist the exigencies of the illumination that is to be obtained and the climate that is to be accepted or combatted. Under the pretext that reinforced concrete is the most malleable material that architects have had at their disposal hitherto, it would be at least paradoxical if its use should result in favoring not an adaptation most closely suited to useful and harmonious ends, but a uniformity of aspects destined to engender very quickly discouragement and ennui. I have touched upon this question in the Introduction to the present work, and I have treated it at greater length elsewhere (see *History of Art*, Vol. IV, Preface to the Edition of 1923). When this reservation is made, I admire the beneficent necessity of such an effort as that of Le Corbusier-Jeanneret. It introduces resolutely into our spirit simple notions that cannot but purify its concepts, regenerate its activity and clear its habits of the ashes that befoul it. Admirable realizations, we know, have already been obtained in the order of industrial architecture by the engineers of America, Italy, France, and Germany, and, on the field of civic construction, by Auguste Perret, Loos, numerous architects of the Low Countries for whom Berlage had prepared the way, and certain German builders (Figs. 35, 215).

and blond, that you have just met in the great park drenched with fog, where the branches of the oaks drip their dew on the emerald of the lawns. And these others, with their gray, sad expanses, where cavaliers dressed in black wander in the dust. And these lakes strewn with sails glimpsed between the zigzags of the maritime pines, where some triangular flight of migrat-

Fig. 54
PLASTIC SURROUNDINGS (Corot)

ing birds emerges from the fog (you can buy a print of this scene in the first bazaar you come upon in some city built of wood, where paper streamers and lanterns swing in the breeze). And this terrible effigy of cruelty and flame, a heap of tusks, claws, jawbones, decayed hands, which you can only meet with in the heart of the desert, after having crushed the head of a viper with your heel, exposed your smarting skin to the burning of the mosquitoes, and torn your flesh on the spines of the cactus.[1]

One cannot doubt this influence of things on the re-actions of the spirit when one sees the extra-visual impressions themselves awakening within us the power-ful sensorial echoes that immediately transpose them-selves into images in the field of our representations, so many centuries old. This perfume, for instance, sug-gests a definite landscape that recalls the circumstances in which it was usually perceived. German or Russian music evokes the aspect of the countries and the customs which, by degrees, have fashioned it. The savor of this food brings before us, on the screen of our memories, the sea, and a definite sea, blue or mauve, violet or gray, the odor of this other food the equatorial forest, and this other one recalls the damp tillage or the pas-tures of the North. If the slightest sensation, far re-moved from the sort of objects among which it first appeared, causes these objects to be suddenly reborn in the memory of the most jaded individual, how much more, in a being as vibrant, as emotional as a poet, will the continuity or the repetition of appearances cause to arise an obsessing image which he will attempt to reproduce, and presently, more or less consciously, abridge, purify, stylize, symbolize? How can he help carrying it with him when he moves from place to place? How can he help associating it invincibly with the new and unexpected appearances that he experi-ences, imposing upon them his own familiar rhythm which, on the other hand, they will modify insidiously in their turn.

Poussin and Claude Lorrain[2] translate into French rhythms the Italian motifs which, in themselves give to these rhythms a part of the significance they would

[1] Fig. 55.
[2] Fig. 56.

FIG. 55

FEVERISH SURROUNDINGS (Mexico)

not otherwise have possessed: it is indeed Italian they speak, but with the accent of their own country. Similarly, Primaticcio translates into the Bolognese language the emotion he owes to the vine-leaves, the branches, the fruits of the orchards of Fontainebleau. Similarly, Carot, toward the middle of his career, imposes the equilibrium and the charm of France on the

FIG. 56

RHYTHM AND MOTIVE (Claude Lorraine)

landscapes between the Arno and the Tiber, and the firmness of these landscapes on the aspects of his country. Similarly, El Greco, so profoundly influenced by the harsh face of Spain, causes to play upon this face the reflections of the long ikons and even a little of the nervous intelligence of the idealized form that characterizes the Greek.[1]

[1] Fig. 210.

Everywhere a strict accord tends to arise between the exterior aspects of the world and the inner realities of the spirit. What one must still discover are the conditions of this accord, its elements, its origins, its frontiers, and the contradictions it reveals to any one who wishes to analyze it.

III

One asks Taine why every Florentine of the fourteenth century is not Giotto, every Venetian of the sixteenth is not Titian, every Dutchman of the seventeenth is not Rembrandt. A foolish and perhaps a meaningless question. Because the flower of an apple tree differs from its fruit, from its leaf, from its branches or its roots, are we to conclude that it is not the flower of the apple tree? Or that it can grow on a poplar, or an oak, or even on a rock or on water? A people, a nation or some ethnic, political, or mystical group forms everywhere an organism that strives to adapt itself to the conditions of life demanded by circumstances. But this adaptation imposes upon the whole organism a complex play of functions the excellence of which is precisely determined by the differentiation of the organs that compose it. It is their hierarchization, it is their reciprocal and interlaced subordination that create out of their own strength the strength of the entire organism: every Florentine of the fourteenth century, every Venetian of the sixteenth, every Dutchman of the seventeenth shares in Giotto, Titian, Rembrandt, as Giotto, Titian, Rembrandt share in the Florentines, the Venetians, the Dutchmen who are their contemporaries, their predecessors, or their ancestors.

Art is a sign, no doubt, a way of speaking. A language, a language that differs from another similar language according to the man who speaks it, according

to the place, according to the epoch in which he speaks
it, and also, let us note clearly, according to the man
who hears it.

But did Taine, who knew this, hear this language
clearly?   Did he find, in its varied accents, the secret
spiritual relationships that express the inner man under
the shell of appearances?   It seems as if he had confused
with the spirit which they conveyed the sonorities, the

Fig. 57

Transposition (Watteau)

nuances, the inflections, the customary bad habits, and
even the orthography that accentuate these accents.
He scarcely saw the work of art save from its picturesque
angle.   He grasped forcibly but almost exclusively its
external relations with the general aspect of the geographical milieus; the history, the passions, the customs
it expresses here or there, that which makes it here
violent or even cruel, there bourgeois or anecdotal,

Fig. 53

DOMINATION OF SURROUNDINGS (Rembrandt)

elsewhere idealistic and generalizing, and also, in this canton, given to translating itself through form, in this other through color.   And indeed, these relations cannot be denied.

If I do not think it either obvious or necessary that man should aspire to reflect uniquely the immediate aspects of beings and objects, I believe he cannot express himself save by borrowing from these aspects all their expressive elements, because he has no others at his command.   If he does command others, brought back from his travels, or from the inner landscapes which atavism obscurely reveals to him, they are those that have struck him first, that still shape him, and that touch almost uniquely those to which circumstances oblige him to address himself.

But there is an ambiguity here.   It is the great creator of forms who knows how best to obey.   But it is also in him that transposition takes place most constantly and most unconsciously as well.   The gray tints of cinder, pearl and silver that tremble over the slopes of Guadarrama, the rose or mauve clouds that graze their summits, the oranges of the market-place the tone of which one finds at twilight in the atmosphere of Castile, the pinks of the rose or the reds of the carnation, are never offered us by Velasquez and Goya in the place where they have seen them, in the order in which they have surprised them: they quiver in this trinket, in the ribbon of this order, in this downy arm gloved in white; they shine in this dark hair, they stain this corsage with a bloody spot, they empurple the mouth in this painted face.

The sky and the sea of Venice penetrate the marbles, the flesh, the satins of Veronese.   The mother-of-pearl of the waters of the Marne throb in this petticoat in which Watteau[1] mingles also the warmth of the woods

[1] Fig. 57.

of Nogent in autumn, just as he catches their spring dews and the pollen that powders the wings of their butterflies. The herrings of the market-place, its rusty scrap-iron, its rags, the flesh-color of the tulips and the russet gleam of the hovels of Amsterdam saturate this man's face, this cradle in which the child-god sleeps, this woman's breast painted by Rembrandt in his poverty-stricken old age. I see clearly the enormous

Fig. 59
Submission to Surroundings (Paul Potter)

distance that separates Rembrandt from Potter, for instance, and even the kind of antagonism that one glimpses between the latter, who reflects his milieu peacefully and faithfully, and the former who plays with it, in order to reflect himself, Rembrandt, as if with the thousand instruments of an orchestra.[1] But I affirm that if Rembrandt, born elsewhere than in Holland, had perhaps been a man of the quality of

[1] Figs. 58, 59.

Rembrandt, he would, admitting the activity upon him of similar historic circumstances and atavisms, have expressed himself by means of a painting different from his own, or perhaps by means of sculpture, or perhaps by means of music, or perhaps by means of the word.

Here, under the mist and the rain, lies a verdant plain. There a rocky expanse burned by the sun. It is not surprising that man does not speak the same language in both places, and I might show, in the manner of Taine, for what very simple reasons the latter will be precise, the former floating and drenched in water. Nevertheless, here as there, the sun rises every morning from the same point of the horizon, disappears every evening into the same point of the horizon, following, between these extreme points, the same curve in the sky.

Here as there, at rigorous intervals, day and night alternate as do the seasons. Here as there, the whole sky seems to turn about an invisible pivot. Here as there, sowing time and harvest time succeed each other. Here as there, wherever man and woman meet, fever seizes them. Here as there, the child is born of this encounter. Here as there, man and woman rejoice in his presence. Here as there, man and woman suffer from his disappearance.

Here as there, man and woman die.

Here as there, all the essential elements are common to all beings in their inner life. Here as there, they experience the same essential phenomena in the external life. It is natural, therefore, that here as there they traverse with more or less the same steps these two regions. But it is also natural that such of the phenomena as differ or even contrast in the external life—the soft earth here, the hard stone there—should ring differently under this same step. Otherwise all our works would be expressed in the same language, without accent, uniform, neutral, useless through excess.

If we do not distinguish until after a long apprenticeship two Venetian, or Florentine, or Roman, or Greek, or Dutch, or Spanish, or Assyrian, or Chinese, or Egyptian, or Hindu works from one another, we distinguish quickly enough a European work from an Asiatic work, later a Roman work from a Greek work, a Venetian work from a Florentine work, an Egyptian work from an Assyrian work, a Spanish work from a Dutch work, a Chinese work from a Hindu work. Why? Because its author has grasped, I think, the most essential relations between the milieu and the language, the thousand subtle exchanges that define the first and indicate the second, and because he imposes them upon us with an irresistible authority.

The milieu is a complex thing, evidently, comprising everything that meets the author's glance, everything that strikes his ear, everything that springs up, unknown to him, from the intimate powers which his near or remote heredity has deposited in his cradle. A milieu in which not only the usual aspects of the country, its geological structure, its climate, its culture, the customary foods it produces, but also the original formation imposed on its inhabitants by the patient modeling of their immemorial life, agricultural or pastoral, commercial or maritime, industrial or military, listless or intense; the events and the laws, the measureless unbridling of the passions or their mastery secretly contributing together to form and even liberate the creator. The creator, I repeat, is he who knows how to obey. If this endless milieu did not exist—a powerful sculptor arresting and fixing the language—a Japanese work and a French work would be absolutely indistinguishable, would consequently lose all accent, consequently all interest, consequently all universal human

significance. It is our differences that unite us, because
we approach one another in order to study them, and
because in studying them we discover our resemblances.
It remains to ascertain why, although our resemblances
increase, these differences exist and why it is probable
that they will exist and perhaps even desirable that
they should always exist.

Fig. 60

SCULPTURAL GEOLOGICAL SURROUNDINGS (Greece)

IV

It seems evident from the first that certain countries
solicit and develop our visual qualities, and others do
not, and consequently that plastic expression is born
more spontaneously and enriched more freely and forcibly in the former than in the latter. I am thinking
of the insignificance, the ugliness or the picturesque
banality of central and eastern Europe, of the monotony, the peaceful or solemn neutrality of Switzerland,
of the mild and empty prettiness of Lombardy, en-

circled nevertheless by so proud a crown—Tuscany,
Venetia, Umbria—of the barrenness of the pampas of
the two Americas—everywhere in these spots are non-
existent, or extravagant, or dissembled forms, a dull
light, a vulgar color.

It is a commonplace, on the contrary, to testify to
the marvel of the entrance into Holland from the northeast or the south; the shining mist, objects, and persons
bathed in it suddenly assuming an unexpected brilliance

FIG. 61

PICTORIAL ATMOSPHERIC SURROUNDINGS (Holland)

at once profound and translucid, the gay display of
geraniums at all the windows, the blue and red wings
of the windmills, the blue, orange, ocher sails of the
boats, the black diamonds of the cattle besprinkling
the polder. A commonplace to mention the surprise
one experiences at Avignon, after a night in the train;
discovering this gray and rose expanse punctuated by
the black of the cypresses, those mauve mountains in
the distance, the sudden passage into the light, the
accent, the vigor, the clearness of the South. To recall

the arrival in an Oriental port where the rocks, arranged in an amphitheater, open their arms that seem brushed with gold by day, covered with violets at eventide, and those waters that seem illuminated from beneath, such sunny, azure rollings in their depths where the phosphorus wanders all night. This Spain, a dead planet, crystallized in the pearl and silver of ashes, through which the red lands assume tones of orange and the rare flowers a funereal accent, their brilliance veiled in all this gloom.

The approach to Ile-de-France with its bending poplars, trembling leaves, roofs and houses brushed with moss, its light vapor everywhere present and suspended like a breath, gilding the walls, gilding the surface of the rivers, lighting with a gentle flame the summits of the monuments. Nature only touches the heart where man forms part of it, certainly. But it might be said that he only forms part of it where it touches the heart. Elsewhere there is silence in a brackish peace, or paltry combinations of consciences and hearts, or, when the race is strong and marked for royalty, the withdrawing of souls into themselves and the springing up of music or verbal lyricism.

In Greece, sculpture, like a hostess, comes to meet the traveler. Bare, without trees, without grasses, even the mountain is sculpture. The stones crop out everywhere, like bones. Enormous vertebræ, monstrous ischiums emboss the soil. On their continuous, smooth, or salient peaks they catch the sinuous masses that spread out in the light, which accentuates their structure and penetrates them, until they enter and fuse themselves with it in the form of the spirit.

Nothing of this exists in Venice, Holland, or the Ile-de-France where the mist lightly veils all forms, but also, through its thousands of millions of little suspended drops, heightens the colors, their correspondences, their contrasts, multiplies the reflections, subtilizes the passages, hatches, in ceaseless exchanges all the enchantments of the air. The skeleton of the planet is the master of the sculptors, the atmosphere is that of the painters, especially when it floats above a damp country where sun and water mingle, close to the sea or a network of canals and rivers, covering the fields and the woods.[1]

I state the facts, the relations, without insisting on the physical causes that are self-evident in their ensemble but whose exact analysis belongs to the domain of the savants.

The Ile-de-France, and especially Venice and Holland, are islets of atmospheric gems and fires, more or less brilliant or subdued, where all the colors of the prism mingle in endless combinations: they are also islets of painting. Not far from the former is Tuscany, a dry country, with a hard and frigid light, very sharp in color, where the little hills, the trees, and the houses stand out like marks on a window-pane. There, painting assumes an aspect that is dramatic but dry and clear-cut, without echoes, without sounds, the linear frames of which no symphonist has ever been able to break. In the neighborhood of the latter, the German mist, thick and gloomy, covering the geological skeleton that is further concealed under a mantle of pines, allows only indefinite or truncated forms to emerge from it, the cries of the poultry-yard, the sounds of big and little bells, the grinding of wheels, the murmurs of torrents: the art-worker, born there, lives in a closed room, his bench under the lamp, and his patient labor is one of sentiment and memory, unless the musician, assembling all these scattered sounds, all these confused sensations, melts their wandering forms in his heart so

[1] Figs. 60, 61.

that the sonorous edifice may sink its roots there before it grows.

When they try their hands at painting, the forms are seen from too close by, as through a mangifying-glass, some placed near others, without any care for ensembles or subordinations. The tones do not mingle. The harmony is never obtained through their reciprocal echoes, but through their juxtaposition. The canvases of Holbein would suffice to define this spirit.[1]

Painting, it is true, is one of the privileges of Spain. And yet, at first glance, Spain is nothing but sculpture. The skeleton of the soil is apparent on all sides, although less compact than in Greece, where it borders and protects all the populated gulfs. Here the settlements border the rivers on the Andalusian plains or on the high plateaus of Castile and Estramadura. The granite mountain chains are far away. One would say they were heaps of roses, or silver wings suspended over the horizon. The warmth of midday shuts the native up indoors, and all life is in the evening, at a strange hour when the setting sun gives the atmosphere a uniformly orange tint, in which the dark clothes, against the white rough-cast of the walls, assume the quality of translucid stones, in which the rising dust—which seems to play here the rôle of the drop of water at Venice or in Holland —gives the fixed or wandering forms a phantom-like air, spots that stand out, of a supreme distinction, and veiled, with a halo on their borders.

Often, in broad daylight, one sees mirages floating above the glowing plains, lakes of tinsel, lakes of pearl across which the warm air vibrates, so that everything seems to quiver, everything bears an unearthly accent. In this milieu Velasquez, Zurbaran, Goya reply to the harmonists of the Low Countries living in their whole-

[1] Fig. 62.
[2] Figs. 33, 185, 186, 210.

FIG. 62

HARMONY BY JUXTAPOSITION (Holbein)

some interiors and their luminous mist and to the symphonists of Venice playing in the enclosed space of that city where everything is dancing illumination, interlaced reflections, reciprocal echoes between the phosphorescent water of the lagoons, the colored fermentation of the façades, the air saturated with vapor, the ceaselessly changing union of the sky and the sea; and the Spaniards reply with their secret, rare harmonies, made up of very few elements, but associated according to an infinity of nuances, not like a hundred instruments in an orchestra but like four or five flowers in a bouquet; nay, more, a bouquet in the twilight, sparkling, austere, abandoned.

The Ile-de-France, so rich in painters, Boucher, Chardin, David, Delacroix, Corot, Manet, Seurat, about whom an imposing procession of lesser masters are grouped, witnesses nevertheless before their time the flowering of a line of sculptors that has no parallel save in the powerful harvest of stone through which the civilizations of antiquity and of the Orient were so forcibly defined. But here sculpture no longer has the traits it assumes in the regions where light plays across surfaces deprived of humus, trees, and humidity, such as Egypt, Greece, Assyria, Italy, the South of France. There, sculpture suffices to itself, is circular, one might say, even when it is *veneered* upon a foundation of architecture, and revolves about its own volumes so that it exists in space like a bone from which all the flesh has been stripped away. Here, sculpture is always *mingled* with its architectural foundations, playing upon them and through them with shadow, light, and mist as one might treat the masses that stand out or sink into the background on the surface of a canvas.

Even on the ensemble of the edifice it imprints the aspect of a great painting, confusedly animated, swarming with scattered life, seeming to stir with the wind's breath like a field of wheat under a breeze, or fine rain, or fog.[1] Is it not remarkable also that we should find such characteristic contributions made to the art of the Ile-de-France by the painters who enter it from other regions? Into this somewhat troubled but very subtle mauve and golden atmosphere that attracts and harmonizes them, Watteau brings the succulent fluidity of his Flanders, which relates him to the Van Eycks, to Van der Goes, to Patinir, to Breughel, to Rubens; with Ingres comes the burning dryness of his dusty Midi which holds him close to the masters of Tuscany, Rome, and the Orient; with Daumier we see the sculptural robustness of his native Marseilles, founded by Greek sailors; with Courbet, the somber harmony of his Franche-Comté, impregnated with Spanish blood.

The case of England is no less characteristic. Here we have light bathed by rain, transparent, limpid; everywhere the forms seen through it are never clear-cut but rounded by the thick covering of the earth and leaves. We find gushing and flowing waters, deep, gleaming mire in which wheels and feet sink. No sculpture. A fresh painting, yes, but soft, spongy, without foundation, clean as a water-color—often the water-color itself is the chosen tongue of its best artists —Constable, for instance, or Bonington. The verbal lyricism that prevails here is awakened and maintained by the moonlight under the trees and over the lakes, by the laments of the nightingale in the warm evenings, the dark manor houses, the ivy-clad ruins, the eternal sea beating the cliffs, the adventure of travelers, the immense fleet leaving the ports, sailing back to the ports, bringing into the fog with it the flora, the fauna, the burning climates.

This lyricism passes into the enchantments of Turner,[2]

[1] Figs. 53, 63, 64.
[2] Fig. 84.

so wild and unexpected, with their cloud palaces, their
sunlight among shadows, their Southern mythologies
amid the smoke of London and the fogs of the North.
But these enchantments are inchoate, uncertain as the
flight of birds in a storm, without muscles, without a
bony structure, without expressive prominences rising
and stamped from within. The art seems a feat of
lyricism, overstressing its visual medium in order to
bewilder us with incoherent harmonies and paradoxical
relations and throw us into a pantheistic disorder that
is repugnant to our sense of the plastic, at least on the
spiritual plane where the Occidental moves. Such an
endeavor could scarcely succeed if some secret logic,
dictated by the traits of the soil, led by the immemorial
play of sentiments and ideas, did not draw from this
soil, deepening these sentiments and ideas, a sort of
moving armature, always unsettled, everywhere provisional, but everywhere present and always in process
of becoming.

It is thus that the genius of India both creates and
solves this problem through the eternal pouring of its
moving water between the dykes which it refuses at
the same time to define or to overflow.

India lies between Shakespeare and Turner.

The one has conquered it for the English people—
whom the other reveals as a little crushed by its conquest. This continuous pantheism, irrepressible as a
flood, which animates the words of the former in the
way we know, only passes into the canvases of the latter
by violating and enervating the methods of painting.
India is the only country to realize this pantheism in
sculpture through the unanimity of its masses which
have hollowed out the mountains, chiselled the cliffs,
given the rocks the palpitating forms of plant and animal. No expression is more completely one with its
natural milieu than these temples that are so quickly the

letter and the very spirit of Hindu philosophy which everywhere mingles fecundity and death and causes them to blossom from each other. Warm rains for six months, flowing in warm torrents to the sea, yellow rains, sometimes red, when the setting sun pierces their thick floods and the burning dust they raise from the soil.

FIG. 63
SCULPTURE MINGLING WITH THE BACKGROUND (Chartres)

Fiery winds, bearing the miasmas of the marshes in a whirlwind of mosquitoes, sowing at haphazard fertility or famine through rain, drought, seeds, and destructive insects. Parched deserts forever alternating with impenetrable forests. Several harvests a year growing untended or annihilated at a blow by a cyclone. Every phase of climate from the equator to the pole lies between the marshy jungles of the plains and the sinister glaciers of the Himalayas. Great rivers sweeping along

confusedly corpses and flowers. The incessant and
stormy interpenetration of all natural phenomena that
follow each other in rapid successions, alternating and
contrasted. Identity of appearance and life of the
three kingdoms blended by fermentation and decomposition, from the bottom of the stagnant waters to the
tops of the dark trees whose splendid flowers distill the
very venom of the snakes that swarm between their
roots—roots that grow from the bellies of the goddesses
or the bosom of the gods.

The magnificence of the wild animals, reptiles, and
insects—striped skins, gemlike scales, flaming insect

Fig. 64

Sculpture Set Against the Background (Arles)

wings, bound, as in a divine servitude, to the most
redoubtable organs of carnage or poison. Pearls in the
sea, topazes, emeralds, rubies, in the sand of the rivers.
Irresistible dialogues between fire, earth, water, sky,
teaching despair and helplessness, the variety, the contradictions, the caprices of which force one to meditation. The glowing rocks upon which the multitudes
stamp the form of the massive monsters that come to
drink at the lakes swarming with crocodiles, or the
flesh-eating animals that prowl in the jungle, are too
chaotic and too varied in appearance to catch and fix
their confused abstractions.

FIG. 65

GEOMETRICAL SURROUNDINGS, CUBICAL SCULPTURE (Egypt)

Man may come, no matter whence, into no matter what new country, bringing with him inner images, habits, obscure reflexes that have risen from his remote heredities, and that will make him see this country a little differently from what it is. Sometimes they will even make him modify it in order to justify this vision. It will remain no less true that as soon as man wishes to speak, the country will dictate to him, with imperious insistence, and will prescribe, in one place, not merely sculpture isolated in an open space and a universe without secrets, but it will even determine the very aspects of this sculpture. In another place it will prescribe an expression intermediary between sculpture and painting from which his most ardent efforts cannot wrest it; and elsewhere again, it will evoke the aerial, almost musical impasto of the painter, fixed or fluctuating, according to the spot that captures the spirit of space because space wills it. If we consider Egypt and India, the painting and music of the North European, the painting and the sculpture of Greece and Italy— Venice always excepted, we can go even farther.

Where the light is fixed, where the forms are few and well-defined, the seasons differentiated, the atmosphere clear, a civilization with static tendencies appears and maintains itself. Where space is confused, jumbled, full of vapors and mirages, where rain and fog prevail, where innumerable forms incessantly interpenetrate one another, an irresistible dynamism dominates and carries away the spirit.

V

Let us not forget, finally, that other elements, almost as remote as the racial determinations, almost as insistent as the rhythmic repetitions of the motives, and certainly as imperious as both, increase the complexity

of the problem almost to infinity, but through this very
thing, it seems to me, demonstrate its nature. Aside
from the weapon, the pot, leather, musical instruments
and music itself, it is difficult to conceive an art belonging to a nomad people. They move at random over
the steppes, never establishing themselves where they
stop to camp. They live under skin tents, rolled up
and carried about, that are the evident antithesis of
sedentary architecture the profile and mass of which are
regulated by the geology and the atmospheric changes
of a permanent milieu. They do not even imagine the
decoration which, through fresco and relief, will give
birth in other places to painters and sculptors.

Where, on the contrary, man establishes himself
amid cultivated fields like a spider in his web, the
industry of the dwelling, then of the household, then
of leisure develops his primitive faculties, and, as with
the deposit of a river, builds up the persistence of his
monotonous daily needs. These needs, although enlarged and complicated unceasingly, preserve the common character which each day nourishes his sight, his
sensations, his soul, and the living tissues that provide
them with energy. Work, food and the manner of
clothing himself impose a tyrannical direction on his
creative energy, through their secular influence upon
his daily deeds.

Take the Chinese farmer, living on rice, fruits, roots,
fish: do we not find the very man in his slow, uniform
art, without convulsive violences, in those great statues,
calm as towers, conceived and realized without haste,
in those paintings, expressing, in their dim harmonies,
prolonged states of soul dominated by serenity and
wisdom, in those tranquil landscapes in which there is
nothing but dew at dawn, the setting of the moon over
sleeping rice-fields, the murmuring of brooks about the

silent villages?[1] Is there not something analogous in the art of the Egyptians, nourished on wheat and dates, an art springing up in the midst of grain, in the proximity of farms, lasting also thirty or forty centuries and never tired of cradling, in an unchanging setting, its sure and monotonous abstractions?

On the other hand, have not meat, wine, and alcohol, by increasing tenfold but also wearing out the nervous force of the European, contributed to mark his poetry, his sculpture, his painting with the dramatic character one finds in all his enterprises? Such great enterprises, but so useless in the opinion of Orientals!

Nevertheless, the contrast between these two imperative materials and the two clear-cut souls that correspond to them, would be much less surely indicated if the influence of daily occupation had not augmented the immemorial effect of food.

Food does not differ sufficiently among these two Occidental peoples—the Egyptian and the Greek—or among these two Oriental peoples—the Chinese and the Japanese—so close to one another through race and habitat, for one to be tempted to see in it too important an effect on the character of their respective geniuses. With the Chinese and the Egyptian this genius is obstinate, slow, all spiritual depth; with the Greek and the Japanese it is rapid, nervous, all direct humanity. In one case, commerce intervenes to precipitate evolution, as agriculture intervenes in the other to slacken it. Here man unceasingly changes his horizons, his interests, his interlocutors. Patient meditation gives place to critical objectivity.

The energies of the intelligence develop, become complicated, but unfortunately also foul and perverted much more quickly than elsewhere. How could trading peoples, established by the shore of the seas escape the

[1] Fig. 41.

Fig. 66

PORTRAITURE AND CLOTHING (Van Eyck)

education of space and the waters, especially when they moved from island to island, every dawn bringing the unknown, every night brooding over the mystery, every new tribe discovered beyond the tide opening liberating outlets which constrain the ingenuity of artists to find in it resources that the monotony of the motifs had perhaps not revealed?   "Nearness to the sea destroys pettiness."

The sea, so apt on the other hand to co-operate with light in order to magnify the aspects of the soil, the sky, the clouds, so alive itself through its eternal movement, its eternal sound, the swarms of creatures it rolls in its depths, has from all time played a capital rôle in change by pouring into the soul of man the taste for adventures, the mystery of departures, the violent joys of returns. The sea means ships dancing under their sails, or trembling under their smoke, constellations never seen before, fiery shores encountered when one first emerges from the fogs, the sadness of the polar regions when all one knows of the world is the shining vault over palm trees and ports, faces, exotic costumes, rich stuffs, unknown monsters, birds of gems and flame unloaded under the eyes of children.   We have the same spectacle in Greece, in Holland, in Andalusia, at Venice, in Oceania, in Japan, on all the maritime horizons of France and England—in every place where a powerful poetry has wrested its secret from the world of the imagination in order to increase to infinity.

It will be objected that Mesopotamia, Egypt, China, India are too massive, too profound to be much affected by the ocean; and, indeed, except for India, where the ethnic revolution is too ardent and repeated to permit a sedentary art to develop completely, it is in these countries that we find the agricultural populations drawing from their vital necessities an art evolving

---

[1] Stendhal, *Mémoires d'un touriste.*

slowly and developing through centuries, if not through millenniums, and following a rhythm so grand that it seems to ignore time. But even here, and however diminished, is there not the pulsation of commerce that has permitted these vast, apparently motionless bodies to maintain the energy necessary to search for the nourishment of their spirit? I find here immense rivers,

Fig. 67
Abstract Surroundings (The Desert)

all running toward brilliant seas, all traversed incessantly by rafts, junks, canoes, propagating the continuous drama of fecundity on their shores and borders, from one end of their course to the other, through the multitudes which their own mass preserves from dispersion.

This is not all. Do we not find always and everywhere the influence of clothing, its density, its neutrality, its luxury, its absence, and not merely in the external appearance of the image but in the very matter of its spiritual determinations? Flemish painting, for instance, is almost entirely at the service of the weaver, the draper, the dyer; and it develops about them in their interiors, full of luxury and shadow, in which tapestries ornament the walls, in which the gowns, the sleeves, the hoods of heavy cloth leave hardly anything uncovered but the faces and hands. Does it not owe in part to these circumstances the force of its portraits, so bony and muscular, with their solid framework, insistent faces, alone in life, one would say, on top of all this somber brilliance of furniture, hangings, and curtains? Does not the embroidered kimono, on which appear all the flowers of the country that is richest in flowers, maintain in the houses, in the streets, on the boats, the taste for the multicolored print? And does not the print, in its turn, influence the whole of Japanese art by complicating, by agitating the drama, turning it toward decorative expression rather than toward its own exaltation?

It is quite evident that the linen robe of the Egyptian fellah has not failed to encourage strongly the geometrical conception of Nilotic sculpture in which the limbs under the material only serve to favor the passage, between the three dimensions, of the subtle wave with which it surrounds the statue like continuous music. It is evident also that the bestiality of African sculpture has not been discouraged by the absence of clothing or by the rare ornaments that serve to emphasize it. Evident also that the spirituality of Arab art from which all images are banned, could not but persist in this singular ostracism when it rested on the protective coloration of the white woolen burnous which from a distance melts into the neutrality of the sand, hides from sight the faces that are often veiled as well, and

Fig. 68

Elegance (Persia)

borrows from the desert its lonely monotony, so aptly
suggesting, on the other hand, the abstract unity of
God.[1]

It is clear that the complications of Polynesian tat-
tooing have only been able to accelerate the blossoming
of architecture and decoration that pursue and lose
themselves in endless scrolls. And that the school
which has determined the art of the whole Occident,
and perhaps of all Asia, would not be explicable without
the national games in which naked man appeared before the eyes of the crowd. This fact undoubtedly
favored the rapid evolution, the sureness, and the perfection of Greek art, but in directing it toward the
anatomical expression of form it engaged it in an impasse from which Europeans have almost failed to
emerge.[2]

Here it is necessary to dispel an ambiguity. The
great position of gymnastics has certainly given its
decisive orientation to the spirit of Greek art, but one
must not confuse this spirit, all proportion, and balance
between the elements of the drama—which gymnastics
by themselves already express well enough—with the
"subject," in which that art seeks its point of departure.
It is too evident that very often the environment dictates the "subject," that this is indeed its least con-
testable but also its least important rôle, for the Museum
of Versailles, where one finds the whole story of the
warlike French epopee, is much less French, in all its
fifty rooms, than this cup by Chardin on the corner of
a kitchen sink.[3]

When we have said, for instance, that the art of
Picardy and Champagne in the Middle Ages reveals
a race of farmers because it speaks especially of harvests

[1] Fig. 67.
[2] Figs. 85, 208.
[3] Fig. 155.

and vintages, that Dutch art, because it preserves for us the sea, pastures, work-benches, and apothecaries' shops, expresses a race of sailors, cattle-breeders, and shopkeepers; that English art, because it takes us out walking in parks with beautiful children and gracious women, expresses a real aristocracy, we shall still scarcely know anything of the art of Champagne or Picardy, of Holland, or England. On the contrary, we shall know much of the Italian people, whose art speaks very little of everyday occupations, if we show its intellectual tendencies, its tense and passionate energy, its will for structural continuity in the drama of movement. Much of the Spanish people if we dwell more on its mysterious harmonies, its remote secret force, its taste for silence, than upon the mendicants, the cripples, and the idiots of whom it so frequently speaks to us. Much of the Assyrian people and much of the Persian people, if we compare the cruelty of the hunting and war scenes shown in the art of the first with the elegance of the hunting and war scenes shown in the art of the second.[1]

Aztec art, I feel sure, has not left us a single one of those scenes of torture which one finds so frequently, for example, in the pictures of the peaceful burghers of Ghent or Bruges: nevertheless, it reveals to us a race of butchers.[2]

VI

Here, then, we have a motif, renewed or always the same, but in any case full of accent. Here is a garment remaining quite as suggestive as it was twenty centuries ago, a food that has continued since time immemorial its slow and persistent action. Here is a human group

[1] Figs. 68, 69.
[2] Fig. 55.

quick to receive images, through the infusion of the black ferment once poured into its veins. Here is always the sea, the great civilizer. We see the eternal light, or the illumined fog. Why is it not legitimate that the incessant solicitations exercised upon man by the environment should always lead man to respond intelligently to the environment?

The human miracle is woven of fatalities so inextricable that the illusion of sudden liberty which it gives us cannot be explained except as the supreme fatality. A prodigious chain of diverse circumstances is necessary in order that here or there, on this day rather than on some other, the flame of creation should arise at the summit of an irresistible wave, borne on by curiosity, confidence, the ardor of living, and the spirit of conquest.

It is necessary that all possible forms of spiritual and practical energy should move groups of men enjoying the unusual privileges of which we have spoken, in order that they should be able to exchange with neighboring groups the products of industry by means of commerce and such collective passions on the march as caravans, fleets, migrations, and armies. It is necessary that the sense of drama should have been preserved in the heart of the individual by the alternation of victory with defeat, poverty with wealth, mysticism with criticism, appearing neither too close together nor too far apart, neither too easy nor too brutal. Imagine, for instance, food appearing of its own accord, a mild climate where no effort is necessary to secure the former or evade the latter, or, on the other hand, a climate too harsh, food too scarce, requiring in order to combat the former and seek the latter exhausting labors that do not leave a second for rest or leisure: where would meditation and enthusiasm have been able to take root?

Suppose again that only a few families people the imperious lands that we know to be indispensable to the complete expansion of the genius of individuals. Whatever might be the solicitations of the secret ca-

Fig. 69

Cruelty (Assyria)

dences that rhythm the flow of their blood, would they have time to increase, multiply, become a city, a nation? Precisely at the hour when the bud was about to open, would they not see some conquering horde appear that crushed it as it passed by? But perhaps at the same

time, through one of those paradoxes that history sometimes offers, that horde would bring to those living on
the other side of the mountains the spiritual revelation
of defeat or domination. Even if these few families
become a city, then a nation, would they be sufficiently
in relation with their neighbors, through books and
merchandise, through trade and war, to develop the
curiosity and inventiveness necessary to make a confrontation between their environment and the universe
within them?

Take some immense space, Siberia or Brazil. Imagine
it endowed, in its ordinary aspects, with every possible
magnificence—austere or laughing, no matter which—
forms, vegetation, dramas of the sky, dramas of the
waters. If these groups, separated by almost impassable
savannahs, by impenetrable forests, cannot come into
contact with one another, if man here remains always
cantoned in the same spot, never hearing the voices of
other men, never meeting their glances, never comparing his products and his ideas with theirs, the monotony
of his representations, the rarity of his images would
fail to give him a new relation or an unforeseen association that could serve as a springboard for his creative
flight. Is not that what happened to the Russians, for
instance, scattered for fifteen centuries on their marshy
steppes until a profound stir, vague but more and more
extended, gave them a wavering consciousness of their
intimate reality through the despairing voices of their
novelists and their musicians?

Why, finally, since it could be born, did the miracle
have to die? Environments change little, men change
scarcely at all. Although it has remained on the same
terrain, the apple tree that was covered with fruit last
season does not bear a single apple this year: have we
the right to conclude from this that it is not the same
apple tree? When one sees the decay of Greece after

Alexander, or only after Byzantium, one may well
wonder by what chance it suddenly blossomed some
thirty centuries ago.

To show its rocks, its light, its women bearing on
their heads the burdens that oblige them to walk erect,
like the caryatides of the Erechtheum, its same people,
turbulent, versatile, mischief-making, ungrateful, in-
fatuated with politics and commerce, is to mention

FIG. 70

MINARETS AND CUPOLAS (Islam)

appearances that have not remained the spiritual realities they once were. To reply that it was at the crossroads of the Old World, at the place that formed the
common highway of all the civilizations—Ionic, Syrian,
Phœnician, Egyptian, Pelasgic, Italic, Celtic—to which
its sailors and its merchants served as courtiers and
middlemen, this signifies only that these conditions
favored a possible flowering. But what other conditions
it had to fulfill!

The instant must have been very fugitive when everything concurred so that the energy of the developing race might express itself by methods that were, as a matter of fact, very natural. There was the weakness of the foreign peoples, all of whom had reached the supreme point of their own civilization and deposited their seed in the cradle of the newly-born. This seed, in contact with its virgin forces, acquired a powerful vitality, increased by contact with neighboring seeds. Then Greece possessed qualities of a singular receptivity, assimilativeness and insistence that could only appear once, at least under this form, one in which chance, that is to say circumstances too complex for analysis, played the capital rôle. There was the encounter of two principal races, one bronzed, the other white, one disembarked from the sea, the other descended from the mountains, that embraced even while they fought, and whose virility and sensuality fecundated one another.

There was unity of religion, philosophy, social, and political aspirations that coincided with the culminating point of the forces of realization, expansion, and conquest. All these are conditions which, if only one is lacking, can cause the immediate collapse of the edifice when it is scarcely begun, a thing that happened, for instance, with the primitive Roman art that was too clumsy to resist Greece, which had come into contact with it too soon. Elsewhere, in Holland, for instance, where the great art did not last a century, we are surprised to find the explosion that occurs. At that moment, liberty conquered by arms, meets with the consecutive development of the individuality proper to a people, and with its economic prosperity, of which it had the right to dispose for the first time. Then, although this liberty, this development, this prosperity continue, artistic energy disappears, perhaps under the influence of acquired wealth, at the same time that the sources of its victorious conquest disappear in the daily drama of war and revolution.

Or else, as in Spain, we see the collapse of the creative faculty along with the collapse of political power and the substitution for conquering virility of an easy enrichment among the vanquished peoples overseas who have been ground down, fleeced, and pillaged. Or else, as in Italy, there is the quick rise of this faculty in the growth of cities delivered over to the most ferocious passions, cities that wore themselves out and were destroyed with the same rapidity and the same violence as occurs in love, leaving nothing but ashes. Or else, as in Germany, there is an event of capital importance —the Reformation—followed by two hundred years of wars that break its spirit in the heydey of its youth and cast it into an abyss of suffering, from which music is finally to rise.

In this domain one can only make statements of what has occurred. It is not possible to follow all the circumstances of the evolution of peoples whose creative inspiration was only a moment of that evolution, although indeed the most impressive moment, and sometimes capable of a power of renewal that seems almost inexhaustible. This was the case of Egypt, for instance, isolated among the ancient peoples in an oasis that could only be reached by crossing immense expanses of water or sand, and yet not so isolated but that, once every two or three centuries, some invasion within the country, some expedition against other Powers, came to agitate the creative sources and give renewed strength to the energies of the spirit.

It was also true of China, whose history is sufficiently similar from this double point of view of relative isolation and renewals as profound as they were rare. And even true of France, the only one among the nations of

Europe to maintain its creative level almost without interruption for ten centuries. Because, no doubt, like Greece of old, France is at the crossroads of the peoples, cross-fertilized in every sense by their spirits, thanks to books, merchandise, war, or through books, merchandise, war, renewing abroad the sources and the stamp of its own self.

Nothing else resembles so much the ripening of fruits, sometimes sudden and followed by a rapid decay, elsewhere slow, almost torpid, but long preserving their savor, covering this tree to the breaking-point this season, entirely lacking the following season, or appearing regularly during several years—sometimes awaited in vain during the whole life of the tree and never appearing at all. Every aspect of earth and sky blend in it, the qualities of this earth and the caprices of this sky, the unexpected flood, exceptional drought, cyclones, the passage of destructive insects, maladies that have come from without, natural senility when there have been no graftings and crossings.

Suppose some religion arouses this inert people, suddenly opens its eyes after having stirred its lungs and its heart, and admits to it, in a great lyric tumult, the solicitations of the country which it inhabits but has not yet considered. Then we have the priests of Buddha spreading over China, Indo-China, the East Indies, Korea, Japan a flood of charming enthusiasms that fills the mountain grottoes with flowers, carves forests in stone, and peoples the edges of the roads with smiling colossi.

We have the horsemen of Islam sowing such rapture among the vanquished peoples that in a few years enameled mosques, sharp minarets, cold cisterns protected by heavy vaults and surrounded with gardens will spring up in the tracks of their horses. We have the peoples of the Occident finding in Catholicism a moral

Fig. 71

Naval Architecture (The Roma)

pretext for glorifying the beauty of their women, the strength of their soldiers, the opulence of their fields, and the wealth of their trades.

Suppose some war stirs the hidden springs of this other somnolent people, obliges it to evolve the drama of creation from the drama of its life: then we have the sudden fusion, when the Medes have hardly left, of the Ionic current, the Dorian current, in the powerful Attic form; we have India awakening after the armies of Alexander have come into contact with it; we have the sudden rise of Holland, Flanders, Spain, of French romanticism.

Suppose some other war occurs, so cruel, so long or accompanied by such carnage that it cuts down to the very roots all impulse toward the future: we have Mycenæan Greece after the invasion of the Dorians, France after the Hundred Years' War, Germany after the Three Hundred Years' War, America after the Revolution.

Or, somewhere else, a more or less rapid rupture of equilibrium that breaks the association of the creative elements and delivers over to wealth, or to intelligence, or to sensuality, or to asceticism, an authority out of proportion to its necessary rôle. We have the convulsions of the Greek city appearing in the dissolution of the unity of the statue. We have Christianity breaking the pagan idol after having adopted its supreme teachings, as, a few centuries later, the Christian idols will be broken by the Christian. We have the slow weakening of the supports of the cathedral as the strength of the corporations decays and diminishes, rent asunder by the economic individualism that grows greater from day to day.

The creative energy of a people taken at haphazard is no doubt only one aspect of its general energy. Art, which is a way of speaking, is also a way of acting, but

FIG. 72

VAN GOGH

there are others—industry, commerce, political domination, the order imposed upon neighbors. The development of the intelligence, of method, security, and well-being can, according to circumstances, produce maturity or impede it. It seems, at bottom, as if all these things were only attributes of a unique force that is born, grows, becomes conscious of itself, bursts forth in the course of the irresistible ascension of a certain group, and commands it to seize and perfect the form of expression that is proper to it.

It has been said, for instance, that a people's most invariable sign of power—luxury—"summons the arts." This is to take the effect for the cause. Luxury is, like art, a sign of ripening. It acknowledges the same origins, grows and develops at the same instant, and, after having favored "the arts" during a brief moment, contributes more than anything else to dissociate and corrupt them. Neither Greek art, nor Italian art, nor French art in the Middle Ages, nor Dutch art, nor English art, nor Spanish art, produced by the growth of those spiritual energies from which wealth arose at the same time, were able to resist the increasing wealth of Greece, Italy, France, Holland, England, and Spain. And yet, while the energy of Greece, Italy, or Spain declined with wealth and dragged art into its decadence, it does not seem as if English energy had sensibly diminished—at least up to the twentieth century— since the century of Shakespeare which is, in the domain of the spirit, the greatest of English centuries.

It does not seem as if German energy had weakened after Wagner and Nietzsche; on the contrary, it seems to have grown greater. And yet, after Wagner and Nietzsche, German art almost disappeared. The energy of Holland has maintained itself since the seventeenth century. And yet, since the unique miracle of that century, Holland has not produced a single great

painter, with the exception, in our own day, of Van
Gogh.[1]

On the other hand, Italian energy, so long languid
and drooping, has appeared during the last few years
as one of the elements that gives modern Europe the
most character. And yet, while admitting that its
industrial architecture—factories, docks, automobiles,
airplanes, ships[2]—is not precisely the new form of expression which its mission is to bring, we could seek in
vain, in its present creations, something equivalent to
the productions of a single one among its small towns
of the Quattrocento.

In the Spain of Charles IV, so ruined, so devastated,
so somnolent, how explain the meteor Goya, if the
energy that hurled Spain against Napoleon at the same
period is not something latent in it, ready to burst
forth into action at the moment when one imagines it
dying or dead? And how define Oriental energy, in
China, in India, and Islam, when it chooses precisely
the instant in which it reaches its peak to proclaim in
its very art, which is its highest symbol, the uselessness
of this energy and the vanity of this art? Mystery!
Nothing can mark in advance the hour when a certain
people will reach the most favorable moment of its
historical evolution and take possession of its geographical milieu, or foretell how it will take possession of it.

VII

The confrontation of the systems of Taine and Gobineau leads us meanwhile to a freshly visioned image of
the æsthetic adventure of man, provided we consent
to retouch them both and relate them, all living and
mingled together, with the extent of time of which

[1] Fig. 72.
[2] Fig. 71.

neither the one nor the other takes sufficient account. Gobineau certainly perceived that the primitive milieu might have modeled his races—the rough life, the cold, the mountain air determining the energy of the white in the wholesomeness of his mutual aid and daily effort, the persistent utilization of the nourishing alluvion determining the practical and surly somnolence of the yellow, the warmth, the light, the fever of the luxuriant forest with its fiery birds determining the sensuality and the lyricism of the black.

But why did he not understand that the ethnic mixture, whose faults he denounces, marks the change toward freer forms of the moral disciplines that were judged by him necessary for the development of his imaginary abstract man? Such a change was inevitable because of the constant influence of the variations of the milieu upon the variations of man. They explain how primitive races may be adapted to the new milieu to which migrations, war, and slavery transport them. Also, it is in order to let the descendants of these races live in the new surroundings that the mixture of bloods in such a milieu takes place almost automatically.

Fig. 73

Surroundings and Work of Sentiment (Durer)

And it is from the very biological drama aroused by these mixtures that not only civilization is born but the civilizations.

The inner struggle between practical interest, will, and sensuality arouses in those in whom it takes place the imperious desire to realize their accord and sometimes brings this desire to a successful conclusion. I do not dream of denying the disorders which a too great and too sudden influx of black blood can arouse in the moral equilibrium of a yellow or white race. But it is enough for this race, after the first shock, to stabilize itself in some favorable environment for a great spiritual impulse to be born and to create in it a superior form of culture hitherto unknown.

The concept "civilization" cannot then long blind us to the æsthetic fact that determines the form of expression of the mixtures of races as we have observed them. The images they leave us are only a harmony conquered between their inner universe and the external universe that has more or less changed. Wherever we look there exists between the milieu and man a necessary harmony that constrains them to reciprocal dominations and servitudes from which its average image cannot but emerge. What makes the image so tormented is precisely the anxiety to maintain this harmony, in spite of everything, while the variations of the ethnic minglings run the risk of confusing or destroying it at every instant. If the race provides the spirit, the milieu provides the image, and the drama of art turns about the point of equilibrium in which this spirit and this image are forced to reach an agreement.

The new arrivals, be it understood, bring from the depths of their race the subconscious landscapes, the passions, and the habits which, in their turn, act, by means of successive generations, on the vision, customs, and passions of the aboriginal population. But nothing

can prevent either from having eyes to see. The white
species remains powerless to
develop a plastic genius if the
milieu does not suggest it
through its light and its visible
framework, and if its black
strain is not sufficiently pro-
nounced for the sense of
rhythm that characterized
the black to be fused in some
way with the sense of
abstract order that char-
acterizes the white.

The example of
Germany is typical
from this point of
view, with its dull and
especially its discon-
nected images, like
the German landscape
itself. But in this
race there is a fusion
of elements flowing in
from distant roots
that have pushed
their tenta-
cles into the
Southern
regions and
the Rhen-
ish provin-
c e s ,
mel-
a n -

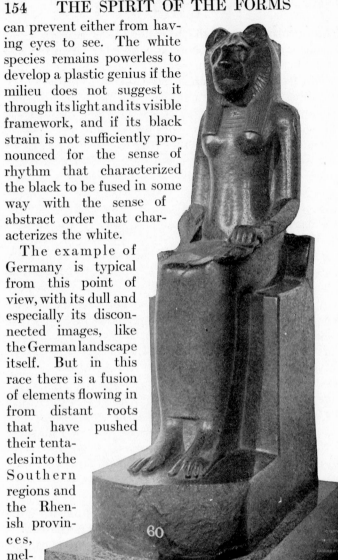

Fig. 74
CRUEL GOD (Egypt)

ized for centuries through the valley of the Danube and the long sojourn of the Legions. And so German fervor forgets the want of harmony of the geographical milieu in order to take refuge in an interpretation of the objects that appeal to the sentiment of man more than to his reasoning.[1] And this is far from being the only case.

We have seen the impossibility of selecting which hampers the Hindus with their too rich strain of black blood and who are moreover swept away by a torrent of colors and forms that are subjected by the climate to incessant changes. The Greeks will teach us their accord with the clearest, the least variable, and the most harmonious of landscapes, an accord conquered over the passions by a race composed in happy proportions of the impulsive violence of the black and the noble sense of order of the white. Amid the incessant drama of revolutions and wars, this harmony occurs even in its symbols carved by the Greeks, Apollo rising from the very carnage to introduce eurythmy into its disorderly gestures.[2]

The Italians, in whom the ethnic drama is at least as terrible, will express it in an art that is more feverish and more tormented and is sometimes wild, carried away beyond its proper limits and moreover marked by Christianity, overwhelmed by the convulsions of cities, but subjected to the discipline of a writing inspired by the bold certitude of silhouettes against the sky, and by the nerve and vigor of the bony structure of the earth. The Dutch, in whom the black share is reduced to a few drops, just enough for their brief and magnificent outburst, will not find any difficulty in bringing into harmonious relationship the enthusiasm which their inner strength gives them and their calm, copious visions, seasoned with the lively colors that play over the mist.

[1] Fig. 73.   [2] Fig. 1.

Among the French, we shall observe a more complex spectacle, due to the situation occupied by their country, which is dominated by the influence now of the German tribes coming down from the North and the East by way of the Oise and the Marne, now of the Mediterraneans ascending from the South along the Rhone and the Seine: on the one hand we have a formal art, very prosaic, which will be called Romanesque or classic according as the chief influence is religious or laic; on the other hand a more floating, musical, picturesque art in which sentiment prevails and which later will be called Gothic—as if one divined its faraway sources, although it is very national; or it will be called romantic, when the German wars once more start the current flowing from the Northeast. But both arts remain in harmony with the aspects of the soil, either through their repressed lyricism, their measure, their sensibly symmetrical cadences that respond to the ordered arrangement of the plowed lands, to the low little hills, the meadows bordered with lines of trees, the moderate character of the climate and the seasons, or through their conquest of space, their moving surfaces, their broken and varied color responding to the majestic, clear height of the forests, to the animation of the leaves and pastures under the passage of the wind and to the mildness of the light over the tiles and waters.[1] Everywhere, in India, in Greece, in Italy, in Holland, in France, there is a triple drama to be resolved in the consciousness of the creator: the conflict of races, the tyranny of circumstances, the influence of milieus.

Now imagine the white represented by the Semite, or thoroughly mingled with him. You will observe, in Europe as in Asia, a similar spectacle, but one that assumes, both here and there, a particular accent.

[1] Figs. 30, 53, 63, 88, 106, 121, 129, 178, 217.

FIG. 75

CRUEL DECORATION (Alhambra)

Cruelty, going frequently as far as self-immolation, characterizes the race. So long as it remains pure, as incapable as the Aryan branch of giving plastic form to the idol, it hates this idol, and perhaps for this very reason.

As soon as a little black blood has penetrated its veins it takes vengeance upon the idol, and through it, by attaching to its aspects, sometimes to its functions, a character of cruelty. The Phœnicians, after having piled up children in the idols, heated their iron gods till they glowed. Wherever it is present one quickly catches the mark of this sadism. Save in the case of the Egyptians, among whom decoration was determined by the richness of the oasis, but whose geometrical characters no doubt contributed to show, in the mass and density of their colossi, in the hermetism of their temples, bare as ramparts, a little of the Semite's zeal to affirm his spiritual royalty, perhaps even a little of his ferocity in the hawk and panther heads of their gods.[1] It is true that we cannot tell whether it is the blood that demands it, or the environment that is everywhere equally ungrateful. In Assyria,[2] an unstable autocracy ceaselessly at war, glories in cutting off hands, tearing out eyes, breaking heads, boiling people alive. Wild animals come down incessantly from the mountains to decimate the flocks. There is a less regular régime of fertilizing floods than in Egypt, an unwholesome slime, polar nights, atrocious heat during the day. About the path of the Arab[3] lie stretches of burning sand in which thirst and sunstroke prevail, for the coolness of waters and palms is reserved for the warlike aristocracy that kidnaps and shuts up the wives and daughters of the conquered. In Spain,

[1] Fig. 74.
[2] Figs. 69, 193.
[3] Figs. 67, 70, 75.

Fig. 76

Musical Painting (Cranach)

we have aridity, the wind torrid one day, glacial the day after, the Inquisition tracking the spirit even into the utmost privacy and silence, political extortion, sanguinary games, a fearful aspiration to asceticism and death.[1]

In all these places the art is ferocious.

In Assyria it parades murder which it describes with a naïve thoroughness—crunching jaws, tearing claws, spears piercing lungs and skulls, wounded animals dragging themselves along on their dead limbs, corpses heaped up and strewn about everywhere. In Arabia, there is the absolute interdiction to express the living form, the enervating arabesque forbidding the dream to take shape anywhere, the cold shadow where sparkles against a background of clotted blood, the carvings and the enamels on the handles of daggers, this raucous song, a leather cord stretched and twisted as if to cut the larynx, and, here in Spain, finally, we have these sinister images of torture and suffering, the cruelty and the sadness of which are even more accentuated by a bleeding rose, a glistening pearl, the shimmer of satin, the down of powdered flesh.

When the Semite does not mingle with the conquered or cannot impose upon them his controlled domination, when he remains apart, on the margin of the peoples, powerless to destroy them, aspiring to direct them, his obstinate apostleship maintains between them and in themselves an atmosphere of combat that forbids them to rest. Aside from his Scripture, the strongest and the most poetic that exists, it is true, we know of no monument, statue, fresco, painting, not even the most insignificant wrought object that belongs to him. One would say that he alone serves as a counterbalance to the need that other men have of expanding and living again in the image they make of their charming or piti-

[1] Figs. 80, 185, 210.

less passions, an image at which he sneers, or which
he buys or sells, as if disparaging it. Wherever the
Semite is, the idol is most accentuated or rather most
irrepressible, whether he pretends to conceive, forbid
or ignore it.

VIII

This search for an accord between his environment
and his race is, for the creator, the imperative necessity
that he pursues through all its forms of expression,
transposing invincibly from one form of expression to
another the essential tendencies which this accord
demands of him. And this is so whether his race is
mixed or otherwise, and whether or not it brings with
it inner landscapes from its primitive habitats. I mean
that if it appears under the form of architecture, the
artist will instinctively carry the accord over into
painting, literature, music, architectural rhythms. That
if it appears under the form of music, everything, architecture, painting and literature, will assume a musical
character, that everything will have a meaning plainly
expressible in words alone if it is through the genius
of the word that the race is tormented.

This, we have seen, is very apparent among the
English, harried though they are by the Celtic dreamer
and the Saxon mystic, who hatch in their rich imagination colloquies of the skies, the forests, the nights, the
oceans. Had they been more truly and wholesomely
painters, they would perhaps have succeeded in introducing these things into their painting, as they introduce
them into their poems in Spenser and Shakespeare,
in Milton and the Lake Poets, in Byron and
Shelley. At least they have unceasingly attempted to
do so. About Turner,[1] as well as before him and after
him, there are enchantments of light and shadow in

[1] Fig. 84.

the ponds, the forests, the muddy roads, and the rainy
skies of Gainsborough, Crome, Reynolds, Constable,
and scintillations, illuminations, specter-like and dying
gleams amid the glooms of Whistler.

We see the same thing everywhere, and it must be
observed that the fact persists in all the harmonies
that occur between man and his environment, whatever
may be the ethnic mixtures that transform the ideas

Fig. 77

Etruscan Fresco

and transfigure the images during centuries, often during millenniums. We know the attitude of Egyptian
art, refusing to change its architectural rhythm during
five or six thousand years in spite of invasions and
distant expeditions, religious and political commotions,
and the crises of realism, idealism, or academism, all
of which are very visible under the apparent uniformity
of the temples, statues, carvings in low relief, and all
the usual objects collected in the tombs.

One may look back to the earliest times of Hindu art and the art of the East Indies, covered over with heavy deposits through migrations, infiltrations, and passing armies, and, throughout their decadences and their eclipses, one still finds their permanent characteristics of pantheistic interpenetration of forms, foundations, lights, shadows, which are common not only

Fig. 78
TUSCAN FRESCO

to sculpture but to architecture itself, and to the poems and the concepts of the mystics and thinkers. Follow, throughout all epochs, the invincible vitality of the German genius for music, since the Nibelungenlied and the Mastersingers, up to the great line, Händel, Bach, Haydn, Glück, Mozart, Beethoven, Schubert, Schumann, Wagner, who correspond to Luther, Herder,

Goethe, Hegel, Schopenhauer, Nietzsche, by interlacing the sonorous arabesques of music with the meanderings of a thought carried, through a synthetic language, into arbitrary symbols, of which pure music is the highest expression.

For countless generations loosely connected images, arousing sentiments rather than ideas and forms, have circulated subterraneously in the German.   When his passion and will gain the victory over the rich confusion of his inner universe, he confides these sentiments to the evocative power of the orchestra.   If he attempts another form of expression, it is still music that one finds in that singular harmony that fills and animates the landscapes of Cranach, Dürer, Altdorfer, those evokers of sounds, vibrations, murmurs, changing appearances.   Their works are filled with scattered episodes where a stray bone, a tuft of grass, a flower, a little creature flying over the surface of a pond assumes an importance equal to that of the mountain on the horizon, the fortress sleeping by the river, the man and woman whose paradise is there.   Like the musical Chinese paintings, these are states of mind—a state of the soul which the play of the ogives, the nerves, the rose-windows in the thirteenth century temple, cannot transform into architectural rhythms save in contact with the French genius.

It is the function of this genius to give to whatever it touches the form of architecture.   Thus for ten centuries —up to the revolution that destroyed the corporations and social architecture—it has been able to maintain in houses, markets, and churches its qualities as a builder.

Observe, from Notre Dame to the palaces of Mansard and Gabriel, its invincible tendency to see a building as a slightly elevated central body, between two higher aisles, where the clear play of the verticals and the horizontals gives life and liberty to the obvious sym-

Fig. 79
Architectonic Decoration (Siena)

metry. Seek this almost miraculous accord between the subject and the object, this familiar communion with the average soul of things, this sort of modesty in effacing itself behind their work that characterizes Corot as well as Chardin, La Fontaine as well as Villon, Corneille de Lyon as well as the Clouets, Fouquet as well as the image-makers of Picardy and Champagne. Here the painters and sculptors that are most clearly French—Fouquet, Froment d'Avignon, Poussin, Claude Lorrain, Girardon, Le Nain, Chardin, Barye, Corot, Seurat—neglect the sensual play of reflected light upon the medium and seek first to establish the form through its essential and average framework, the form that endures and is evident the moment one wishes truly to see it.

The gardener realizes an architectural plan with his straight alleys bordered with clipped trees, his circles in the woods, his geometrical ponds, his cascades and water-jets as regular as the walls. The Alexandrine of the poet, with its alternating rhymes and its monotonous cæsura, as well as the three unities of tragedy, give to the verbal expression an apparent symmetry that forces the drama of the passions to remain behind its façade.

Philosophy directs all thought into the paths of a rigorous method with which even the reasoning of even the freest minds have remained impregnated ever since the balance of Montaigne, the well-rounded aphorisms of La Rochefoucauld, the diametrical aphorisms of Pascal, up to the luminous edifices of Voltaire, nervous, scintillating with innumerable little windows like a palace by Gabriel. Nothing resembles a wall of Vauban like the impeccable logic of a work of Turenne or the powerful cadences of an opera of Rameau.

Observe now the persistence of the ancient Etruscan genius, although enervated, broken, meager, tracing sinister scenes, in the "Triumph of Death" of the

Campo Santo of Pisa, the Spanish Chapel at Florence,
the tormented, drawn, violent forms of Della Quercia,
Donatello, Lippi, Botticelli, and Verrocchio, in the
bizarre visions of da Vinci, the hell into which Signorelli
and Michael Angelo hurl their flayed figures.[1] Note
that all this, even when shut up in the darkness of a
tomb, is almost always painted on a wall, so that the
eye can seize at once, and altogether, the passionate
imagination shown in the crowds of dead and living.

The Italian is a decorator, but in the most human
sense of the word. I mean that he is not satisfied, like
the Japanese, for instance, or the Polynesian, or the
Egyptian, or the Greek of Pompeii, or even the Greek
of Byzantium, to ornament the walls of public buildings
or private dwellings with symbolic motifs borrowed
from creation or from the prevailing myth.

Nor is he content to surround the spirit with an
atmosphere agreeable, or pious, or cruel, in any case
obeying a ritual, or customary preoccupation, or to
consecrate a unanimous social or religious order. It
is the spectacle of his soul, and of that alone, which he
imposes on the spectator, without seeking to please
him, or convince him, or obey him. He reveals to the
crowd, by means of the image that haunts him, the
permanent drama that moves him to the depths. Until
he lets the profusion of the ornamentation ruin his
architecture through its search for effect, he has evidently the passion for naked surfaces, brutal as axes,
dominated by aggressive towers, pierced by those naked,
regular openings, separated by straight columns, all
things that give his palaces an appearance of such wild
grace in spite of their sadness and air of fury.[2] And it
groups these palaces, although they are rivals of one
another, around public squares whose arrangement as

[1] Figs. 77, 78.
[2] Fig. 79.

a whole marks an irresistible sense of formal harmony
and decoration.

The music of Monteverde, Corelli, Marcello unfolds
with a unilateral passion, sonorous as brass, with hard,
sinuous volumes, which one sees rather than hears.
In the literature of Italy, one finds this obstinate care
for plastic and decorative expression that makes it
cover with frescoes not only the chapels of the churches
and the walls of the cemeteries, but the façades of the

FIG. 80
TRAGEDY (Goya)

houses; Dante's poem, D'Annunzio's novels are a succession of images that leave the strange impression of
works of art made to appear in space and not to unfold
in time.

The Spaniards are almost at the opposite extreme
from this spirit that projects the most complicated
drama into the image and the setting, since on the
contrary their theater restores this drama to the oppositions of sentiment which are, moreover, easily trans-

posable into the image and the setting. Their dramatic instinct appears, at first glance, not only in the eternal antithesis that makes their greatest book one of the three or four great books of humanity, but also in the gold that shines out of the shadows from the naves of their cathedrals. It appears in their Christs of painted wood, torn, bleeding, stained by their sores, opposing spiritual grandeur of sacrifice to the most ignoble matter; it appears in the unforeseen contrasts of the most tragic painting that has expressed the Occident.[1]

[1] Fig. 80.

Fig. 80a

The Column (Egypt)

FIG. 81
THE MELODIC ARABESQUE (Giotto)

Chapter III. THE ACROBAT, IMAGE OF GOD

I

NEVERTHELESS, when the spirit of some illustrious work has vividly touched us, we
discover one day or another a contrast between
it and its origins that sometimes reaches the point of a
radical antagonism.   For the artist in whom sounds
the most emphatic accent of his epoch, for him who is
distinguished and who will endure, expression is like
a cord stretched between the two extremities of an arc.

One of these extremities is unquestionably the action of the social and historical milieu. The other, the re-action of a heart. Between the two there is established a system of equilibrium suspended between the errors or the sentimental excesses that characterize the epoch and the secret protest they awaken in this heart. We cannot understand the fundamentals of any capital work if we ignore this. We shall slide over the surfaces; we shall forever fail to appreciate its heights and its roots. The work of art is a drama, and all the more poignant because of the grandiose serenity which char-acterizes it from the outset. It indicates, without establishing them, the spiritual limits of the desire to live according to the dominant instincts of the sur-rounding crowd, limits that condition both self-expres-sion and self-restraint. To depict life is nothing if this chaotic, indistinct, diffuse life which constitutes the adventure of almost all men on this earth is not upheld and corrected by a strong inner structure that manifests both the consent and the intervention of the spirit.

How shall we understand the order and the calm that prevail in a group or a statue of Phidias if, after having shown that this order and this calm can be found in the form of the hills, the gulfs, the immense luminous space, we then observe the turbulence, the lack of discipline, the impulsive violence, the sudden changes of humor and conduct of the Greek race in general and the people of Athens in particular? How shall we understand the moral energy, the prophetic power, the grandeur, however convulsive, of the style of Michael Angelo if, after having recognized the fury of the passions that mark the Italian race, we then observe the universal baseness of character of that time, the complete dismemberment of the religious edifice, the political corruption of the towns, the low estate of morals? How shall we understand the silent drama

FIG. 82

LYRICAL ORDER (The Parthenon)

revealed by the slightest sketch of Rembrandt, his smallest etching, his most indistinct outline, by any of his portraits whatever if we forget the war of the beggars, the gibbets and stakes, the pillories at the crossroads, the sores of the Amsterdam slums, the strange play of light at the back of the hovels and the skies hung with shining mist if, instead, we see only the coarse Dutch life, its healthy out-of-door existence, the cleanliness and prosperity of the houses, streets and fields, the joy and verve of the crowds, the ingenuous feasting and the indisputable morality that maintain all this? It is useless to go farther. The costume alone identifies Phidias, Michael Angelo, Rembrandt as a burgher of Athens, Rome, or Amsterdam. The soul escapes from the milieu which it draws with it and uplifts as if it wished to condense and separate its crystal essence. Everywhere and at all times, between the ordinary history of a people and the evidences which it leaves, there exists the identity of substance and the difference of density which one observes between dust and granite.

The greatest works of art resemble a vengeance of the spirit and the heart that have been martyred by universal custom and seem a complete paradox to the eyes of the crowd. I know quite well that this paradoxical air gradually disappears as one grows accustomed to it, but it reappears vividly as soon as one begins to explore the times that gave birth to great works and to plumb the passions, the customs, and the laws that apparently support them. And it is the more accentuated the more individualized the epoch is, the more religion is debated, the less morality and law are respected and followed, and when the man of ability stands erect, facing a crowd that is at once anarchic and silly, in order to affirm against it the persistence of the spirit. The individual can only define himself by adopting the same scale as others, by placing himself under the same standard as others, by constantly comparing his ideas and his actions with those of others.

Democracies, for example, authorize and even impose comparisons. It is therefore natural that even a superficial examination should almost always reveal, where democracies prevail, a sharp antagonism between the environment and the artist. But in the most coherent, the most hierarchized, even the most hieratic epoch, if one will take the trouble to study the inner meaning of the great collective works in which the crowd itself, following a universal rhythm, expresses its highest tendencies according to its most living methods, one discovers a veiled contrast, veiled by the crowd, with its passions and its customs. At whatever moment one isolates it in its flow, all life is at bottom a vast æsthetic system which maintains a precarious equilibrium between its divergent tendencies. The task of the spirit is to discover and make plain this system. Because the work of art has no other function than to establish this equilibrium, it constitutes its most moving, if not its most perfect image, and it alone has been as useful to man as bread.

It is not plastic expression alone that at one bound can thus reach our spiritual pole and turn our animal pole in its direction. The acrobat marvelously symbolizes the position of man confronted with the problem of giving order to the universe. He overcomes the weight that drags him down, and the weight itself acquires, by a sublime paradox, the ease, the lightness, the freedom of his movements. One will understand art and history at once if one never loses sight of the acrobat.

The whole of Greek art, for instance, displays this invincible tendency that drives profound souls to create in themselves a style that seems the shining antithesis of the average appearance of customs so as to express it later in the dance, the temple, the statue, the ode, social and military action, and tragedy. There is no need to describe the sanguinary versatility, the fantastic and futile spirit, the moral and political anarchy which, for six or seven centuries, characterized the adventure of the Athenians. There was constant disorder, there were continual changes of constitutions

Fig. 83

Lyrical Order (Versailles)

and methods, there was endemic war that was cruel and sadistic as well, every city ten times destroyed and raising itself ten times more truculent than before, every strong man experiencing repeatedly in his career apotheosis and exile. There was a violent and universal impulse towards responsibilities too high and ends too inaccessible that ended in the execution of the leaders who had taken up and defended them and the philosophers who had been drawn into them. There was no security in the relations between men all of whom were in pursuit of gain, no security in the relations between cities all of which sought to live at one another's expense. There was an atrocious spirit of domination dissembled under idealistic pretexts, otherwise sincere, that included the justification of destruction, felony and carnage. . . .

Fig. 84
LYRICAL DISORDER (Turner)

Opposed to this there was such order in the arrangement of the elements of a tragedy or of the temple, a harmony so imperious and simple in their proportions, a rhythm so constantly and so strictly subjected to the control of the most limpid reason and to its most logical deductions that for centuries the temple and the tragedy represented to us, through a sort of falsehood, the whole Greek civilization as the continuous and complete mastery of the spirit over the passions.[1] In reality, it

[1] Figs. 1, 82.

was the spiritual residue of this civilization which, establishing itself as a conqueror over the ruins it had made, brought it forward as one of the determining elements of the future, in spite of its inner lacerations and antagonistic violences. In this case the illusion has finally vanquished the truth, as always happens whenever a race—however base, quarrelsome, and unjust it may be—bears in its heart an image capable of surviving all storms, crossing all seas, and abolishing distances. Plastic and philosophic harmony has cloaked the horror of the abyss, like those corollas that cover the surface of poisonous swamps in which their roots are buried.

France offers an almost analogous contrast, from its position of almost geometrical precision, at the other extremity of the spiritual axis that starts from the banks of the Ægean Sea and traverses Rome and Florence to end in the tragedies, gardens, and palaces of the classic century. Over an almost waste land between the Zuyder Zee and Versailles and the Cévennes, there still prevailed a military and social orgy, license of manners, the repellent grossness of a gorged aristocracy, as well as the merciless wars, tortures, and massacres that had marked the conflict of the religious orders of the preceding age. All these powers were confusedly jumbled together and confounded under the autocracy at the very time when there arose Cartesianism, the three unities, the Alexandrine, the trimmed trees, the formal fountains, the bridges, roads, colonnades, and high walls, a whole spiritual construction that extended to all the regions of the intelligence and masked the disorder of appetites under its cadenced and regular appearance. In addition, and especially, an almost divine moderation, a feeling for the proportions of things and of the universal and constant relativity of phenomena, introduced through reason an indispensable counterweight to the deep-seated nobility of sentiment.[1]

The stability of art was here an immediate result of the instability of opinions, and the æsthetic discipline was invented by the most undisciplined of all the peoples then living. For it was necessary to reduce to a common scale the excessive impulses that characterized this people and so often cut it into two diametrically opposed camps. It was necessary incessantly to repulse or bring into accord the mutually exclusive influences with which the surrounding peoples penetrated this flat land living at their crossroads. Romanticism, they tell us, escapes this singular function of acting as a stabilizer. But it only seems to do so, because, coming in from outside, from England and Germany, it spread and developed at a time when the abstract order that sprang from the Revolution and was introduced by Napoleon into law, was assuring the positive reign of the French bourgeoisie against which, precisely, its lyric tumult unceasingly reacted.[2] Thus, from one end to the other of the French spiritual epopee, the phenomenon is constant. These variations, these successive and extreme experiments, these sudden changes of front belong even more to the Celts than to the Hellenes in whom the spirit, equally mobile, is more impure, less disinterested, and in whom a more strained and calculated moderation appears as eurythmy, or order. But the contrast is of the same nature and assumes very similar aspects.

Let no one object that in the epochs when France prepared and realized its classic order amid public disturbances, English manners presented a still more brutal character, without however imposing upon English art, as a counterbalance, an equally well-ordered aspect. Here, in spite of everything—in spite of the axe that

[1] Fig. 83.
[2] Figs. 2, 157, 163.

fell, in dungeons, upon the necks of young women—or perhaps thanks to the axe—here a spirit of continuity prevailed, in the political organism, a spirit that was altogether unknown in France. Once the moral discipline brought in by the Reformation had been imposed on the passions to maintain a social equilibrium in which the aristocratic caste and the commercial caste henceforth played a rôle unanimously agreed upon, the political convulsions gradually slackened and permitted the English to pursue obstinately the conquest of the freedom of parliaments and the seas. For three centuries in France the country was exhausted with political and religious struggles. Idealistic apriorism always got the better of economic realism. And finally the lack of moderation appeared in the absolute abstractions of equality and fraternity, while, on the other side of the channel, the positive idea of liberty limited by the neighboring liberties absorbed and reunited the effort of all. In opposition to what took place in France, the order in England was practical and the disorder intellectual. And in contrast with this practical order which was confined on all sides by the Puritan matrix, and augmented, perhaps, by domestic well-being and egotism, English lyricism suddenly flowed out from these cramped souls. Its moving waves mirror the starlight. It listens to the murmur of the winds, follows the fall and the flight of the leaves, seeks the enchanted palaces in the architecture of the clouds, draws from men's hearts the grandiose disorder of Shakespeare, Byron, Shelley, and Turner,[1] fantasies of fantastic fogs and, through its informal gardens, establishes in the sinister order of the towns, the mystery of the lakes, the shadow of the nocturnal woods in which the nightingale sobs and that wild countryside appears, haunted, under the moon, by sorcerers and enchanters.

[1] Fig. 84.

If a methodical system appears, in Greece in the ancient world and in France in the modern world, in the two peoples upon whom their lack of method imposes the most despotic need, it seems that the intoxicated expansion of the lyrical and pantheistic sentiment of the world has protested, through the voice of the

Fig. 85

ANATOMICAL IDEALISM (The Parthenon)

English race, against its universal mercantilism and its practical religion, whose inner springs are constantly bent on the repression of instinct. We observe in Germany a phenomenon of the same order. When the obedience of the multitudes to the law and to rule assumes there an almost mechanical aspect, makes one uniform block from which nothing diverges, in which all efforts turn in a unilateral sense, a man suddenly looks within himself and closing his eyes refuses to notice the teachings of experience and the object, takes no account of the hundred thousand facts of the library and the laboratory that autocratically rule the militarized savant and give to the great musical expansion the intransigent form of his will alone.

Fig. 86

THE HARMONIC ARABESQUE (Raphael)

II

Does this mean that the great man, always, everywhere, in all circumstances, affirms himself only by placing himself in diametrical opposition to the spirit of the people whose flower he is? By no means. First of all, he speaks its language. Embedded like it in a geographical and historical milieu from which he can-

not tear himself without condemning his original gifts
to green-sickness and early death, he expresses, through
radiant words, its obscure desires for continuity through
action.   He is one of the voices of the multitude and
like it he experiences, through his passion and his need
to satisfy them, the imperious need to organize them
so that he may discover and understand the principle
that will sublimate them and give a heroic unity to their

Fig. 87

The Symphonic Arabesque (Rubens)

disorder. I have read in the words of a Spanish writer [1]
that the realism of his race is only "the wholesome reaction of a people against its own tendency to dissemble
the unpleasant aspects of its life."   And this is quite
true. For if the beggar drapes himself in his tattered
cape as in a royal mantle, Velasquez, who resembles
him, has depicted this cape without forgetting a single
gap in it. No doubt Don Quixote leaves his niece and
his friends to purify the world, but his horse is a jade

[1] M. de Madariaga.

and the sublime knight wears an armor of pasteboard and a shaving-dish on his head.

These powerful contrasts, which emphasize the profound desire of the race, are carried at a stroke into the domain of plastic art by Velasquez, Zurbaran, and Goya, who throw over the frightful aridity of the earth the aerial veil of wandering harmonies that give the Spanish atmosphere through the dust and twilight the quality of jewels—silver, pearl, and trembling dew. Thus their world is not concealed but transfigured.[1] Do we not see the same thing among the Greeks, who never go beyond their prodigious faculty of ennobling and idealizing the exclusively physical form which is the indelible mark, of their narrow realism in the domain of practical life and material interest? The same thing among the French, whose moderation in rhythm, while concealing their lack of moderation in opinions, betrays their incapacity for great lyrical flights? And among the English, whose most liberal spirits—Swift, Hogarth, DeFoe, Byron, Stevenson, Bernard Shaw, sometimes Shakespeare himself—even while the grandiose disorder of the poem is reacting against the powerful order of practical and domestic life, are obsessed by the principle of morality? Among the Germans whose forcible escape through music from the monotony of obedience and the heavy materialism of manners, leads, in the world of sound, to an absolute obedience to the commands of the most independent of arts and constrains the least material means of expression to give the Dionysiac forces—the hunger for food, war, and sex—their most formidable support?

The Italians present a still more impressive spectacle. They invented the arabesque in painting whose spiritual significance is the most profound possible. The Greeks had hardly suspected it. We might even wonder if the

[1] Figs. 33, 185, 186.

form of their pediment did not give us merely an illusion that they knew its secret virtue were it not for the Combat of Olympia,[1] whose sculptor has obeyed the dominant care for continuity in action, revealed through continuity in deed, in which the great Italians would have recognized their own dominant preoccupation. Nevertheless, this is only an isolated work. Even as individuals, the Greeks made use of the temple and the myth in order to unite them. With the Italians, on the contrary, from the fourteenth century onward, the myth is attacked, the temple shaken on its mystical bases, gods foreign to Catholicism appear from all sides, the individual flings himself passionately and confusedly into the search for his own reality. The most complete passional anarchy arrays man against man. Street warfare is endemic. The amorous frenzy breaks and scatters families. The frenzy for lucre, the frenzy of political ambition divides cities and drenches them in blood. Poison and the dagger are the natural and have become, so to speak, the legitimate weapons of the wild passion that devastates the heart of the individual.

Now even today when one enters an Italian church, one is struck by the disorder that reigns there, if one chooses to compare it with the North. The crowd there is scattered at random, talking in groups, often with their backs to the altar, men and women confused, lovers, laughers, the curious, children, even tradesmen, mystics with their foreheads on the flagstones, all mingled together and each for himself. Splendid, and also fatal scattering of wills, pleasures, and sufferings! To bring order into this crowd a long sinuous line must unite this upright child, whom a kneeling woman folds in her arms, with this man who supports himself against a pillar in order not to fall from anguish, this couple

[1] Fig. 2.

isolated in their passion, cheek to cheek, this old woman
with the eagle's face looking fixedly at God.

Only a line such as that of the arabesque can impose
a common law on these scattered beings each of whom,
all his life, vainly seeks his own law. There is no question here of the cinematic eurythmy of Athens in
which the disorder is much more in people's hearts than
in their heads. There is no question of the static
moderation of France whose errors hold more of intellectual fantasy than of sentimental imagination. It
is a question of establishing between the antagonistic
passions, expressed by these forms, without apparent
cohesion, a dynamic equilibrium which the suppleness,
the confusion, and the variability of the lines can, at
every instant, break, reform, assemble in new combinations—to break again the next moment. The arabesque,
which Raphael carries to its most perfect degree of
continuity and of modulating and enveloping expres-
siveness, is the weapon invented by the mind to unite
these scattered forms separated gradually through the
disaggregation of Catholicism during the last two or
three hundred years, and to carry them simultaneously
to the conquest of a spiritual unity which, having been
destroyed in the human heart by knowledge, was
awakened by the same agency in man's brain. It is, so
to speak, a moving articulation. The Venetians, while
awaiting Rubens,[1] will finish his task by making the
earth, the sky, the waters, and all the reflections
wandering between earth and sky and water, the universal accomplices of this communion which will serve
as a counterbalance, in the æsthetic domain, to the
frantic individualism of the social domain. Who can
fail to see that, here also, this contrast only emphasizes
the dependence of the great Italian upon the most
elementary instincts of his race, by obliging him to

[1] Fig. 87.

Fig. 88

The Bone Structure of the Guilds (Chartres)

establish, through his will-to-order, a unity that persists while refusing him its heart?

III

The arabesque—at least the arabesque that includes
real and concrete forms in its continuous rhythmical
modulations—is so completely the necessary expression
of the Italian soul that at the height of the Middle
Ages, from the end of the thirteenth century onward,
it already inscribes itself in the church frescoes with a
firmness that excludes neither candor, nor love, nor the
tender exaltation that at first characterizes them. At
this moment, however, there is still a profound and
general communion of souls in Catholicism at its height,
in this Italy where Dante is writing his poem, where
Thomas Aquinas has just disappeared, where the influence of Francis of Assisi is only beginning to be dis-
cerned in people's hearts. The day when Giotto painted
his "Descent from the Cross,"[1] the Christian moral
unity was destroyed by a Christian and the spirit of
continuity was transformed from mysticism to knowledge. This in turn acted as a restraint upon that individualism from which the world nevertheless was to
obtain its ferment. At this instant, in a certain man
in a certain work, in which the great sinuous line of
enthusiasm and knowledge causes the soul of the dead
god to pass into the kneeling women who hold his broken
limbs, we can grasp the precise point where the past,
centered in a common faith, and the future scattered
in the search for facts, face each other unseeingly, I
think, in the candid intelligence of a hero. From the
day when he began to follow the progress and the detours of his linear consciousness over its blood-stained
roads through the present passions and sorrows which

[1] Fig. 81.

the human form symbolizes, always present also and living, the arabesque becomes the most powerful lever of the plastic organization of the Occidental spirit.

Three centuries later, on a terrain plowed by Raphael and seeded by Venice, we shall witness an encounter between the North and the South that will be decisive for the Occident. The giant Rubens[1] will succeed in crowding a prodigious mass of matter and living forge into the melodic line that orients the very spirit of the passions. There is another contrast here between the grossness of the instincts of the Germanic world animated by a diffused pantheism and the trenchant clearness of the Latin intelligence which, abandoned to itself, would ignore this living flood but alone can provide the means of uplifting it.

Suppose we turn to Giotto in order to follow the development of the aristocratic line which, beginning with him, penetrates the North in proportion as individualistic fragmentation dissolves the religious unity of the Middle Ages in the democracies about to be born. The first thing that strikes us is the progressive organization of a unity of the intellectual consciousness that is destined to replace it. Here is a contrast no longer Italian but already European between an élite that is incessantly dispersed and an amorphous mass that tends to dissolve, since mysticism confesses itself powerless to bind it together. Nowhere, in the Occidental Middle Ages, save precisely when Giotto appears to close these Middle Ages, and at the same moment inaugurate the personal quest, nowhere does one find this powerful fashion of at once uniting and exalting people's minds. No such thing was needed since the faith and the formal symbols of the faith sufficed for this task.

Art then, in Europe as in Asia, possesses a character of enthusiastic universality which causes it to spring

[1] Fig. 87.

from men's hearts almost without touching their intelligence. It seems at first as if there were no intermediate agent between the formidable unity of the
popular passion and the impulsion art receives from it.
In order to find a contrast between these diffused poems
and the voices of the multitude that ascend together
and answer one another in a common sentiment, we
must first observe that this contrast occurs repressed,

Fig. 89
THE MYSTIC REFUGE (Rome, Mosaic)

as if determined to keep silent so as not to hinder the
eruption of the general energy which it is of prime importance to effect. It is the contrary of what takes place
when the individual has the floor and when it is very
difficult to grasp an accord that nevertheless always
exists on some point between the desire of his race and
the revolutionary interpretations which he pretends to
give it.

Here, then, we have the choir of the people. Listen to it. The cathedral lifts with it, as it soars, all the hopes, struggles, and sufferings of men, all their joys mingled with the sounds of trades, the sounds of the fields, the sounds of the streets scattered by the thousand forms of the markets, the kitchen-gardens, the rivers, the woods, from the top to the bottom of the edifice which is shaken by the sound of bells and traversed by the light of the stained-glass windows, in a world of painted statues, sculptured capitals, and garlands of leaves, vegetables, and fruits.

The contrast, though no doubt less evident, is just as powerful as it was two centuries earlier, when the thick-set Roman temple, almost naked, huddled on its short limbs, placed like a dyke at the center of the frightful convulsions of war, amid the bloody instability of temporal powers, the theocratic framework of its continuous vaults which its massive walls united immovably with the earth. Since the cathedral is free and animated like a merry crowd, since the long slender fingers of its pillars lift it lightly above the pavement, the corporative bony structure[1] is as clearly defined in its skeleton as are the universal beliefs which it balances and cadences on every side. Through its buttresses, pillars, and ribs, it maintains their formidable pantheism within the rigorous limits of the most steadfast reason.

At the other extremity of the Christian world the spectacle, though no doubt less touching, is quite as impressive. The Byzantine statues that open their fathomless eyes on the inner enigma, the Greek temple that spreads its exterior to the light, but turns its architectonic force toward the interior of the structure, the marvelous mosaics evoking the freshness of seas, the variegation of meadows, the glitter of the stars, are only a mystical refuge against the sexual orgy and the

[1] Fig. 88.

brutality of the punishments through which the Christianized Hellenic autocracy marked its horrible power.[1]
As for the endless arabesques and geometrical combination of Islam, which still cover the walls of palaces that rise beside clear and shadowy waters, they know that nothing durable can unite tribes shaped by the empty desert, separated by solitudes, unceasingly devastated

Fig. 90
The Work of the Fields (Egypt)

by fierce appetites. They assume from this a value resolutely and exclusively abstract[2] and seek their spiritual continuity in silence and immobility.

It is necessary, in this connection, to point out immediately that at these great epochs when art shows this confused unity and this universality which bear the stamp of mysticism and give it such power, a strong hierarchic element is always present in the social body,

[1] Figs. 89, 172, 204.
[2] Figs. 75, 114.

supporting and usually oppressing it. It is this which
checks, in the temple and the statue, through the intervention of the temporal and religious or sometimes—as
in France—corporative authority, the outburst of popular energy and faith. On the contrary, following the
fourth century in Greece, the Renaissance, the Reformation, or the Revolution, those very strongly individualized epochs in which the theocratic or feudal authority
is hardly more than a façade, it is the great individual
who is the only aristocrat, charged by the obscure instinct of the species to curb and purify its passions.
This explains the system of equilibrium, silent but so
firm and strong, which is necessarily conditioned by the
Occidental cathedral, the Byzantine church and the
mosque, the three orders issuing from Semitic spiritualism. But whenever one goes outside of Europe, in
antiquity or in the Orient, wherever a powerful autocracy, aristocracy, or theocracy prevails—in Egypt, in
Mexico, in China, in India—one observes a spectacle
almost identical with this.

Egypt, physical and moral, seems at first exclusively
defined by pure colossi affirming, in their rectilinear
universe, the metaphysical despotism and the social
consequences of the religion of the land. Nevertheless,
the pitiless rigidity of the profiles and the heavier
accumulation of granitic masses and walls do not succeed in stifling the charm and freshness of the popular
realism—young women shaking down blossoms or pick-
ing them, the sound of wings in the wheat, the sound
of the wind in the palms.[1] Rather they give this realism
its striking character, incorporating it alive in the
most sustained style possible.

China does not belie the immemorial patience of its
cultivators, its slow meditation accumulating like a
rich pasture, in progressively heaped-up masses, the

[1] Fig. 90.

heavy monsters that border the avenues of its tombs.
But its sages are present there through their meticulous
elegance of thought, which maintains their formidable
profiles in a morality that is hermetic, circular, subtle,
singing, dense as a vase of bronze, unctuous as a jade
jewel. The suave serenity of Buddhist art in Java, in
Cambodia, the peaceful light that it radiates, will never

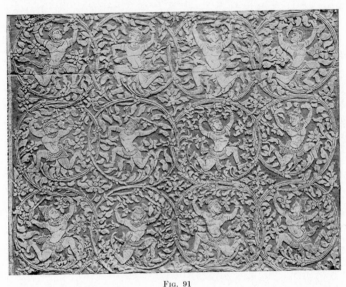

Fig. 91
The Orgy of Happiness (Khmer)

prevent an orgy of dancing and flowers from flooding
these countries constantly with an intoxication that
at the same time stupefies and lulls them, but disintegrates them.[1] The bleeding Aztec statues,[2] those
amputated fragments, those composite monsters made
up of bloody mouths, decayed hands, tusks, and claws,
only accentuate the expression of anxious expectation

[1] Fig. 91.
[2] Fig. 55.

of the god Tlaloc, who longs for the rain like a poor
man whose field has been burned to lime by the sun.
It is easy to discover in negro or Polynesian art an
extreme contrast between the ingenuous and disordered
violence of the appetites of those races and the schematic simplicity of their intellectual organization.[1]

And as for India, if anything is as permanent in its
immutability as is the art of the Indians in its eternal
flow, it is indeed their system of castes the implacable
frontiers of which can never be crossed. But the metaphysics of Brahmanism, while determining them for
all time, delivers to him who sculptures the caverns
and the mountains the liberating doctrine of transmigration: and as every form, however fixed it may be, can
thus pass into another, this contrast—perhaps the
sharpest possible—is not evident.[2]

IV

Let us go further and conclude. The artist appears
to us as the conscience of peoples, charged by them to
react against both the disorders and the excesses of their
instincts, and to find in these very excesses and disorders the sign of their most constant and their most
real desires. In short, he organizes them, which he
could not do if he did not first accept them. And
through the footprint which he leaves upon the soil
where his race has lived, suffered, worked, he remains
its principal and most irrefutable herald. But let us
give a more generalizing look at these temples, these
statues, all these serried rows of objects which the
artist leaves as landmarks along the desert routes to
show the men who are coming that others have passed

[1] Figs. 47, 49, 198.
[2] Figs. 39, 131, 132, 177, 202, 207, 216.

that way. When, after having studied their grain, their density, their form, we seek to evoke the customs, ideas, and faces of those who built them, they lead us to the larger and more profound sympathy of history.

Even when plunged into drama and war, history calls them into being, as a man who lifts his plow with his bleeding hands. A great people leaves a work of art after it, and just this is its history. A civilization, however undistinguished it may be and whatever may be the horrors and the sufferings that have overthrown it, is in its ensemble a poem which the temple, the statue or the symphony epitomizes. This is what makes them so moving, so decisive, so necessary for us. This tragic equilibrium everywhere conditions or constitutes the work of art, and if we examine it and seek to find in it the echoes of the vast social poem which it has survived, we find that at bottom the equilibrium is the very law of this poem, which would not exist without it. It establishes itself from one end to the other of the spiritual life of the ruling people, no matter how tormented, devastated, full of shame and blood this life may be, and gives to its adventure an heroic form that endures into the future.

Madame de Staël has said: "The Germans, who cannot endure the yoke of rules in literature, would like to have their entire line of conduct marked out for them in advance." If the illustrious blue-stocking had mentioned music as well as literature, would this not sum up the whole story of the Germans? Indeed, if we look keenly, would this not give the whole course of history? All history in which the art of war and armies has been conceived in order to stylize and canalize violence, revolutions created to give play to the rigidity of political forms, laws devised to restrain the convulsive disorders of the instinctive expansion of man by an unremitting attack upon this expansion,[1] religion formed to raise over the mire of the heart some air-tight reliquary to hold a nosegay of the flowers that cluster there so thickly that they render the atmosphere unbreathable, even to themselves, and all the forms of marriage imagined to stifle the voice of love under cares or comforts.

The prophet-character of the Jews, for example, from which moral Europe has sprung almost entirely, was an iron brake destined to arrest in their descent the dissolving critical spirit and the sordid immorality of almost the whole race, at the risk of destroying that race. There was need to castrate the Semitic goat, to break the teeth of the usurious hyena so that it should release a few shreds of lean meat. Besides, this was a roving people, without a material home-land. All the more need, then, that they should build themselves a moral home-land, enclosed by thick walls, whence they could throw boiling oil and molten lead on the heads of the besiegers. And this land was full of individuals, all furiously analyzing, dissecting, and destroying themselves. Therefore they required a unique god and they fought to display his terrifying face to the world and to themselves. The formidable strength of the language cut, like an axe, the gangrenous bone or, at need, the neck supporting the listless head that faltered from tenderness or skepticism. Thus while elsewhere races accepted without a murmur the armatures of a law designed to lend them moral support, here the great individual attempted to toughen and to salt down the spiritual backbone of man himself, so that it might take the place of legal armature.

At all times the great man is merely a pitiless regulator of the passions, whether in the social, military,

---

[1] The *written* Law appeared in those Southern countries where instincts are freer, customs less rigid, impulses less repressed, and good faith rarer

judicial, or political field. The passions of the multitude, of course, to which he gives the grandiose form
of his own passions that he has brought to the light
and examined until he can discern their contours, mass,
impulsion, and creative weight. The great man introduces an æsthetic state of the intelligence into the world
by means of the law which he dictates, of religion which
he animates, of the success which he assures, of the
statue which he sculptures, or the drama which he
writes. He evades now the environing order, now the
environing disorder, here, by establishing a new order
in his heart, there, by forcing his heart to correct the
disorder. Thus all history records the antithetical
struggle of the individual against the social body that
tends to absorb him or which he tends to destroy, their
alternating victories and the provisional equilibrium
that each maintains for an hour by absorbing the
powers of the other.

This ceaseless balancing dominates epochs and even
races. It extends to the longest periods of history,
those of which neither the origin nor the end are visible.
The great immemorial rhythms that inspire our metaphysics are unintelligible to those who take no account
of its always present and perceptible reality in all the
incarnations and excursions of the spirit. Thus we
observe that Oriental philosophies attest the perpetual
flux of things while Oriental races remain fixed. And
that while Occidental philosophies strive to establish
stability in customs and manners, the peoples of the
Occident know no rest from one end of life to the other.

Only in this way can we explain the conquest of
plastic art by the religions that spring from pure mind
and the conquest of pure mind by the material arts.
Hence the extreme contrasts and surprising antitheses
between, on one hand, too rigid moral disciplines together with a sensual ferment which, far from destroy-

ing them, stamps them with an immense humanity, and
on the other hand between very free or even altogether
ignoble customs and an æsthetic armature so strong
that it wins for these customs the consent of the loftiest
reason. It is impossible to explain the art of the
South, the art of the North, or even their politics if
we lose sight of the origins of the ceaseless struggle

Fig. 92

THE PLANE—SOUTHERN INTELLECT (Piero della Francesca)

between the strong modeling expressive of sentiment
which reveals the Northern, Christian, and Romantic
character, and the architectural, intellectual character
of the planes which define what is Classic, Pagan and
Southern.[1] In one case, the individual tries to separate
himself from the herd through the opposition of lights
and shadows, unexpected movements that push surfaces outward, a breathless lyrical expansion, and in

[1] Figs. 92, 93.

the other case he attempts through distinct profiles, regular cadences, a severe and logical organization of the sentiments, to give the bewildered sheep a common direction. Though the man of the South is the helpless prey of his passions, which separate man from man and arouse rending conflicts in himself by separating the mind from the heart and the heart from sex, as soon as he approaches an æsthetic object or idea he tends to

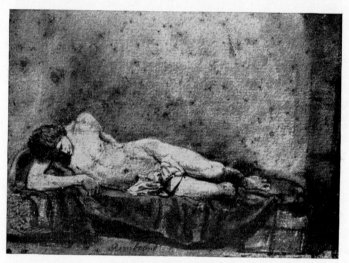

Fig. 93

The Projection—Northern Expression (Rembrandt)

generalize, to idealize, to unite. The man of the North, who generalizes about morality because he tends unceasingly to place mind, heart, and sex in accord, never approaches an idea or an object save with an invincible desire for analysis and characterization.

So we have temples springing abruptly from a chaos of senses and hearts enclosed in a theological matrix, we have mind arched like a vault above a blood-stained pavement, we have multitudes hollowing out mountains, aqueducts striding over the plains like pursued monsters, forests growing on heaps of ruins that once were sanctuaries; mingled forces through which shines and moves that fire of the mind, music. . . . Music in which all the voices of consciousness and space unite to bear along confused souls in the victorious course of a single dominant soul.

We have the migrations of starving peoples across deserts, the tears of the unsatisfied in the warm nights, broken heads, rape, the blood-stained mud of war, the fever of the dance, the might of summer. Here a man's head lifts up because all these things have been. In another case we find millions of men, none of whom excel, but among whom an immense harmony breathes and reigns because a single man existed perhaps a thousand years before. The beating of so many hearts to create a single intelligence, the humility of so many intelligences to awaken a single heart! Every civilization seems to possess an intransigent unity, in spite of the permanent conflict of interests and passions that tend to dismember it, or precisely thanks to that conflict. We have had to rend our own selves in order to dissociate the elements of this civilization. It is one, unquestionably one, like a cry of love rising from a breast pierced by a sword. Nietzsche was more right than he knew. Was this true only of the Greeks? It is true of all of us. Nothing can exist anywhere, nothing, I maintain, unless the light of the intelligence springs entirely from the flame of the instincts.

In all ages and everywhere there is the struggle between Dionysius and Apollo, a struggle with no possible issue. None, I mean, unless it be the conquest, always pursued and never attained for more than a generation in the life of a people, for an hour in the life of a man, of an equilibrium, unstable and tending to destroy itself, between the mystical powers rising from the intoxication of the senses, involving a torrent of troubled images and ceaselessly reborn desires, and the intelligence that welcomes these sensations to enchain them on its heights. According to whether the spiritual balance inclines to one side or the other, whether in one place the great pantheistic flood, finding its order in itself, brings to its surface the mind that has risen from its depths, or whether in another the intellectual order traces through the harsh lights of the confused universe harmonious masses, rhythmical movements, and sure roads, one can grasp at a glance the art, religion, and history of all peoples, their flux, their reflux, and their reciprocal penetrations. . . . The adventure of man is a continuous oscillation between his irresistible desire to become an intelligent animal and his insatiable desire to remain a confused god. His victory is to be both, in the highest degree, but neither exclusively.

FIG. 93A

NEGRO SCULPTURE

Fig. 94

Pietro Lorenzetti

Chapter IV. THE SEARCH FOR THE ABSOLUTE

I

ART and man are so intermingled that they seem to us, in the last analysis, the same pulse, beating the rhythm of history. Now, there is no question of man when one speaks or writes on art, even if one relates his life without omitting one of its details. Since the events of his life reverberate in himself alone, what purpose does it serve to tell them, if one does not hear what he says of them? See how people complain of not knowing Shakespeare, after *Hamlet* and *Othello*, *The Tempest*, and *King Lear*! The poem is the only sign by which the poet may be recognized, and it serves better to explain the adventures of the poet than these adventures serve to explain the poem and its creator. It is possible for one who has known Cervantes to fail to understand Don Quixote, but whoever knows Don Quixote understands Cervantes. The effort that man makes to reconcile in his work the contradictions that the chaos of appearances reveals to him defines the effort which he makes to conciliate in his heart the contradictions which are aroused there by the chaos of his feelings.

The mark of our passion is to wander without rest in the search for ourselves. The mark of our power is not to discover ourselves. Whoever has penetrated the mystery of himself no longer has to resolve the drama by projecting it into his work, with that heroic force which intoxicates the spectator. For a humanity that is conscious of its destinies, the spiritual world congeals immediately in death. It is poetry that saves it by organizing unceasingly the rhythm of its movement, of whose end it is ignorant. And through this it defines its misery and its grandeur. The hermetical quality of painting must be very profound for such a man as Pascal to have reproached the art with that "vanity" which "attracts admiration to the representations of things the originals of which one does not admire." Aside from Pascal himself who tells us what he thinks of them, are the "originals" of Pascal themselves so admirable? Strange blindness that finds a sound of humanity, feeble as this sound may be, in the conversation of his wig-maker, and refuses it to the language of Michael Angelo because he did not wish to learn it or did not know that he ought to learn it! If Pascal refused to speak to Michael Angelo, was not that so much the worse for Pascal?

The impression of security that the poem brings us measures the loftiness of the poet who has conceived it. But this impression is reserved uniquely for those who can grasp the relationship between the depths of the drama which he expresses and his power of expression.   Painting, which does not exist aside from the heroes of painting, can reveal this relationship in an apple of Cézanne[1] placed on the corner of a table for all eternity, because the echoes that attach it to each point of space preserve the sound of the sentiments

Fig. 95
Drama (Cézanne)

that have modeled the artist's heart.   The degree of heroism to which a man may lay claim is proportionate to the violence of his passions.   It is not for any of us to ignore them or subdue them, but to utilize them.   If the creator is secretly devoured by envy, ambition, greed, lust, pride, or even vanity, we will put up with it.   On one sole condition.   This is that he recognize

[1] Fig. 95.

and that we recognize in him the resolute persistence of one incorruptible element: the will to disengage from the drama in which those passions rend themselves a form that is his own, that of a man like all the others in everything that defines man, save in this form. . . . This is not the place to make the portrait of the man. But I would begin with the portrait of the man if it were my intention to make the portrait of the creator.

This incorruptible element is at the heart of each of us. But scarcely one of us is capable of finding it there. It sleeps under too many age-old alluvial deposits, religion, laws, education especially, which is bent upon burying it, and those passions, secret demons, which the creator faces boldly when almost all of us yield to them with closed eyes. We have no difficulty in discovering it in the most paltry acts of interested activity, trade, the deed, the word, silence itself, the automatic acts of daily life, all the monotonous forms of the mysterious virtue that resists despair and leads us for better or worse to the avenues of death. Between the element which distinguishes the wig-maker and the one which distinguishes Pascal or Michael Angelo there is, after all, scarcely anything but a difference of quality. If I sketched that of Pascal or Michael Angelo, I should wish that their wig-maker might recognize in it the face of his own.

Every creator is a monstrous egoist. The only superiority before which Beethoven bowed—"goodness"— is not incompatible with the insatiable power that marks this egoism and is not without that natural radiance which we call generosity. But beware lest he pursue in a sort of clairvoyant hallucination an inner image to which he is obliged, in order to safeguard his original purity, to sacrifice everything if necessary—family, friendship, interest, if interest, friendship, family have the misfortune to place themselves between this image and himself. Balzac has written on this subject a book, *The Search for the Absolute*, since which no equivocation is possible. Neither the morality nor the goodness nor the innate nobility of Balthasar Claës can be disputed. The drama, on the contrary, lies in the contrast between his natural virtues and the intransigent passion that makes him Balthasar Claës and makes him even more cruel toward Balthasar Claës than toward anybody else, if something in him opposes his own satisfaction; for this passion is the incorruptible element that he must draw forth from its matrix, even if his children and his wife must suffer for it, his fortune must disappear, his health and his joy must be lost, his friends, either too docile or too severe, draw down upon themselves his disdain or his hatred, even if the whole world goes to ruin. . . .

This same element, I know, may inflict terrible ravages upon many poets whose "absolute" is only a very poor "comparative." But the greatest poet is inconceivable without it. When his life, seen from a distance, seems to us harmonious, we must give credit for it to his pride which advised him to undergo the martyrdom of solitude, or else to his entourage, where also no doubt there existed an incorruptible element that found its path in sacrifice. I do not see why the dominant passion of a superior nature should be less tyrannical— or even less respectable—than the other passions and should yield before them or before those of others. It alone, precisely, has the opportunity, by leading the others in its direction, to create a center of life against which a few are crushed, but about which millions of beings will gravitate some day. Because he followed to the ultimate consequences of its own logic, making no concession, the incorruptible element that he had discovered and developed in himself, Jesus Christ seems to me at once the most complete of egoists and the most accomplished of creators. It is impossible for a man to offer himself to his family or his country or his friend as a sacrifice, if he offers himself as a sacrifice to his vision of the universe.

This pitiless need that rises from the depths of the unconscious in order to people the mind with images and give to the will the command to realize them is the true salt of the earth and the food of heroes. I am thinking of the destinies of the majority of the masters, so diverse, but in whom one almost always discovers this fury to experience life through and through, whether one leaves one's flesh behind or takes the flesh of others, in order to follow a phantom which becomes insubstantial the moment one touches it and which, as soon as it has escaped, resumes a fixed form, always the same, always new, never leaving one any rest until one has seized it to experience a brief intoxication and one more disappointment.

I think of Ghirlandajo, weighed down with children and orders, always behind in his work, talking of covering all the walls of Florence with paintings. I think of Signorelli disrobing the corpse of his son in order to paint it, suppressing his tears, his heart contracted in an anguish composed of creative fever and sorrow. I think of Tintoretto living in a torment of continuous fecundation, shut up for days and nights, painting by lamplight, in order to people convents and churches with the tormented forms that unceasingly germinated in him. I think of Michael Angelo locked up for fifty-four months in the Sistine with his bread and his jug of water, coming out staggering, emaciated, drained dry, blinded by the daylight. I think of Rubens whose colossal creation cleaves life like the keel of a ship, his pomp, his embassies, his love affairs being nothing but the spray of the wake behind him. I think of Rembrandt leaving everything, success, friendships, fortune, a method of painting legible to all, to allow ruin, poverty, intoxication perhaps to establish themselves in his household, because one day he had surprised in himself an image of the world that was like nothing but his own self. I think of Poussin refusing the presents of the King of France because he saw every day, on the threshold of his little house on the Pincio, the motives of his emotion renewing themselves for him. I think of Goya, green with fear, suspected by the Inquisition, suspected by the Bourbons, suspected by the French, but rather than not paint with his jets of fire or attack his copper with vitriol, peppering the Inquisition with arrows, boxing the ears of the Bourbons, butchering the French. I think of Gros, old and illustrious, pursuing his fugitive form to the very reeds of the Seine and plunging his mouth in the mud in order to drink it there along with death. I think of Constable to whom the verdant humidity of the fields, the growing shoots, the sprouting herbs repeat without ever wearying him: "I am the resurrection and the life." I think of Cézanne, bent over his ungrateful work, deaf to all the sounds of the world, shut up for thirty years among fools, painting like a madman for the relief of the monster whom he feels in himself alone, forgetting his canvas in the fields because he has caught sight of some flame rising before his soul. I think of Renoir, a human ruin, ossified, warped with rheumatism, unable either to get up or lie down and creating incessantly the breasts, the bellies of women, roses and anemones, from the brush fastened to his fist. I think of Hokusaï, the "old man mad over drawing," affirming that at the age of one hundred and ten he would at last know how to give life to this point, to this line.

I think of those artisans without genius, the sick Cellini, dragging himself from his bed to cast his pewter vessel into the mold where the bronze of his Perseus

Fig. 96

Toward the Fleece (P. Breughel)

was liquefying too slowly, of the poverty-stricken Palissy burning the wood of his floors and his furniture in order to heat his plates. I think of all those Italians wandering from city to city, Giotto, Taddeo Gaddi, Uccello, Gozzoli, Lippi, Piero della Francesca, Pinturicchio, Sodoma, without a roof to cover them, paid by the piece, mad with science and painting, for whom it was a passionate adventure to decorate some little chapel in a forgotten village, as jealous of one another as lovers, exhausting their genius in the effort to conquer that clenched their passion about an idea like a hand about a dagger.

I think of those good companions of Flanders or France, setting out on foot for Italy where glittered the golden fleece, painting sign-boards on the way for a living, Fouquet, Breughel, Van der Weyden, Van Orley, Courtois, Mignard, Bourdon, Coypel, Duquesnoy, Puget, Girardou, of the child Callot following a band of gypsies, of Claude Lorrain becoming a cook, then a household servant in order to live there, of Parrocel taken prisoner by pirates while seeking to land there. I think of the engravers of Egyptian hypogeums, making the shadows blossom with feminine forms, palms, shimmering water, of the Chinese or Hindu sculptors scooping out their mountains, peopling their immense caves with their swarming gods. I know very well that in these cases it was the mystic passion that drove them to bury themselves alive or roast themselves in the sunlight on the vertical wall. But is not the search for the incorruptible element that constitutes his inevitable form precisely, even in the atheist, a mystical passion before which all the others are forced to abdicate? Mystical, that is to say, eager to confront a mystery that is common only to himself and God. I think of the confession of Pascal who, after having denounced literary vanity, wonders, if he does not hope that his notes

will be found at the bottom of some drawer. The poet
must teach men sooner or later that something essential
to the development of their quality as men comes from
his quality as a man, the only one which belongs to
himself alone.

II

There is only one passion that can thwart the development of the peculiar purity that is in each of us and
which the rôle of the poet is to discover and define in
himself. Love is our purity, the only certitude that
imposes on our entire being deeds for which we are not
responsible, since they blend completely with its nature
and its methods. The cruelty of the poet is only the
carrying over into the spiritual plane of the cruelty of
love in the sentimental plane, and as the cruelty of
beings who are a prey to love ceases when love ceases,
the cruelty of the poet ceases at the cessation of the
resistance of the obstacle between his image and himself.
The poet is the fatal force that maintains in the intelligence the necessary continuity which love is charged to
maintain in the species for ends which neither the species
nor the poet, nor even love knows. There is between
love and the creative power an identity of substance
which all poets feel, because these two forces contradict
themselves by turns or annihilate one another or exalt
themselves through one another, following circumstances
and the moment.

Michelet said one should only write to "put love off
the scent." Hence that incomparable intoxication when
love appears, because the certitude of being in the
eternal verity of one's own purity still further surpasses
that which one tastes in the creative fever—which is
only its transposition. Hence those terrible conflicts
when love, swallowing up all the powers of the being as

well as its spiritual reserves that have been drawn vio-
lently into the zone of the conflagration, gives us the
impression of absorbing with them our faculty of creating and all its possibilities of future development.
Hence, when it passes, the prodigious fecundity with
which it has endowed our hearts by sowing in them the
inexhaustible seeds of grief and pleasure. Nothing
resembles more the passage of one form into another
form, of one sound into another sound, of one idea into
another idea, than the passage from one embrace to
another, from one voluptuous sensation to another, and
this constant proximity in the depths of pleasure, of
sentimental despair and the physical intoxication that
one finds, on the heights of the mind, in the permanent
association of lyrical intoxication with the anguish of
death. People have tried to see a revenge of the soul
in the victory of ideal form over the so-called bestial
powers that shut us off from access to our ideal. Why
revile in this way the most imperious of the instincts,
that is to say the noblest, and veil in sublime pretexts
our self-interested recoil before the sufferings and the
disasters which it inflicts? An admirable unity presides
over the perpetuation of animal life of which thought
and art are only the supreme flower. The idea is
essentially sensual and the animality of the poem is the
fated and efficacious function of its spirituality.

The proof of this is that all the religions are organized
about the sexual problem. All the myths of ancient
paganism are concerned with love. Brahmanism accepts the drama in all its consequences. The ethics of
the Persians, the Jews, the Chinese make of the entire
social order a system designed to master its violence.
Islam offers it as a reward in death for a life that has
submitted to the law. Christianity, on the contrary,
sees in the conquest of salvation the eternal ransom
from original sin.

Fig. 97

Sexual Spirituality (Java)

And art is almost constantly, in the course of history, only the illustration of these ideas through their confirmation even when it believes it is combating them, or their refutation even when it pretends to be supporting them. It is thus that the spiritual force which ends in Buddhism disengages itself from the sexual orgy with which Brahmanism has covered the rocks of India and that the spiritual force of Buddhism provokes in its turn, in China, in Java, in Cambodia, an orgy of form that fills the forests and peoples the deserts with temples where the dance, love, naked women under the leafy trees form the almost permanent motive of decoration.[1] It is thus that Christianity appeared in Asia as a reaction against the sanguinary sensuality of the Phœnician and Syrian cults, and could spread through Europe only by proclaiming itself the antithesis of the cult of physical beauty of which the people were weary. It is thus that the Jewish-Christian prohibition of the idol, the receptacle of carnal love, ends in the paradox of introducing Christianity into the heart of the Occidental peoples through the Byzantine, French and Italian idols, the swarm of which led, with the Renaissance, to the rehabilitation of love.

Thus, in the species as in the individual, every great creative vein exhausts itself in the way that love does when the senses and the feelings separate from one another and the creative act, more and more skillful, becomes less and less ardent and more and more forced. By degrees it prostitutes itself. It turns into a habit which divine modesty speedily deserts. A wearisome practice, mechanical and monotonous, gradually replaces the natural and radiant expansion of love. Where the man lived, where the idol was only a passionate image of the man, the "artist" appeared, he who manufactures the idol because the idol sells—the "artist"—

[1] Figs. 97, 202.

he who makes of art an illustrious and fruitful career,
whose work responds henceforth to certain formulas
that are learned and transmitted and gradually lose
from sight even the remote pretexts that have given
birth to them. Art can do nothing but take refuge in

Fig. 98
Humility (Fouquet)

a few solitary hearts when the "artist" arises, the
artist, that parasite, unknown to civilizations during
their period of strength, he who appeared in Europe
toward the fourth Greek century, began again to play
his deplorable rôle after the Renaissance, and in our
day has transformed academies and schools into asso-

ciations of private interests, surrounded by a servile multitude from which the official mandarinate of each generation is recruited.

It is certainly difficult to indicate the line that separates the "artist" from the poet, the more so that it fluctuates, and as there are differences of quality, or even of quantity in the domain of living creation. One cannot place on the same plane, whatever Diderot may have thought, a cabinet-maker, however admirable, and Rembrandt, or even Moreau the Younger and Rembrandt. A sincere heart may beat in the breast of a man whose spirit is only agreeable or distinguished. We cannot pretend, on the other hand, that no creative force ever surprises us beneath a weary skill or an affected sentiment half-heartedly displayed. Van Dyck and Reynolds are aware, at certain hours, of their mundane servitude. Greuze does not always display shamelessly his sentimental merchandise. The eloquence of Le Brun is not always devoid of muscles. It sometimes happens that the Dutch anecdotists catch a charming relationship between the glove of the physician and the vial of his draught. Often a tender desire is lit at the tip of a breast touched by the brush of Fragonard. Tiepolo's sleight-of-hand does not wholly prevent him from perceiving the silver that quivers in a cloud like the feathers of a wing or the petals of a flower. The great illusion never gives way all at once, it has moments when the flame revives, which very often indeed render its failure all the sadder. . . . One can only say this, which would suffice, if the majority of us had eyes to see and ears to hear: where love is, however light, however superficial, however fugitive, there is man. The "artist" is elsewhere.

A state of innocence, without which the amorous illusion cannot exist, characterizes any one who discovers in himself the more or less powerful means of

Fig. 99

VISUAL CLARITY (Michael Angelo)

confessing his quality as a man, and this is true of the humblest sort of creative work, that of the potter and the upholsterer, the carpenter and the glass-maker, the jeweler and the dressmaker, the florist and the currier— in whom this state of innocence is spontaneous, without deep anguish, without a glance thrown upon death and the uselessness of everything—as well as in the highest summits of spiritual grandeur, in Michael Angelo, Shakespeare, Rembrandt, Pascal, Beethoven, in whom this state of innocence is a conquest without respite over doubt and despair. It appears that unusual spirits exist midway between the two classes, especially in the art of France where unstudied moderation, discreet confidence, a sort of familiarity between the object and the mind, an indifferent disposition toward great lyrical expansion have always marked, at each and every epoch, the most perfect creators.

With the image-makers of the twelfth and thirteenth centuries, with Fouquet, with Chardin, with Corot,[1] one finds this joy of confessing a charming emotion, the emotion of a child who is always marveling at his discovery of the world, and a constant simplicity in telling the circumstances that everywhere else defines the humblest worker in wood or clay, in flowers or glass, in wool or metal. This is the case with La Fontaine who belongs, like Shakespeare, to high literature but prefers talking with his gardener about the sprouting of his lettuces and the habits of snails. A unique gift, it seems to me, when—quite possibly—a man is not unaware of the drama of creation but possesses the very rare and miraculous faculty of masking it completely, while all about him is the turmoil of wings in the storm, a panting effort, a constant tension toward a dizzy equilibrium in which primitive innocence is only recovered for the space of a flash of lightning. Here in this pitiless

[1] Fig. 98.

FIG. 100

INGENUOUSNESS (Henri Rousseau)

lucidity, that never loses sight of the abyss while it dances on the heights, does there exist more depth than there where the feet move over grass and the glance seems to find only limited horizons, made up of woods and rivers? I do not know. But there is as much love in it. And it is love that matters, first of all. The custom-house officer, Rousseau, is much closer to Michael Angelo than his most perfect imitators ever approached.[1]

III

This being said, it seems to me that a second growth of ingenuousness, that of a Michael Angelo—that which resists the clairvoyant interpretation of facts, that which is fortified by suffering, which the intelligence, far from wearing out gradually achieves, has a higher quality than the careless ingenuousness of experiment that is little sensitive to disappointment and over which the intelligence never dreams of exercising any control— the ingenuousness of a Rousseau.

No doubt nothing can replace the pure force of instinct, the confused fervor that rises from the whole being upon contact with the sensible world and seizes the brute image in order to fecundate it. But when it springs from its roots, intelligence is the flower of instinct. The intelligence chooses, redresses, eliminates. It establishes between events and objects the proportions that stand out against a choice, if the hesitant instinct is feeble, but reinforce it if the instinct is strong. There, again, it is like love. A passion at its height is exalted by the greatest obstacles. In its decline the smallest obstacle makes it doubt and yield. The intelligence feeds on the bones and viscera of instinct and then, having purified the nourishment it has

[1] Fig. 99, 100.

received, renders it back whence it came. Nothing can compare with this common ascent toward the peak where lives the phantom tracked and pursued by these two entwined beings. A lucid intoxication becomes the portion of the man who has discovered his natural medium by the light of an incessantly active meditation and, thanks to it, frees it from the dross and the foreign deposits that hide it from him. As he knows that his tears and his pleasures nourish it, he accepts his tears and his pleasures with a light heart. If you doubt the fecundity of this intimate association, compare the "Syndics of the Drapers" with the "Lesson in Anatomy"[1]; in the former, the academic grouping, the even and waxy material, education interposing between the universe and the painter to

Fig. 101

DECORATION (Korin)

conceal his emotion from him, and in the latter these men of flesh and blood watching, this poignant matter triturated with blood and fire, the painter standing alone and facing the drama of living and discovering himself in it.

When this slow, anxious discovery of himself is necessary, when, instead of divining in the shadow the moving forms which one can only outline gropingly and define stammeringly, one can also, thanks to the increasing

[1] Figs. 102, 103.

light, dovetail them into one another to make a single block which the spirit models and cements, it seems as if the second threshold of the mystery had been passed, before which the simple-minded stop without even seeing it. I believe it is very great to obey with enthusiasm the most imperious of the instinctive forces that lead us toward an end where we alone can walk. I believe it is still greater to justify and increase this enthusiasm by discovering that the mission of the conscience is to disembarrass this force of everything that does not belong to it. Driven out of paradise through knowledge, we aspire to enter it again through love. The faculty of projecting life in an imaginary form is the animality of man raised, by a sublime operation, to the dignity of the spirit. Everything that expresses the simple man, the poor man, the beast scarcely emerging from his most thwarted impulses and his elementary need to create for himself a shelter, tools for work, primitive cadences to facilitate this work and give it rhythm, finds itself solely in the highest consciences which do nothing, after all, but spiritualize this need. This is not found, half-way along the road, in the "cultivated" man, nourished on erudition, rotten with education, frozen with science.

I recall once arriving at Piræus, where the delicious little houses with their triangular pediments, tinted red or blue, gave me the sudden and irresistible impression that this had been the popular architecture of this place for three thousand years, and that it was more closely related to that of the Parthenon which I saw, a few leagues away, on its natural base, than the skillful reconstructions that housed the universities and the banks of modern Athens, not to speak of the Madeleine, the British Museum, or the various Pinacotheks of Munich. And precisely the same day, I heard on the Acropolis a young Greek student translate for me the probably immemorial peasant laments in which I recognized the accent of the curses of Prometheus. Who does not know, for that matter, the close relationship of the popular songs to the greatest music which borrows their themes and rhythms at every moment? This dish, this pot modeled by earthy hands and placed in the oven with the bread—yesterday or a thousand years ago— reproduced the motifs and the harmonic relationships that are found, like an invincible command of the soil, the sky, the cultures, the race, in the rarest harmonies of the most powerful creators. Are not the image-makers, the glaziers, the lead-workers, of the cathedral artisans comparable with the ballad-writers of all nations, with the potters and tapestry-weavers of Persia, China, Africa, the old provinces of Europe, with the painters and sculptors of the Egypt of antiquity? Has not a great master of the spiritual synthesis, Korin,[1] given for three centuries his formulas to all the decorative work of Japan? I have seen sheaves of flowers, painted on the black varnish of a hotel bed by a Florentine workman. They reminded me at once of the bouquets and garlands of the canvases of Botticelli, Lippi, Pollaiuolo, Ghirlandajo, with which the most medaled pictures of the professors and the exhibition artists of the region, who imitate them, have absolutely no relationship. These are facts of everyday observation, almost a commonplace for those who consent to give heed, and they express the organic continuity of "tradition" much more authentically than all the educations, all the formulas, all the groups, all the recompenses imagined for preserving appearances. It is not by his collar that one recognizes the dog.

The question of the creative conscience has always been badly stated. Due to a false point of departure people have confounded or tried to confound with the

[1] Fig. 101.

search for effects called "literary" in so many bad
painters, that sense of the universal which every work
expresses and cannot fail to express and whose continuity and logic define in some degree the existence,
the absence, or the degree of quality. Every work of
art, as well as every intelligence, is and cannot be
anything else than an abridged system of the world.
Whatever the value of this system of the world, or

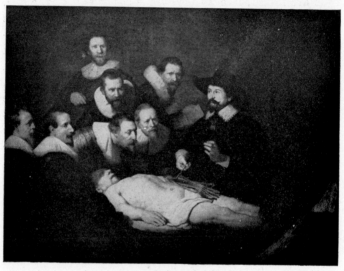

FIG. 102
SCIENCE (Rembrandt)

rather whatever the value of its coherence and the
depth of its relationships with man as he has appeared
at all times—that is the value of this work. The pagan
system, the Christian system, the pantheistic system,
the spiritualistic system have produced by turns or
simultaneously works of about equal value that depend, in the last analysis, less on the value of the system
than on the passional value of the man, or the men whose

faith and intelligence have been determined and oriented by this system, or who had the power and the
courage, during the period when this system fell, to
imagine another for their personal use.

Plastic language is even more of a language than one
might suppose. It is a manner of speaking because it is
a manner of thinking. It is even probable that it adjusts
more strictly than verbal language its manner of speak-

Fig. 103
CONSCIOUSNESS (Rembrandt)

ing to its manner of thinking. It can express ideas and
the relations of ideas which the sculptor or the painter
would be altogether powerless to translate into words.
It is even desirable for him not to know how to do it, for
he would cease to be a sculptor or a painter and become
a writer and would lose, in the meanderings of discourse,
the simplicity, the coherence, and the vigor of his
thought. The grandeur of a spirit is not bound up with
its faculties of discourse, but with its greater or less

power of expressing, in whatever language, that which it conceives. And because Cézanne would not always understand the language of Hegel, I do not see why Cézanne should be a less great spirit than Hegel, who, I imagine, would have understood no better the language of Cézanne. Philosophy itself is only a manner of speaking. The inaptitude of Rubens for general ideas seems to me as difficult to sustain as the aptitude of Teniers,[1] and from this point of view I perceive a distance between the two comparable to that which separates, for example, Spinoza and Crebillon *fils*. A personality of this stature is an indivisible thing in which sensation, idea, and expression are firmly united, intuitively and without possible debate.

Here an ambiguity appears that must be removed. It seems to me useless for Rembrandt to read Spinoza, and it seems to me deplorable that Greuze should have read Diderot. General culture seems to me useful to a painter as soon as he passes beyond the unconscious stage, if at the same time he possesses a sufficient mastery over his methods as a painter to be able to incorporate that culture in his painting in such a way that the passage is not noticeable even to a trained eye. But the direct influence of philosophy on painting has never been very valuable, the painter, if he has a weak soul, being tempted to force the language of painting to make it utter the things that philosophy alone has the power to utter in its own language and cannot utter otherwise. If Phidias resisted the influence of Anaxagoras whose discourses he followed, it was because he did not try to express in his sculpture the ideas of Anaxagoras, but because he recognized in his own ideas the ideas of the other, because he bathed, like him, in a spiritual current which the historic moment and the phase traversed by Greek thought at this in-

[1] Fig. 104.

stant determined both around the two men and in them.
The same thing happened in the case of Descartes the
philosopher and Le Nôtre the gardener who, very
happily, had not read Descartes, not being capable of
understanding him, and because of this came much
closer to him.

I do not say that it
is enough to have read
Æschylus to under-
stand at the same time
the *Centaurs and the
Lapithæ* at Olympia,[1]
or that it would be use-
less to read Æschylus
when one has under-
stood the *Centaurs and
the Lapithæ*. I say that
it is impossible that
one or the other of
these works should not
emerge from a common
matrix of ideas and
sentiments, each being
like the other the sum-
mit of the spiritual
drama, unique in Greek
thought, where one

Fig. 104
MEDIOCRITY (Teniers)

may see the will of man emerging suddenly from a
murderous and intoxicating sexual orgy in order to
attempt to master it. One easily finds similar correspondences between the thought of Aristotle and the anatomical sculpture of Lysippus, between the thought of
Saint Benedict and Roman architecture, between the
thought of Abelard and the sculpture of the thirteenth
century, between the thought of Voltaire and the paint-

[1] Fig. 1.

ing of the eighteenth, between the thought of Auguste Comte and Claude Bernard and the painting of Ingres and Courbet, between the various anarchistic systems and French Impressionism.

It would be a little puerile to pursue these parallels, which have been made too often, and sometimes awkwardly, and which can be found everywhere and at all epochs. But it is necessary to point out their origins and meaning and that they almost always appear, to safeguard their vigorous progress, in the plane of the unconscious. Philosophy, like art, comes from the necessities of the hour. Food must be found, ramparts must be raised, the spiritual current must flow through the arteries of the race. These necessities command the concepts of philosophy quite as much as they drive art to raise up on the cross-roads our great puppets besmeared with ochre, blue, and vermilion. Philosophy is no more conscious than art of the determinations which, in a given place and a given time, cause them both to respond to the imperious appeal of certain general needs. Art is not less conscious than philosophy of the means it employs to satisfy these needs.

IV

The poet, in the last analysis, is the realizer of the sum of superior energies created by the humble efforts of multitudes of men to earn their bread. He expresses the general aspect of this effort—and better than the philosopher who explains it.

He is the immediately extinguished consciousness of life that realizes itself, the affirmation of the victory of organisms newly-born over organisms that have worn themselves away. He is the eternal sage, who has the hardihood, amid fools and weak men, to transpose all the exterior forces into a personal form that is a new

world, articulated from one end to the other, in which
all men of his time should recognize each other and in
which a few men of all times should do the same. The
dramatic search for his inner unity, in which his sensuality and his consciousness meet and reach an equilibrium in spite of continuous lacerations, and no doubt
thanks to them, is his very reason for being, since, in
the measure that he raises himself in the mystery of
this unity, his sensuality and his consciousness increase
and the end to be attained continually recedes. His
desire is made up of scattered sensations, in each of which
he finds only a fragment of the definitive image which he
believes he can seize in every new work and of which
every new work, through its very realization, delivers
to him only a vain shadow capable of attracting others
but fading away for him. It is he who resists indefinitely the successive crumblings of the illusions he
pursues. It is he whose passion survives in experience
and who maintains a state of love in the universe by
maintaining it in his heart.

He is the bond through which the inner life of men
appears to us uninterrupted. It is in fact impossible
for him not to bear witness to that which has constituted
the capital spiritual event of his time and his species,
one that neither his time nor his species seems to have
perceived. As the nourishment derived from the air
and the rain rises from the soil to swell and ripen the
fruit, so he carries in him the atavisms and the dispersed
energies that mark him as the most moving testimony
of an epoch. And it is through him and through him
alone that this epoch reaches us.

When we say of such and such a poet that he is great
in having understood his epoch, we take, at least partly,
the effect for the cause. In reality we see his epoch thus
because he has commanded us to do so. Lyricism never
describes the event of the hour. It does not recount

memories. Its presentiments have no need of exteri-
orizing themselves in the pretext of an imagined
adventure. Memory, the hour, presentiment, everything transforms itself unknown to him. It is they that
make the reds of this canvas more cruel, its blacks
sadder, its greens more biting, its grays more subtle,
its blues more aerial. They that render more trenchant
or more sinuous the profile of this statue, impaste it
with more or less of shadow, make it stir through the
expression of its sharp reliefs or radiant through the
simplicity and the silence of its planes. No recent
event, no ancient event is foreign to this profound
anxiety which is in the very substance of the poet, to
the sudden flashing of the desires and enthusiasms that
rise from his anguish, to the waves of suffering that pass
over his pleasures. The ancient landscapes that he
has passed through influence the sensations that stir
him now and these present sensations are closely bound
up with the loves that have fashioned them and the
bereavements that have rendered them strong.

Will you tell me that it is thus with every man? No
doubt. And as I have said from the first line, one does
not find the poet if one does not look for the man in him.
But we cannot recover any footprint but that of the
poet, since he is the only one among us whose step is
vigorous enough to leave its print upon the road. I
know very well that there are all-powerful men who
walk there stealthily, as if they feared to shake the
pavement. I do not think their influence will be lost.
It passes, from place to place, in pure, silent echoes in
neighboring consciences, to expand some day in some
poem occasionally very remote from it. So also passes
what we consider the lost effort of the humblest folk, the
humblest beasts, the plants, the very minerals, light,
and waters. But it is this poem, alone, which consti-

Fig. 105

VISAGE OF ACTION

tutes visibly the reversions of history, unimaginable without it.

There is also, no doubt, action, the great adventurous action that traverses the inertia of crowds to attract them to it as a magnet draws steel filings. Action through word or deed, that which determines and orients the allegiance of hearts, that of Zoroaster or Moses, of Sakyamuni or Confucius, of Rama or David, of Sylla or Jesus, of Saint Paul or Tamerlane, or Mahomet or Napoleon.[1] Action, to which men subject themselves with joy in order to live symphonically about it, as the colors about the painter, the sounds about the musician. It does not differ from the poem save through the language it speaks, and there is, between the two, a permanent exchange and intercrossing of influences, the conqueror springing from the Bible or the Temple which in their turn spread abroad and legitimize his action. Action, which is beneficent through the material or spiritual edifices which it, raises, malignant through the ruins which it makes, like the poem itself, both the supreme expression, intensified and monstrous, of life, devastating and fecundating, but necessary for propagating that formidable indifference to maintaining an illusion without which it could not exist.

Do you doubt perhaps this fecundating action, you who have heard the tempest of the Sistine, whom Shakespeare has lulled in the surge of the worlds, and who have felt the royal-heartedness of man over things in the music of Beethoven or the epopee of Balzac? But if you doubt this devastating action, count the victims of Phidias, who were and still are almost as numerous as the victims of Jesus. See in what state Michael Angelo left his Italy, Rubens his Flanders, Rembrandt his Holland. The country where such beings have passed seems ravaged, empty of its forms,

[1] Fig. 105.

condemned for ages to sterility. They have the power of fire. They leave nothing behind but ashes. But these ashes constitute the richest of fertilizers.

If life has a meaning, then it is the artistic feeling of man that imposes this upon it, beyond Good and Evil, beyond the Beautiful and the Ugly, beyond the True and the False, by creating with energy and enthusiasm the spiritual forms to which the multitude rallies with all the more facility because its masters impose upon these forms a sentimental significance in order to facilitate its approach to them. Whether he destroys or whether he spreads despair to attain one of these forms, his own proper form, the poet is he who never ceases to have confidence precisely because he does not attach himself to any port, does not fasten himself by any anchor, but pursues this one form that flies through the storm and is lost unceasingly in the eternal becoming. He attempts to substitute for the human and natural disorder that wounds him a divine order that he will never find, fortunately for his confidence,—the divine order being nothing but the definitive adaptation and consequently the death of a definitive man to a definitive world. Man is condemned, through the play of his very spirit, to clench his hand about granite and feel the sand flowing between his fingers, but it is this frightful drama which constitutes precisely the majesty of his spirit. Outside this illusion, there is nothing but love of ruins, discouraged respect for that which dies or is dead, fear of dying, fear of living. The Greeks piling up the statues mutilated[1] by the Persians in the earthworks of the Parthenon of Pericles seem to me to have lived the symbol of this ardent research which will not, which cannot, which should not be arrested. In the general movement of a humanity that seeks to survive itself, every generation is a wave that seeks to

[1] Fig. 8.

survive itself, every man is a drop of water that seeks to survive itself, and it is this, perhaps, which is the principal aspect of God.

Which of us does not make, by means of his own power, a gigantic effort to endure one instant more, an instant which he imagines to be rich in possibilities? The priest, opening to the faithful the gates of eternal life, opens them to his own hope. The conqueror and the legislator seize a fragment of time which they call history to quicken their action. The savant marks off a fragment in which he inscribes a law to eternalize his own. The humblest girl, through maternity, believes she is taking possession of the future. The peasant enlarges the property that he will leave behind him. The imbecile builds for himself a mausoleum. Frostratus burns the Temple. The poet, who tries to incorporate time and space in his inner life so that they will merge with it and in this way pass with it into the future determination of the intelligence and the sensibility of men is undoubtedly not the least illusioned among them. But it is possible—and probable—that his illusion may be the most fruitful and the most noble of all, because his realization orients the reality of the spirit.

Fig. 105a

RENOIR

Fig. 106

CHARTRES

Chapter V. THE POETRY OF KNOWLEDGE

I

ONE step more and we are at the threshold of the thought of Baudelaire in which the apparent antinomy between art and science is resolved in a few words: "The imagination is the most scientific of the faculties, because it alone understands the universal analogy." This poet was not unaware that the savant is the poet, and it is not the fault of the savant or the fault of the poet if we ourselves begin to become conscious of it. The savant scorns the poet, the poet fears and respects the savant, both with their eyes closed. The former is not far from viewing the mystery as an ensemble of phenomena reducible to mathematical

238

FIG. 107

THE DEMIURGE (Lamarck)

relations, which is true perhaps but proves that he does not feel this mystery. And the other, if he believed this would cease to feel it. I speak of the poet as one would of a bird that has alighted somewhere along the road, or in the fields, or in the town waiting, like an Æolian harp, for a breath from the sky—the singers of England, for instance, or Verlaine among ourselves.

For the metaphysical torment is not always in the heart of those who desire passionately to catch the scattered harmony. To know the despair caused by the idea that a geometrician alone can attain a limitless absolute, to dominate this despair when as one sees that this absolute is within the reach of a student of special mathematics, one must be a Michael Angelo, a Shakespeare, a Pascal, a Beethoven, a Goethe, or, precisely, Baudelaire. Even Pascal did not feel life sufficiently to conquer the obstinate anguish to which he was condemned by the need of assigning to life an uncompromising moral finality, and thus rejoin Baudelaire on the summits of the imaginary world where plastic art, music, and poetry tend to associate themselves with mathematics in the intoxication of an objectless harmony.

I say "tend," for geometry, to my mind, can be "pure poetry" only on condition that, outside the poet, it ceases to exist as an implement—Pascal would say as a "métier." It does not attain to the dignity of the poetic state except in very rare creators and as an intuitive instrument of harmonies that are always being born. It was rigorously applied geometrical formulas that brought Arabic decoration and, in consequence, architecture to their death.[1] They lead us directly to an automatism that is more severe than that of the workman sinking a rivet every three seconds into a plate of cast iron that passes mechanically before him.

[1] Fig. 114.

At school we have all known various puppet-students who did their mathematics with machine-like accuracy, and we are not unaware of what they have become after their taking the required courses, in a state college.

The drama of art unrolls—for the poet within, for the geometricians without—the scope of geometry properly so-called, even though the drama may tend unceasingly to an extreme-limit of idea, the conquest of which would drown it in the Nirvana of its silent axiom. . . . If we went down to the deepest roots of our spiritual impulses we should see that neither geometry, nor analysis, nor calculus dealing with the infinitesimal, which gives us so perfect an impression of security, would exist without Euclid or Descartes or Newton. Has not Kepler told us how certain of the most commonplace circumstances of his life permitted him to foretell and, in the end, formulate several of the laws that laid the foundation of astronomy? We are doubtless not yet ready to discover in the personal work of the great geometrician those events of his inner life that must have led him to geometrical invention. But I defy any intelligence that is in love with the language of the geometricians not to dedicate to Euclid, Descartes, Newton, Kepler a passionate gratitude. In order to express themselves they imagined material signs and suggested images in which the music of the spheres, the cadences and the volumes of space assumed a physiognomy which they had not possessed before.[1]

I have said elsewhere[2] that the mathematical harmonies are not more independent of the moral terrain whence they spring than are the sensuous constructions of the painters and the musicians. Einstein could not

[1] Has not four-dimensional geometry given to the thought of Riemann and Lobatchewski a *visible* form, very different from that which clothes the thought of Euclid, and does not the cosmic relativism of the thought of Einstein obey a rhythm that is very different from the Newtonian rhythm?

[2] *History of Art*, Vol. IV, page x.

have been born in the age of Descartes, nor Descartes in our days. A mute tragedy presides over the elaboration of the most impartially established algebraic formulas, and this tragedy is not the same in every man, in every species, nor under the pressure of the events and circumstances of every epoch or environment. The pure geometrical verity, immutable and transmissible, is no other than the residue of a few great passions.

Baudelaire wrote some extraordinary lines that resolve the conflict by going back to its sources, about the same time that Claude Bernard published his *Introduction*. For three centuries an obstinate prejudice obsessed and dominated the European spirit, gradually modifying it and, in my opinion, betraying it. Organized by Cartesianism, tending to an increasing tyranny by its positive conquests, it appeared as an unconquerable adversary of a good half of the human soul, determined to destroy it—I mean an enemy of its faculty of feeling, imagining, and creating poetic forms.

M. Le Dantec has written on this subject some very sad things—or joyous, at least for those who do not think as he does. But with that unconscious irony which God[1] imposes on us, to revenge himself upon those who strive to destroy his unity, after having decreed that art is at the antipodes of science and that the latter intends to exterminate the former, he gave a definition of "science" to which art accommodates itself marvelously: "What we call 'things' are the elements of the *human* description of the world, and these elements depend, not only on the nature of the world, but also on the nature of him who describes it." Had M. Le Dantec inadvertently read Spinoza?

The efforts that have been made to render the partition water-tight have convinced so many people that

[1] Or, if you prefer, the universal dynamism.

one wonders if this is not one of those phenomena of collective intellectual indolence created by the mystical craving for certain immediate and urgent gains. That art and science translate, in the superficial regions of the spirit, two orders of different activity is so evident a fact that no demonstration is necessary. But I could not conceive that these activities should end in creating two intellectual structures that can never agree. One cannot define science by reducing it to mathematical relations, since geol-ogy, anatomy, botany, biology—sciences nevertheless—are irre-ducible to these rela-tions, and since music —although an art— and probably painting as well, submit to mathematics in the end. As for the other argument of weight, which bases the so-called antagonism on the personal character of art and the imper-sonal character of science, it drives

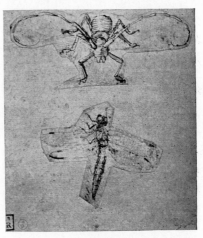

Fig. 108

Anatomy (da Vinci)

Claude Bernard into a flagrant contradiction, since he affirms, in the same illustrious *Introduction*, that science varies and art does not vary, for the impersonal tends to the law, which strives to be invariable, and the per-sonal to opinion, which varies unceasingly.

That which is impersonal is not the spirit of science, since it is the creation of man—and even, in the last analysis, of a few great personalities; it is its language. This character conditions science and assures its transmission. But we perhaps mistake for "science" a *state* of science that would destroy its achievements if both persisted in confusing their aims. The present impersonality of scientific language is perhaps only a step toward surmounting the mass of the unknown,—one achieved by the determined needs of intellectual curiosity. And it has been necessary to limit these needs on all sides, to specialize and define them in order to assure their efficacy. Mathematics, for example,— which today is doubtfully regarded as a science and which is probably only a precise way of speaking, or rather of dreaming,—mathematics two centuries ago a u t o m a t i c a l l y adopted toward the natural sciences an attitude that is almost similar to that which science assumes today in regard to art. Which does not prevent us from supposing that art will succeed one day in conquering some impersonal instrument in the presence of which the personality of the sculptor or the painter will preserve the same importance as does the personality of the scientist armed with the algebraic symbol, the scales, the microscope, and the crucible. The cinematograph already offers the example of a dawning art, in which the mechanical means reveal neverthe-

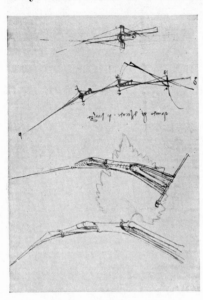

Fig. 109

FLIGHT OF BIRDS (da Vinci)

less—and with an extraordinary accent—the personality of the stage manager and the actor.

The most rigorous partisan of the impersonality of science really knows no more than I—and probably less than François Villon—about the end which is sought by our universal exploration of the world. It is perhaps nothing but curiosity about the useful, a means of adaptation, or even a game gradually incorporating its discoveries and its intoxicated creations in an incessant becoming—in any case a passion common to the artist and the scientist. Science no more than art—less than art, I imagine—attains "the thing in itself." It establishes the relations between "things." The faculty of first reflecting and then of generalizing is all that shapes the depths of our intellectual action, whatever may be elsewhere the elements of its enquiry and its modes of expression. Science, like art, is only a system of self deception, that is to say, of conquest.

It is in a domain superior to that of literal and transmissible science that art and science show a constantly renewed accord. At different points where science, having reached the limits of its proofs, finds itself on the verge of the unknown that withdraws before it, art appears to grasp the new intuitions upon which other proof will be founded. The great scientific hypotheses, gravitation, transmutation, atomism, so fruitful from the point of view of results, so apt to arouse creative experience and attract other hypotheses, are no more demonstrable through experimentation than art. They belong to the poetic order, like the transcendent mathematics that has nothing to do with experience and moves freely entirely outside the domain of facts. Now, what is poetry if not the intuition of the possible? How can one say that Newton is so remote from Rembrandt, if one sees clearly the abyss that separates Newton from his astronomer-pupils who have not been able to handle as subtly as himself his impersonal method, or separates Rembrandt from his painter-pupils who imitate him exactly without ever penetrating his personal virtue? Can one imagine, on the other hand, a poet destitute of the implement of knowledge, of that blood-relationship which unites him to the object of his desire, makes him, so to speak, savor with his finger the special quality of the stone and clay, touch with his eye the passages from light to shadow, arrange with his delighted intelligence the sounds and noises that reach him confusedly?

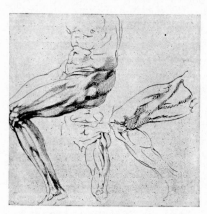

Fig. 110

ANATOMY (Michael Angelo)

There is in the poet as much rigorous knowledge as there is in the scientist himself, but he only formulates it tacitly, giving sudden shape to the lightning-like hypothesis that is born of its slow assimilation; he makes use of the object to prove his hypothesis. There is, in the scientist, as much synthetic intuition as there is in the poet: he starts from the hypothesis in order to define the object. Lamarck,[1] enlightened by the analogy which he established between universal forms, affirms their original unity and delegates to Geoffroy Saint-Hillaire, to Darwin, to Huxley, to Spencer, to Haeckel, to Cope, to Samuel Butler, to Bergson, to the interminable future, the task of pursuing the proof from form to form, from the protozoan to the spirit. Rubens seized upon these forms, scattered everywhere,

[1] Fig. 107.

and summed up the universal analogy in a space that
could be caught at a glance. Newton pursued the musical
curves of his intellectual architecture to the confines of
the invisible universe itself where he based them un-
shakably on the material bodies of the stars and the real
orbits which they trace in the sky. Sebastian Bach
brought them back to the dimensions and the scope of
an orchestra that inscribes them on the heart. Aside
from men of this stature, who are not very numerous,
aside from the instinct of certain illustrious peoples
who have given to the rocks and built on the desert the
form of their illusion, I see everywhere materials loyally
united by the grinder of colors and the biologist, by the
lute-maker and the geometrician, by the chemist and
the mason. Michael Angelo is much more of a savant,
Laplace a very different sort of poet from this very
erudite or very sensitive professor of this faculty of
sciences or that School of the Fine Arts. Intuition has
its certitudes which proof does not know.

II

The Italians of the fourteenth, the fifteenth, even of
the sixteenth century, although they were more responsible than any other European people for the rupture of the spiritual unity of the Middle Ages, felt the
danger of the adventure in which they made use of an
intelligence determined to separate science from art in
order to forge the weapon necessary to the European
spirit. Aside from a few Platonists who were careless
of disturbing the framework of practical knowledge and
whom da Vinci could not endure, it was a strained,
desperate, constant effort to maintain the conquests of
intuition in a setting of the strictest technique and the
most exact science, to prevent a momentarily inevitable
divorce and to reconstitute in reason the lost unity of

faith. An almost universal tendency manifested itself in them to transform into experimental and transmissible knowledge not only architecture but sculpture, the fresco, and even the painting of easel-pictures.

We know, moreover, that Uccello, Brunelleschi, L. B. Alberti, Verrocchio, and Piero della Francesca passed their time solving the problems of perspective[1] and attempting to apply the solutions to the rigorous composition of their buildings or their pictures. We know they wrote treatises on perspective, arithmetic, geometry, mechanics, geodesy, at the same time as treatises on architecture and painting in which they obstinately pursued the concentration of the means of knowledge in the same systematic and rational view that could unite them to all the forms of expression. We know that da Vinci, Signorelli, Michael Angelo,[2] Cellini were anatomists, passionately interested in dissecting corpses and drawing from nature muscles, bones, viscera, systems of arteries, and nerves. That da Vinci, who wrote a work on human anatomy, another on the anatomy of horses, pursued the study of the universal analogy on the nerves of leaves, the membranes of insects, the spread wings of bats and birds.[3] That this same da Vinci considered painting only as one of the processes of demonstration and of technique which permitted him to dig canals, establish locks, construct machines, and cast metal.

And we know, again, that plastic art is naturally oriented by a scientific conception of its mission since it springs from the great unknown fountain-head of the Middle Ages, where the painter and the sculptor rub elbows with the glassmaker, plumber, carpenter, and mason men who construct their own molds and

[1] Fig. 110.
[2] Figs. 108, 110, 111, 112.
[3] Fig. 109.

their braces, cut their own marble, granite, and sand-
stone, and prepare their own mortar and plaster for
their frescoes. The same phenomenon appeared in
Germany, especially with Dürer, who was trained in
the ateliers of Nuremberg where they forged iron,
hammered steel, pol-
ished glass, filed the
wheelwork of clocks,
and passed their
springs through the
rolling-mill. It ap-
peared in France also,
with Jean Cousin,
Palissy, and a few
others.

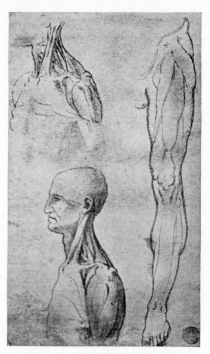

And from this fact
one grasps one of the
fundamental princi-
ples of the Renais-
sance, especially in
Florence. At the most
temptestuous hour
that human passion
has known, art
assumed an ener-
vated, restless, even
tortured character be-
cause it attempted in
vain to bring the
beating of the heart

Fig. 111
ANATOMY (da Vinci)

and the fever of the intelligence into rhythms dictated
by those laws of articulate movements which were being
studied on the skeleton and on the spacial order established by geometry and astronomy. The drama lived by
Michael Angelo consisted wholly in this antithetical
struggle between a heart, which the frontiers of the real

are incapable of containing, and an absolute science that attempted to fix them. Moreover the struggle was successful, causing the realization of one of the most extraordinary of the miracles of man, but at the same time precipitating the whole of civilization, bent upon reproducing it, into an intellectual dualism still more tragic than the mystic dualism in which the Christian drama grew up.

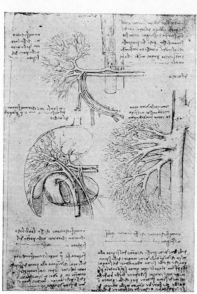

FIG. 112

ANATOMICAL DRAWINGS (da Vinci)

The capital error of the Renaissance, in other ways so great, is to have believed, in its universal enchantment in discovering science, that art should be subordinated to science. On the contrary it seems to me, that science would recover all its virtue if one saw it as depending upon art, or rather, like it, as an attribute of the æsthetic genius of man seeking to introduce into the universe, by these two essential means, an incessantly pursued dynamic order. The power of the scientist will be increased tenfold on the day when he understands the real nature of the poetic intuition that leads him to conquer the world, as the power of the artist will be found complete and ten times increased on the day when his understanding has completely assimilated the elements of poetry and mystery that science has gradually incorporated. The Christian order at its peak—say toward the twelfth century—knew this fundamental unity, since science, infinitely more advanced in the Middle Ages than one thinks, but using other methods than those of today, was entirely wrapped up in the cathedral, at once rationalistic and living, in which it was united to art through sculpture and stained glass and so became, like art, an image and means of universal symbolism.

It is certain that the alternate rhythms of synthesis and analysis which appear in history as soon as one seeks its pulsations under the outer surface of events, are in great part nourished by the association or dis-association of attitudes of mind that we have tried for three centuries to separate from one another and which seem today to be once more coming into accord. In all Egyptian art the monumental expression is merged with the utilitarian and this assigns to the Pyramids,[1] for example, a rôle of triangulation. The industrial and agricultural encyclopædia is written in the thousand low reliefs, all quivering with beating wings, opening flowers, budding breasts, while hieroglyphics in-corporate the mystery of articulate thought in an ani-mal or vegetable form that is as close as possible to geometrical stylization. In all probability it is the geometrician and the engineer who build the temple. In all probability in Chaldea the priest-astronomer is also the builder. Chinese meteorology regulates the symbolism of all buildings. Greek art, up to Phidias, is inspired by a naturalistic mythology and rests upon a utilitarian philosophy to which it owes its unity, which it loses with the philosophy of Socrates, the point of departure from which the poet Plato and the savant Aristotle go their different ways. In India, Pantheism reconciles the hermetical science of the

[1] Fig. 113.

initiates and the feverish art of the multitudes in the
intuitive knowledge of universal relations.[1]

In the great moments of art science is completely
dominated and drawn by it into the triumphal movement of a force of creation that absorbs it for the good
of the universal lyric order. Whether this order dwells
under the brow of Apollo, in the heart of Jesus, in the
blood of Brahma, or under the breast of Isis, it is al-

Fig. 113
PYRAMIDS

ways this order that expresses the unity of divine knowledge of which science and art are attributes. When art
declines under the blows of criticism or under the weight
of fatigue, science, assuming the upper hand, drags to
its ruin the previously imagined social poem. Thus,
unfortunately for all Mussulman art, the arabesque of
Islam tends gradually to enter and finally succeeds in
entering the geometrical form with which it plays

[1] Do not the contemporary works of the Hindu scientist, Jagadis Chundra
Bose, tend to demonstrate the biological unity of animal, plant, and mineral?

henceforth endlessly until its force is rendered sterile.[1]
We have seen that this was precisely the influence of
the disciples of Socrates in regard to the Greek edifice.
We have seen that, in spite of the effort of the Italians,
it was the influence of their universalists, incapable of
uniting enthusiasm and method anywhere except in
a few brains, that
precipitated the ruin
of the temple even
while trying to pre-
vent it. The Renais-
sance, thanks to the
too wearing restraint
of Cartesianism in
France, was to lead
the two poles of
European genius
toward a progressive
discord which the
Revolution would ap-
pear to render irreme-
diable by destroying
the corporations that
maintained, at least
among the artisans,
the union of imper-
sonal technique and
individual lyricism.
In the nineteenth cen-

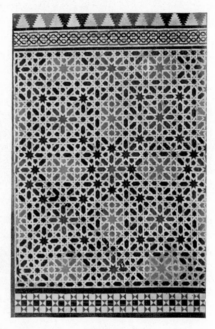

Fig. 114

GEOMETRICAL ARABESQUE (Alcazar)

tury the divorce was consummated, art sinking from
day to day, in spite of the heroism of a few, into sentimental preaching, and science, in spite of its incessant
and most beautiful conquests, into the most degrading
positivism.

Happily a dynamic conception of the world was born,

[1] Fig. 114.

unperceived, in the very heart of the movement that attempted, in the sixteenth century, especially in Florence, to shut up all art in the narrow frames of a static science in process of formation. It tended to subordinate this science, victorious in appearance, to the conquest of a lyricism that was indifferent to all immediately useful ends and that was being inaugurated by a few minds. Feeling instinctively the lost Christian unity, Venice introduced into the rigid armature of primitive Italian art a new circulation of spiritual forces which great painting was to organize through Rubens, Rembrandt, Velasquez, Watteau, entrusting its completion to German music.

It is no mere chance that the greatest works of Beethoven and the *Philosophie Zoologique* of Lamarck are contemporaneous. The meeting of the symphonic poem, organized by painters and rendered more perceptible to the multitudes by the musicians, with the biological poem that continues to develop in our days, marks probably the decisive moment after the ancient framework had been decisively broken by the fall of the corporations, when a nucleus of force appeared, capable of drawing back to its center of attraction science and art that had been separated from one another by criticism. And then also appeared the method that was to reunite the materials after the collapse of the Christian edifice. Everything from this day is passage, becoming a progressive harmony of contradictory forces. Form, which up to then scientists had thought they could delimit and describe in all its aspects and for all time, became—as poets knew, as they have always known—a momentary and fugitive expression of an inner, unstable, and yet continuous movement. Biology and mathematics meet one another in this concept, in which the dance, painting, and music have preceded them, and from which spiritual unity is undoubtedly destined to spring.

III

Thus in spite of the appearance, after Phidias, of Greek criticism which opened the enquiry necessary for changing the rhythm of our march, in spite of the Renaissance which pursued a similar end, we have never ceased to be surrounded by a confused universe in which the divine begins at the limits of knowledge. Art, science, philosophy, the social order, all are poetry at the outset. Everything becomes poetry again as soon as knowledge, after having saturated the mind, is obliged to appeal once more to the synthetic

Fig. 115

Motor

intuition to break the rigid circle that every system is fated to create when it exhausts its virtue. Experience, almost always if not always, has confirmed the great lyric synthesis of which it has been able to rend only the veil, woven of symbols. It burns the charcoal, it does not touch the diamond. But it is true that in burning the charcoal it leaves a residue of cinders so rich in nourishing substances that it adds, at every cycle, new fires to the flame of the diamond. Greek analysis, in ruining the ancient myths, has thus precipitated in the Jewish focus, innumerable facts, sentiments, forms that have permitted the Christian myth to flourish. Occidental analysis, in ruining the Christian myth, has accumulated in us such unemployed forces that we can foresee their approaching organization on some mystical plane under pain of being destroyed by them if we refuse to utilize them.

In fact, the belief that modern science brings moral progress or is even the same thing, has nearly ruined man's confidence in it and led him to break the new idol that failed to crown his hope. The optimism that is born in the sentimental reaction of the weak against the cruelty of social realities always represents a serious danger to the effort of civilization—I mean the effort to organize the illusions, the symbols, and the images and not that which desires to moralize every force of man at the risk of neutralizing him. On the other hand, it is curious to find that the critical spirit had reached the point, in our time, of confusing the fact of its growth with what is called "civilization"—which means, to almost all men, the impulse to apply science—when at all times, on the contrary, it has appeared at the decline of successive civilizations which it has contributed more than any other force in the world to destroy.

The notion of progress, vulgarized by science and confused with the evident development of the general well-being, has spread the idea that it is at last going to bring the reality of happiness, as if happiness could be anything else than a state of unstable equilibrium, as if the first effect of science had not always been to destroy this equilibrium and illuminate cruelly the inmost recesses of our illusions! At the stroke of its wand, has not science suppressed the inner analysis, the drama of love and the consciousness of death, which on the contrary it has deepened by multiplying the means of exchange and the terms of comparison? It is remarkable to find that the cruel myths of India, Syria, Judæa, or Greece have not sown more despair in the world than the consoling myths of Buddhism, Christianity, Islam, or the humanitarian religion of today, of which science constitutes the central myth. The pitiless development of science,[1] that universal mechanization, fated as the course of a star and which man could not stop if he wished to do so, exceeds perhaps in ferocity the most sanguinary mystic symbols of Phœnicia or Mexico, not only because of the beings whom it destroys in industry or war, but especially because of its geometrical progression, which drags people's minds into a whirlpool of ever-increasing swiftness. Every change of idol is expressed by murder and suffering, and quite as much in individual consciences as in social realities.

The idea of progress is always fatal to art, and to it Hellenic and Renaissance

[1] Fig. 115.

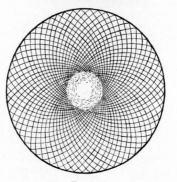

Fig. 116

Stereodynamics of Life

1. Nummulite (Spiral of Archimedes)
2. Fossil Ammonite
3. Orbitoid (Logarithmic Spirals)

art notably owed their rapid decadence for having confused the idea of expression with the idea of perfection.
It can be maintained in the field of science only on condition that while it labors to develop mechanical systems, it also develops the will to establish over this
mechanism the domination of man.   Until now he has
been merely its victim. On the day when he holds this
new weapon firmly in his hand he must make the most
terrible effort that God has demanded of him. If thereby
he can regain the equilibrium which was broken by the
too sudden invasion of applied science, he will be able to
plan, not the resumption of his way toward an indefinite
progress, but the realizing through his intelligence of
a new form in which art will once more attain its
rights.   It is increasingly apparent that science, without modifying the depths of man, is engaged on a
thoroughgoing renewal of the bases of his illusion.

The Italians certainly felt this.   Their art would
have amounted to nothing if their learning as geometricians, anatomists, technicians had not offered them
the occasion for a new enthusiasm, much more than a
precise end which they had cold-bloodedly set out to
attain.   Without a passionate love for geometry would
Piero della Francesca have discovered in the human
structure those monumental forms, those spherical
skulls, those pure and solid faces, those torsos, those
column-like limbs, all that formidable majesty that
makes one think of a race of gods descended in prayer
and struggle?   And would Uccello have achieved those
harsh rhythms that resound not merely in vigorous
movement and the mass of groups in action, but in
somber harmonies of black and red that reveal the
rectitude and the force of calculus?[1] If da Vinci had
not applied an ardent curiosity to the study of the
muscles overlying the bones, of the arborescences on

[1] Figs. 141, 142.

insect wings and leaves, of the networks of veins under the skin, would his drawings quiver with that animation, at once distinct and mysterious, which causes the living surfaces to vibrate as if under the continuous caress of the influx of the nerves and blood?[1]   Michael Angelo is haunted to such a degree by his own learning that he comes to hate it, like a too tyrannical love which by turns exalts a hundredfold or annihilates our power of action.

We must not forget that in the sixteenth century the sciences were still mysterious and inexact. They formed part of the divine domain of the always renewable unknown, they had not yet assumed that fixed position from which their rising dynamism has torn them during the past few years, and the persistence of which would have risked destroying the hypothesis as much in the hearts of the poets as in the brains of the scientists. It is in this dynamism itself, and not in the daily increasing applications of science that we must seek its incomparable poetry, in which art can acquire renewed strength.

Never more than today has the contact of the spirit with reality, patiently and methodically scrutinized, forced upon us the impression of this infinite and undefined enlargement of the mystery that gives our lyric force its eternal freshness. At the same time that industrial mechanics and architecture are laboring to restore to the intelligence of artists a logical skeleton that articulates it in all its parts, the thousand new relations that science creates, the thousand old relations which it destroys, confront the spirit with an unexpected and profoundly moving universe. The immense poetry of transformism, after having revealed to us the original identity of the organisms scattered over the earth and in the waters, has made out of time

[1] Figs. 108, 109, 111, 112.

the spiritual architect of space itself, though this is
no doubt only one of its incarnations.

A metaphysics—I should say a mythology—in process
of constant formation teaches us that the spacial illusion enters, with all its implications, into an incessantly

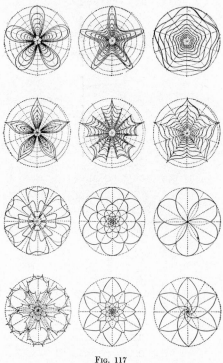

FIG. 117
STEREODYNAMICS OF FLOWER FORMS

creative development in which rigorous scientific instruments—the cinematograph, for instance—project the
moving image under aspects that mingle like musical
rhythms. The opacity of forms disappears, revealing
beyond the hardest surfaces and the densest volumes
that one had thought were defined for all time, forms

that sink deeper and deeper into the secret of a life that is in process of elaboration. Distance no longer exists, since the thought and the word are transmitted instantaneously from any point whatever of space to all its other points. Objective psychology reveals moral labyrinths that were formerly covered or rather masked by morality. We are beginning to grow intoxicated with the idea that the infinitely small, obedient to gravitation, opens up within us, through the dance of the atoms, the same mechanical abyss in which the

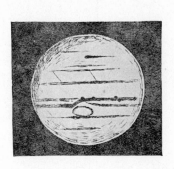 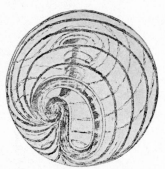

Fig. 118

ANALOGIES (Whorls: 1. Jupiter.   2. A Drop of Water)

vortex of the stars surpasses in extent and complexity the limits of intuition.[1] Never perhaps has such a mass of poetic material appealed to our enthusiasm.

And, in the last analysis, a similar impression, I think, derives periodically from the meeting of two elements: our candid but invincible need of "progress" and our imperious feeling that art and science, springing from the same source, going toward the same destiny, accord, at their great moments, in a unity so close that one could not destroy one without destroying the other at the same time. If, as I believe, the universal order

[1] Figs. 116, 117, 118.

is not moral but æsthetic in essence, it seems that the only progress that can be realized in it is the continually growing power of the spirit to rediscover the virgin sources of its natural emotions, to break through the deposit of sentiments, ideas, and sensations left by generations and centuries, and to give to these natural emotions the form of a new organism. The effort which this exploration demands seems more and more painful, no doubt, but as the inner nature of man grows more and more complex it is possible that this effort will weigh upon him less in the future than that of creating fire, for example, or than the making of the first flint hatchet weighed upon his ancestor. In any case, it is in this effort that his grandeur lies. If the world exists for a thousand million years more, it will still be the poet, after these thousand million years, who, on the image that he shaped of himself, will impose the order established among the spiritual materials accumulated by the knowledge that had existed before him.

Fig. 118a

Egg of Epiornis

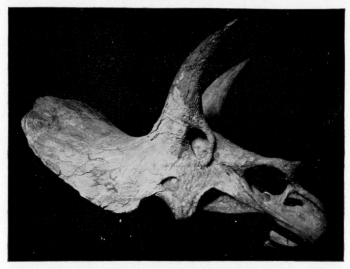

Fig. 119
TRICERATOPS

Chapter VI. THE KEYBOARD

I

THUS, far from shrinking, the keyboard incessantly grows larger. The more the complexity
of the spirit increases, the more the elements of
its creations accumulate. For its own safety it will not
escape them. It will never be suspended in the void.
It feeds on solid things as a fire feeds on oil or on wood.
And the poet has charge of providing it with this food.
History, religion, civilization, the conquest of the universe by man, his pathetic creation of God, all this is
nothing but poetry—that is to say, the incorporation
in the spirit of the matter that creates it and which it
recreates itself and transfigures in a continuous exchange. Nothing is conceivable for man without some

his senses for blood—or their aversion to it, his anxiety in the presence of women, his bitterness at being despised and his joy at being understood, his revolt against the yoke, blinders, and the rod, his refusal or his consent that society, the country, and the world should be what they are, down to the very influence of the air he breathes and the food he digests upon his health, his waking and sleeping, his cheerful or sullen humor.

Then in the very heart of the stone there is established the identity of his spirit with the profound movements that determine the surfaces of the stone, the incidence of light and the play of shadows upon it, its grain, density, sonority, savor. It seems inconceivable, but it is natural, that a dark bronze should assume the ruddy tone of flesh, an icy and compact marble the pulpy firmness of fruit, solid granite, the fluidity of running water. It seems inconceivable but it is natural that a block of formless stone, worked over by loving hands, should become a spiritual wave, an infinite quivering of imponderable vibrations, a play of scarcely sensible nuances that spreads over its entire expanse the commandments of its mute depths, whereas this same block, worked over by mean hands, wastes the splendor of its mass in disjointed gestures, loses the living quality of its natural density and color and becomes colorless and empty, even if those hands polish it, even if they are bent upon increasing its importance. Spiritual nourishment, like material, becomes part of the man himself who imparts to the product of the exchange the qualities he receives from it.

One can only imperfectly imagine, I believe, the depths of the reverberations which the very nature of the material, its density, its hardness, the degree of resistance it opposes to the implement—that is to say to the hand, which means the intelligence—can awaken

in the soul of an artist by way of the thirty or sixty or
one hundred generations that have worked in it before
him. Why should not wood, which is so soft and can
be cut in all directions without being chipped, give
to the German or the Polynesian[1] who attacks it and
whose knife pierces it at the will of his sensual or sentimental impulses, a taste for the complications of winding

Fig. 121   Fig. 122
Work in Stone (France xiii Century)

lines, for picturesque irregularities on the surfaces, for
scrolls, volutes, and rhythmic repetitions? Egyptian
basalt,[2] which wears away so slowly, rocking meditation
on its wave during the long hours of work—why should
it not bring about a taste for great simplified planes
that merge into one another without shock or sudden
fracture, like a silent music of endless modulations

[1] Fig. 120.
[2] Figs. 27, 39, 197.

which no eye can interrupt? Stone, less soft than wood,
less hard than primitive rock and which iron easily
chips in decisive strokes that can not be altered later—
how should it not indicate to the Frenchman or to the
Hindu[1] the path of high relief and expressive movements, half way between immediate impulse and the
great immutable systems, and so produce what is both
most general and most perceptible in the drama of
humanity?

It is the same everywhere, from the most utilitarian
architecture, in which our permanent needs are logically
formulated and expressed by bold surfaces and flowing
parts, to the most personal of paintings pursuing, in the
most complex play of reflections, values, and passages,
the psychological tragedy which the poet sees unfolding,
withdrawing, hiding, or springing up within him. It is
not by chance that this Florentine, in whom gesture is
the natural prolongation of an activity patiently and
passionately prepared, paints with a kind of violence
on the plaster of walls that dry quickly, the severe
tones and vigorous contours which he never retouches
later.[2] Or that this material-minded Fleming, nourished
on beer and meat, seeks in the fluid and fugitive luster
of oil the sensual correspondence of his rich, sonorous,
abundant visions, mingled and triturated like the thick
paste in which his brush revels.[3]

Or that this German, with his precise mind, juxta-
posing his sensations like selected objects to confront
them with the most vague and floating of reveries,
bending near-sightedly over his steel plate, engraves
the metal with a hundred intercrossed strokes of which
he does not see directly either the color or the arabesque,
and whence the shadow and the light surge up as if

[1] Figs. 121, 122, 178.
[2] Fig. 123.
[3] Figs. 28, 32, 66, 87, 96, 140.

without his knowledge.[1] Or take this Chinese with his magnifying glass who, a thousand times, has copied all the little animals, all the grasses, all the ripples on the water; it is not by chance that he suddenly forgets the external universe and paints his own states of soul, in which everything that he knows so well appears only as so many signs to transmit to the changing silk, in harmonies as fragile as pollen, trembling like dew, crisp as snow, vanishing like the perfume of a flower, the limpidity of dawn, the hum of summer, the cruel silence of winter.[2]

To every wrought material there attaches a special pleasure that corresponds to the intimate emotions of the individual and the species. The beauty of the craft blends with the lyric intoxication which increases in the measure that the form, growing clearer each moment brings meaning out of chaos. Here is a man who would remain insensible to the work of the thumb in clay, but he takes delight in casting in a mold his mixture of tin and copper. Another, who does not feel the subtle joy of mixing pure tones in order to obtain, in the undulating and glistening vehicle of oil, the imperceptible nuances that betray the confessions of the passions, will watch with delight the slow baking of the earth, as it renders the freshness proper to this leaf, the velvety depth proper to that corolla, the metallic brilliance which belongs to the corselet of this scarabæus, to the scales of that fish. No one has the right to intervene between the desire of the poet and the object of this desire, for he himself does not know from what extraordinary accumulation of obscure atavisms, fortuitous correspondences, indistinct memories, sensual fatalities, has issued the unique flash that bursts from their encounter.

[1] Fig. 73.
[2] Fig. 41.

Fig. 123

FRESCO PAINTING (Filippo Lippi)

The poem of matter saturates our flesh to such a point that, to follow its unfolding in a work of art, it would be necessary to begin with one's mother's milk, when a liquid matter models our very form, touch upon all the contacts which the education of our senses (food, clothing, lodging, play) imposes upon that form, and end with the amorous embrace which reveals, in the indefinitely prolonged exchanges of pleasure and suffering, the most subtle researches of the imagination and the spirit. Our seats and our beds are stamped by our physical appearance. Our threshold is shaped by our steps. The objects of the table and trade obey the anatomical arrangements of our mouths and our hands. It is not possible for us to escape the haunting multitude of things that force upon our notice the endless form of the world so as to turn it into spirit. The wall which we make and which introduces into our mental habits so much rectitude at the same time that it shelters us, is made of stone that is cut or brick that is baked by us. The money that we coin for the exchange of our goods and our passions assumes the aspect of our geometrical abstractions and the myths upon which our history rests. All the spiritual conquests through which we think to escape from this material flood that surrounds us and rises with us—even while we try to raise ourselves above it—are inclosed in the enormous heaps of parchment and paper stamped with ink which the font or the block has imprinted. We only capture light on condition that a metallic support consents to it. And the sonorous waves that traverse space without our perceiving them only reach us through the intermediation of antennæ, plates or shells of metal. It is a subtle and continuous education that matter exercises over our faculties of comparing, eliminating, ordering, and choosing, even, and perhaps especially, when we

Fig. 124

GEOMETRICAL ARCHITECTURE (Albi)

imagine that our spirit revels in an abstract space of which it has nevertheless determined the dimensions.

II

The plastic means through which the poet is able to know these dimensions is not contented with the geometrical symbol. It reaches our mind by making use

Fig. 125
ARID SURROUNDINGS, OGIVES (Avignon)

of our senses, to be sure, since neither the absolute straight line nor the absolute circle exists in nature; the geometrical symbol is merely the schematization of the grossest sensations, those, precisely, which show us an absolute straight line on the surface of a distant expanse of water, for example, or an absolute circle in the appearance of the maritime horizon, of the moon or the sun. But the symbol does not enrich the sensual imagination, through which the relations of feeling between man and man are discovered; it ends by creating instruments of merely material organization in which we can find, for that matter, a thousand pretexts for intensifying and multiplying these relations. The marvelous industrial implement which it has created in our epoch is not capable of spiritually augmenting man, like poetry, painting, or music, but it creates the new circumstances and the unexpected dramas in which poetry, painting, and music can renew their nourishment.

Architecture, which approaches most closely, through its sources and appearances, the geometrical symbol, is the most universal plastic means, and the first in date, I imagine, which may have offered itself to the poet to order the universe on the plane of his emotions. Through it matter was immediately and practically utilized. Primitive man who was physically and mentally poor, got from the branches of trees or the vaults of caverns the suggestions which resulted, later on, in the invention of cross-pieces capable of completing this branch-work on the wall that would stop up the vault and keep out animals and the elements. For this very reason I do not believe that there exist, between geometry and architecture, relations as close and necessary as people have said. It is possible that at the moment when a race attains the possession of its highest equilibrium, the confused sentiment of the harmony that dwells in it coincides with approximate or even absolute mathematical symbols. These, far from lying at the origin of the harmony, express, on the contrary, its least conscious direction, mark the end it is approaching, and succeed, only by a brief miracle, in mingling with it.

But even at these moments, or especially at these moments, there is not, I think, in the rigor of the geometrical relations we discover in some monument, more of a conscious will to express these relations than exists in the rigor of the arithmetical relations that are found in music and ignored by musicians. All nature, to my thinking, is only an approximate harmony that tends to become a perfect harmony but which, happily for its own conservation, only succeeds in doing so momentarily. Mathematics itself is a creation of our mind, objectively non-existent, but made to fill the need of an absolute about which our miserable life turns

Fig. 126

PELASGIC WALL (Italy)

for its consolation. Mathematics, in short, the creation of the intelligence, is a postulate of instinct, like musical, plastic, or even chromatic harmony, with the difference that it tends to demonstrate the postulate which harmony is satisfied to live. But simply by virtue of the fact that it is harmony, it is right. Mathematically right. Against all systems, against all methods, against science, against law, against morality, against a divinity reduced to the rôle of a policeman. It remains for us to know whether this harmony, at the very instant when our instinct creates it, does not itself entirely transfigure the rigorous numbers to which it can be reduced, by assuring to these numbers life and movement through a mysterious and irresistible labor. I mean: it remains for us to know whether the dancer moving over the bit of earth on which he dances does not measure it more infallibly than the surveyor armed with his instruments.

Going back to the rudest sources of instinct, those that impel the negro or the Papuan to seek ornamental motifs in the circle and the line, the architect, reaching the summit of creative power, experiences, like all creators, the need of rationalizing the emotions that lead him there. But Pascal, at the moment when he takes up the pen, no longer knows geometry. Which does not prevent his most eloquent phrases from borrowing from the subterranean persistence of his geometrician's temperament that sort of solidity which one finds wherever great architecture has apparently borrowed from calculus the most exact of the harmonic laws, those that seem to preside over the apparent symmetry of the Greek temple, over the rhythmic alternation of the ogives of the Papal Palace at Avignon,[1] over the harsh monotony of the Italian civic palace,[2] over the measured proportions of the buildings of the French seventeenth and eighteenth centuries.[3]

Nevertheless we know that in no Greek ground plan are the columns rigorously parallel, that Byzantine cupolas or French ogives differ slightly in dimensions, like the deviations between the summit and the base of the buttresses and the pillars that uphold them, that

[1] Fig. 125.
[2] Fig. 79.
[3] Fig. 36.

the rhythmic alternations borrow their illusory aspect of reality more from the play of numbers than from the symmetry of forms, and no more in the Italian palace than in the French palace are the distances between the solid parts and empty spaces exactly the same anywhere. If architectonic harmony were supported by definitely fixed laws, they would not be lost sight of so frequently and in all places. But it is only when the sentiment, at once practical and mystical, of great construction gives way that no one longer finds them. The exception of the formula to be found in the arabesque offers the single example, precisely, of the way in which rigorous calculation ends not in a saving architecture but in destroying it after having lost its principle of ornamentation.

In truth, architecture offers the moving spectacle of a living geometry,[1] something which can only be obtained on condition that one does not observe an absolute rigor in distance, measure, and proportions. The fact that every well-constructed building is conceived in what are approximately circles and rectangles, belongs to eternal architecture. When our geometrical instinct maintains this formula, at least roughly, it is only necessary to animate in one's own way the significant surfaces, which is the proper task of the epoch and the moment. A revolution, in whatever sphere, has no other aim than to animate the surfaces of the social body. When it takes place it is because the depths are ready. On the day when Constantine issued his edicts was not Christianity already formed in the hearts of the Occident, as was Buddhism in the hearts of the Orient when Asoka became a Buddhist? And consider the French or Russian revolution when the Third or Fourth Estate instituted its dictatorship over the whole of the social body. I find in the Parthenon, in the

[1] Fig. 124

Fig. 127

Roman Wagon—Vault (Tivoli)

Mosque of Omar, in Saint Sophia, in Notre Dame, in the palace at Siena, all different or even antagonistic in appearance, an inner skeleton of a structural logic strictly similar, though responding to diverse needs, and outlines and surfaces where there play eternally, in different rhythms, the circle, the square, the ellipse, and the triangle.

Architecture marks the passage of geometry from the intellectual to the perceptible plane. To give the illusion of movement to matter disposed according to the crude appearance of the geometrical order—that is architecture! The fact that architecture seems to start with the geometrical symbol and end in a living organism, while painting, at the other pole, sets out from living emotion and tends toward the geometrical symbol, takes us no farther than the most rudimentary sense-illusions. They show once more that painting expresses the individual at grips with experience and seeking to substitute his reason for the lost social principles, while architecture expresses the multitude rationally enclosed in those social principles from which the needs of individuals seek to free themselves. One finds in plastic art all possible correspondences between these elementary tendencies and the ensemble of the social body. Even though painted, for example, the Egyptian relief is based upon architecture while the Hindu relief, even when it is not painted, tends to be painting.[1]

Even if, as I have read somewhere, everything is a matter of proportion where the Greek temple is concerned, an affair of mass in the case of the Egyptian temple, a matter of space-mastery with the ogival French temple, we know all this only from the expression, serene, imposing, or enthusiastic, which the dominant passion imposes on the face of the temple. Architecture always arises, in the intention of the archi-

[1] Figs. 39, 91, 97, 131, 136, 137, 177, 188, 202, 207, 216.

tect, according to the impersonal principle it draws
from the needs of the multitude; but the gigantic
personality of the multitude imposes on each building
a signification such that one recognizes immediately on
seeing it the race, the epoch, the religion, or the drama
that built it. Architecture is, from first to last, a science
rather than an art, the science of materials, the sci-

Fig. 128

Cupola on Pendentives (Saint Sophia)

ence of weights and pressures, the science of the strict
adaptation of an instrument to its end.

The great inventions of architecture—the wall, the
Egyptian column, the Assyrian vault, the Roman
vault, the cupola on pendentives, the ogival transept
of Occidental Europe[1] are comparable, from this
point of view, with the inventions of modern industry
—the boiler, the motor, the metallic framework[2] and

[1] Figs. 126, 127, 128, 129, 180 bis.
[2] Figs. 35, 71, 115, 168, 215, 218.

hence structural exactness appears most necessary in these organic parts. The bridge, for example, where the vault and the wall unite, is a scientific work of the first order, and the entire formidable Roman architecture makes one think much more of the industrial constructions of today than of any plastic art of Europe or Asia at any period whatever.[1] But by a unique miracle these very organic parts, a column springing up, a cupola imprisoning space, an ogive capable of sustaining on its frail skeleton the most enormous pile, a vault paradoxically suspending tons of stone above the abyss by means of their own weight, succeed in giving us such an æsthetic emotion that after having known it we cannot tolerate any longer the least ornament upon them or about them. We demand them, therefore, in their scientific purity, like a visible, aerial music that makes us, so to speak, *see* the song of the spheres in the ether, the organ voice of giant trunks in the forest, the incessant murmur that lulls the vault of the woods. The Romans have taught us that their utilitarian constructions represent an æsthetics superior to their ideological constructions and that their aqueducts are more impressive than their temples. It is thanks to them, I firmly believe, and thanks to the example of contemporary engineers who are returning to the principles of architecture (ruined by architects) that we have come to seek in the most beautiful ideological works of the Egyptians, the Greeks, the Arabs, the Italians, or the French the structural nucleus that determines them, as the skeleton determines the form of the animal.

And first of all we have come to eliminate ornament as if it were a parasite, no longer using it save as a servant, a means of stressing the function of such and such a lever or portion of a skeleton, that we seek first

[1] Figs. 34, 127, 213.

of all to discover. The entire Parthenon, for example, is contained in the earthen house supported by four posts at the corners, on which rest four horizontal posts, which still shelters the peasant in certain regions of Ionia or the Isles.[1] This will teach us to analyze the statue, perhaps even the picture and certainly the piece of furniture, which last is architecture and nothing but

Fig. 129
GROINED OGIVES (Chartres)

architecture. Seen from without, an edifice or a piece of furniture expresses its inner structure. Its façade is the projection on the vertical plane of its functional reality on the horizontal plane. The splendor of the Egyptian statue, or of peasant pottery in all countries of the world, acknowledges this origin.

Those, then, who do not forget the function of the building and of the skeleton that secures, articulates

[1] Fig. 130.

and sustains it, can clothe it with all the vestments possible, and pass without effort from the most severely naked Roman vault to the most heavily decorated French cathedral while recognizing in them both the same eternal principle. Everything that obeys this principle, whatever its exterior aspect may be, expresses an essential moment of the human soul, simple or complex, positive or mystical, humble or terrible, but one that consents to start with a careful knowledge of the material and of the end to be attained through it, and tends toward the most magnificent expression of the collective life of the spirit at that moment. All revolutions challenge the religious edifices because these represent most clearly the ancient ideas held in common that are opposed to the new ideas held in common.

They could equally well challenge civil monuments. For in reality they aspire to substitute, in architectonic symbols, a spiritual architecture eager to express itself for a spiritual architecture that has exhausted its virtue. That does not make it any the less true that they only reject the symbols of the older order because they confuse them with the inner reality which every edifice must obey if it wishes to remain living. There is much more difference between Saint-Sulpice and Notre Dame, which pretend to express the same religion, than between Versailles, the palace, and Notre Dame, the church, because Saint-Sulpice sacrifices the structural basis of Notre Dame to a false principle of religious pomp which Notre Dame ignores absolutely, while Versailles, like Notre Dame, recognizes this same basis.

The differences betrayed by buildings as far apart in appearance as the cathedral of Rheims and the Trianon of Gabriel, the palace of Angkor Vat and the Sansedoni Palace at Siena, testify much more to a state of mind

peculiar to such and such a people or epoch than to
a fundamental discord in the science of their builders.

Architecture does not change its mind but its soul.
While remaining, in contrast to painting, the common
expression of an ensemble of knowledge, beliefs, and
systematized ideas, architecture may tend, like painting,
toward the symphonic character it reveals in India,
in Europe from the twelfth to the fifteenth century,

Fig. 130

GREEK HUT

and in Cambodia, or it may tend toward the melodic
character it reveals in mediæval Italy and in France
during the two centuries before the revolution.[1] It is
a matter of relation between universal mystic sentiment and individual reason. In the first case universal
sentiment predominates to such an extent that it
leaves the individual free to express, within his limits,
his measureless sensuality and his confused passions.

[1] Figs. 30, 36, 53, 79, 88, 131.

In the second case, the reason of the individual is so sure of its supremacy that it includes in its logic, its will, and its measure the ensemble of the sentiments and beliefs of all individuals.

III

Egyptian sculpture,[1] so completely architectural, seems to me to demonstrate, even better than architecture, that the relationship between the purest plastic art and geometrical abstraction is merely a relationship between neighbors. Or rather there exist parallel tendencies that meet at an indefinite but very living point of consciousness, where the spiritualized plastic art approaches the numerical absolute and where humanized geometry aspires to assume a material form the better to touch our hearts. Its symmetry is only in appearance. The pretended *law of frontality* that is supposed to characterize it is only a commonplace and very crude approximation. The two parts of the Egyptian statue, if we imagine it as bisected, cannot be placed side by side. Asymmetrical, they maintain their equilibrium through very slight but incessant vibrations that assure life and continuity to the ensemble.

In this case, also, the surfaces are animated. With such an animation, indeed, that at no point of it can we say there begins or ends the continuous wave that envelops it and lulls it, so to speak, in its own immobility. One would say it was modeled like a planet, by some force at once mathematical and living which, seen from a distance, gives it the appearance of a clearly geometrical creation, but which is seen, from near by, to recognize details that contract its surfaces or smooth them out again; thus almost imperceptible wrinkles come to have the force of valleys and moun-

[1] Figs. 27, 38, 65, 175, 197, 199.

tains, a slight change of accent tells of the billows of the forests, and the obedient mass of the atmosphere and the waters rolls with the movement of the sculpture.

Fig. 131
SYMPHONIC ARCHITECTURE (India)

It is possible—and probable—that we must seek in the influence of geological conditions the origin of the particular vision of form that gives to the Egyptian sculptural block the aspect of a cube,[1] to the Chinese block[2] the aspect of a sphere or cylinder, and to the Hindu block[3] a sinuous aspect that evokes an eternally agitated sea.

But it seems, nevertheless, as if in all these imposing forms, in which sculpture appears still half caught in the architectural matrix, there lives a central force which obliges the significant surfaces to turn about it with a fatality as invincible as that of gravitation. What has made the success of Greek art is perhaps its divergence from this, a divergence very clear-cut in its dynamics and very eclectic in its aspects; I mean that, while remaining submissive, at least at its apogee, to this central force, the diverse elements that constitute it appear to emerge from the spherical and sinuous model, if one considers, for example, the Ionic sculpture that comes from Asia—I am thinking of the *Hera*[4] of Samos—and the cubic model that comes perhaps from Egypt, and in any case is more congenial to the keen and categorical mind of Occidentals. I am thinking of the Doric[5] Apollos.[6] We see in them traits that still persist slightly in Myron and Polycleitus or, on the other hand, in the anonymous sculptor of Olympia, until they fuse in attic art where they are summed up in Phidias.

From this moment Greek art is strongly marked by the pursuit of the anatomical modeling which makes sculpture deviate from its architectural rhythm and at the same time turns Occidental civilization toward a too narrow rationalism. And this pursuit seems con-

[1] Fig. 65.
[2] Fig. 133.
[3] Fig. 132.
[4] Fig. 135.
[5] Do not Greek legends make Danaos, the founder of the Peloponnesian or Doric-Hellenic civilization, come out of Egypt?
[6] Fig. 134.

FIG. 132

SINUOUS MODELLING (India)

ditioned by the encounter of the cubic mass with the spherical mass in the sinuosity of movement. I do not ignore its splendor at the outset. It is a unique moment of history, one which brings together the inner structure of the motionless form and the external appearance of its relations and interchanges. At that moment actuality and change, instinct and intelligence, subject and object, life and style, the particular and the general fuse in a universal and average expression. At the instant when anatomical perfection is attained in a fugitive equilibrium one does not think at all of anatomy but of the appearance of nature, of bodies full of blood, bursting with sap, of these human torsos and limbs thrusting themselves up from the soil like roots, mingling their branches, with veins and tendons going through them as the fibers run through the bark of a tree, one notes the knobby knees, the shoulders, the bony skulls stirring under the rough, stretched skin.[1] Anatomy for its own sake appeared only with Lysippus and was henceforth to lead sculpture astray through the academic Greco-Roman art.

On the contrary, as if frightened at the impasse into which they were being led, the more sensitive sculptors who followed Praxiteles were to seek, through the play of light over form, to approach painting whose reign was about to begin. In Greek Egypt, soon afterward in Byzantium,[2] and thanks in part to the vague but growing and assertive Christian sentiment, this art will gradually forget anatomy and turn toward music through the mysterious play of the relations of flat tones and spaces, through bold deformations tending to moral expression: large eyes, narrow skulls, sparkling jewels, contours melting into the penumbra. Thus sculpture, the most material of the arts, will have

[1] Figs. 1, 12, 14, 85, 208.
[2] Figs. 37, 89, 172, 204.

Fig. 133

Spherical Modelling (China)

created the intelligence which, ending in painting, will recreate sensuality through it. And painting, through sensuality, will lead back to the mystic sentiment that anatomical rationalism has destroyed. Admirable circulation of the spiritual forces in the interior of matter which they animate and which animates them in a

continual interchange! When its wandering musical waves have encountered on all sides the space where they are to expire, painting will rediscover in that space the common plastic field which architecture will then take up again.

Thus sculpture dies at the moment when it tries to overstep its function, which is to define the structure of the object, as that of architecture is to define the structure of society, as that of painting is to define the structure of the individual, as that of music is to assure the passage between the individual and society. Sculpture's field of oscillation between architecture and music remains immense, on condition that it does not lose from sight the source of its strength: the function that I have just mentioned and that assures the gravitation of its significant surfaces about its central architectural principle.

Fig. 134
Doric Modelling

Thus we shall see Chinese sculpture, and especially Egyptian sculpture, evoke, from their crude beginning, the eternal, circular movement of music[1] precisely be-

[1] Figs. 27, 38, 40, 133, 173, 175, 197, 199.

cause, since the mythical
body remains almost identical
with itself, it is in the interior
of the statue—art of permanent, objective, material
reality—that the musical
passage between painting and
architecture takes place.
Thus we shall see mediæval
French sculpture participate
with architecture itself in a
universal and profoundly
touching movement toward
the mystery of painting, because it never ceases to
anticipate the appearance of
the individual in the Occident.[1] Thus we shall see
Hindu sculpture never emerging from an eternal mobility
in which form, the social
body, the individual fuse and
blend in a mingling of architecture, painting, the dance,
and music.[2] Thus we shall
see this same spirit declaring
itself with inexpressible
clarity in Cambodian sculpture, where the universal
communion is still more
strict, better ordered and, as
it were, rationalized, and
where the *apsaras*[3] repeat the

[1] Figs. 30, 53, 63, 88, 106, 121, 165,
178, 191.
[2] Figs. 39, 97, 131, 132, 136, 177, 178,
216.
[3] Fig. 136.

FIG. 135

IONIC MODELLING

Egyptian miracle, no longer in immobility but in movement, through the apparent symmetry of the two wings
of their dance, which is nothing but perfection in rhythmic equilibrium. Thus we shall see Mexican sculpture[1]
snatching sanguinary and palpitating fragments from
form, grouping them in expressive masses about a
moving center, as if the social myth forbade it to define
its nature, the nature of the form and that of the individual; we witness the disturbing cruelty of a civilization, that is inscrutable to us I imagine, whose steps
reel, whose periods are undefined, but in which the
feeling for painting, sculpture, and building, as powerful
as it is confused, succeeds in maintaining itself in an
intermediary form of expression from which nothing
can be detached without ruining the ensemble. With
the negro,[2] the architectural tendencies of whose sculpture are more rudimentary, but perhaps more clearly
indicated, something quite different is produced. The
fiery colors with which he besmears his statues define a
brutal, impulsive, candid individuality, plunged entirely
in the social body which does not exercise any restraint
upon it and seems, quite on the contrary, to repeat its
accents.

I have told what it is that characterizes the genius of
the black man of Oceanica or of Africa, and within this
genius is the secret of his art. In his idols, his jewelry,
and his weapons, he renders through modeling the
rhythmic reality which characterizes him beyond all
else. Not that his art lacks objectivity. It is, contrary
to what most æstheticians believe, fiercely realistic:
it accentuates the dominant essentials of the object to
the point of caricature. In one case a certain bird is
defined by its beak, in another a wild beast is represented
through its jaw, a woman through a torso or the breasts,

[1] Fig. 55.
[2] Figs. 47, 49, 93 bis, 198.

Fig. 136

Rhythmic Equilibrium (Cambodia)

or a man by a muzzle thrust forward with the complete innocence that means hunger or desire.

But the black never concerns himself with descriptive "truth," as does European art in general—that is, with the average anatomical relationships of the different parts of the object. The immemorial stability of the black civilizations is translated directly by those rudimentary sculptures in which (as far as our ignorance of their chronology permits us to judge) there is not the slightest hint of evolution toward either of the poles of artistic expression—the collective or the individual.

From this point of view, their art is even freer than that of the Hindus, or possibly, indeed, that of the Aztecs. The secret cadences which animate their centers of receptivity and of representation sweep with them everything and give order to everything. The one element that stands out is that of the rhythmic relationships. The arms or the legs may be shortened, or indeed suppressed, the organs, the accidentals, or the lines of the face may be disposed without respect for their natural functions; the musical exaltation, incorporating in the divine void both the individual and race indiscriminately, reveals to the spectator a second reality which is absolutely new. With reference to this exaltation, the sculptural masses are as freely disposed as are the musician's conception and expression when he imposes order on the masses of sound. For the negro, more than for any other man, nature is only a dictionary, consulted with as much of fever as of candor. There are works of art of a higher type, but none more authentic than these, which, apart from all social considerations, would suffice to define the essence of the work of art.

IV

Painting also presents, according to the epoch, the race, and the painter, the predominant tendencies

Fig. 137

Sculptural Painting (Signorelli)

that will clothe it in one case with an architectural aspect, in another with a sculptural aspect, elsewhere with a close and harmonious association of all the plastic elements of which it is the flowering in the heart of the individual. I shall never grow weary of repeating that it is indeed the individual that painting expresses, everywhere, through its power to restore, with the aid of the innumerable combinations at its command— contrasts, oppositions, complementary blendings, light, shadow, half-tints, values, reflections, passages—the complexity of the human soul and the eternal or fugitive components that reveal it to us. Nevertheless, in the case of Giotto one finds painting almost entirely sheathed in architecture. With the Florentines, the Umbrians, and the Romans, da Vinci, Signorelli, Piero della Francesca, Michael Angelo,[1] it quits the monumental order to crystallize in the sculptural form. With the Venetians[2] it appeals to all the voices of space to realize the great visual symphony and tends toward music without losing sight either of the form that firmly unites the elements of the chromatic poem or the architectonic rhythm that assures their cohesion.

It is true that the more one withdraws from the mythical or social fictions to plunge deeper into the labyrinths of the heart the more do successive epochs in the same country stamp their characteristics upon painting and lead us perceptibly, in Italy for instance, from architecture to music—as from Giotto to Veronese —passing through the intermediary stages of line, mass, the relations of masses, and the relations of colors— Angelico, Masaccio, da Vinci, Raphael, Titian.[3] But, independent of epoch, reasons of race and environment impose upon this art here, linear tendencies that persist

[1] Figs. 92, 137, 142.
[2] Figs. 31, 144, 146, 162.
[3] Figs. 43, 86, 138, 139, 143, 162.

Fig. 138

Transitional Painting (Masaccio)

to the very end, elsewhere, orchestral tendencies that have been present since the beginning. I am thinking, in the first case, of the whole of Italy outside of Venice, and of France before Watteau and romanticism, in the second case of Flanders, Holland, Spain, and especially of Venice and the French romanticists.[1] And I remark the tendency of Oriental painting—especially the Chinese[2]—to remain within the limits of a symphony that is reduced as to the number of instruments but very rich as to their quality; chamber music, in a word, which expresses the slight desire felt by even the most individual Oriental to leave the agreeable edifice which atavism, tradition, myth, dogma, and the social environment have built for him.

In any case painting, even on reaching the verge of music, should escape no more than sculpture from the force that maintains it in the orbit of a logic that derives its vigor from the example of living organisms. It is scattered and dissolved if all its organs do not recognize as their center a united skeleton whose presence is felt even in their most extravagant motions and which is forever constraining them by means of the arabesque (on the surface or in depth) to recognize its secret mastery. Almost all painters—I am speaking of the true painters—develop away from the colored surfaces toward which the impulse of their senses draws them and to which, unfortunately, it most often confines them. The greatest, and the greatest alone, returning to the organic connection of forms in function, seek the bony framework of these forms under the relief which light and shade produce; they seek the contours of the forms hidden by the gradations of atmosphere and the succession of values. This is the recent history of

[1] Figs. 31, 32, 87, 140, 144, 157, 162, 163.
[2] Fig. 41.

Fig. 139

MELODIC PAINTING (Fra Angelico)

Renoir. It is that of Delacroix. It is that of Rembrandt.

It happens more rarely that the mind, instead of returning painfully to its sources, departs boldly from them as occurs, it seems to me, with Corot or Velasquez, who based their work on irreproachable composition and very compact form, only little by little to discover space and to unite in it all the surface points of their forms in action. I do not speak of Titian or Giorgione, creators of great painting, who were obliged to follow this course, since sculpture and architecture immediately preceded them, nor even of Raphael, who would have followed it, no doubt, if he had lived longer. In general it is the musical sense of painting that leads back to construction, and it is therefore remarkable that this musical sense grows more delicately perceptive in proportion as the painter's understanding approaches the structural foundations of painting and, by approaching them, advances toward the depths. The spiritual adventure of Cézanne is typical in this respect; in proportion as form becomes dense and turns on his canvas as if to carve the flat surface of the picture, it seems as if color ascends from this picture to ornament the surface, and as if, through the play of what he himself called "modulation," a stirring music rises from it, binding together all points of the painted expanse. When the painter has recovered his pure instinct, when he seems to have forgotten architecture, sculpture, and painting itself to listen to the silent orchestra that accords its thousand voices in his musical imagination, it is only then that he is truly a painter, a sculptor, or an architect, that is to say, an individual.

Painting, then, expresses the subtle, essential, and multiple passage of sculpture into music. It attains its greatest expressive equilibrium in the instant when it still contains a maximum of musical significance.

It is this and nothing but this that separates painting symphonically organized by the Venetians and represented at its summit by Rubens, Rembrandt, and Velasquez, from painting melodically realized by the Primitives. In geometrical language, the latter express themselves through a curve and the former through a sphere—two very different arts, one of which may be preferred to the other but which cannot be compared. Between Angelico and Rubens[1] there is, if not identity, at least similarity of method. There is a radical difference—almost an antagonism—in spirit. The primitive has given way to permit his successors to grasp better that space which the sculptor and the architect believed they had already conquered but which they had only imprisoned. The two dimensions of which he disposes on his canvas have the privilege, by a touching paradox, of leading painting to such an effort of the intelligence that, on a single plane, it will suggest the third dimension which the sculptor and the architect really command, and, going farther than they, it will discover, in this reconquered third dimension, sensations that will demand time in which to manifest and express themselves fully. This in turn will lead to music by a geometrical progression having its permanent source in the senses and the heart.

Quite evidently, it is thanks to geometry that Occidental painting has succeeded, often to the detriment of its freshness of feeling and its ingenuousness of sentiment, in delivering to the individual methods hitherto controlled by architecture and sculpture only, so that it might people its artificial space with a thousand subtle impressions and ideas that architecture and sculpture are incapable of expressing. The invention of perspective distinctly separates the modern European from the mediæval European and the Asiatic,

[1] Figs. 139, 140.

and expresses the antagonistic character presented by two such men as Rubens and Angelico or any great Persian, Chinese, or Japanese painter.[1] In the evolution of Italian painting from Uccello to Raphael we surprise the astounding phenomenon of the intelligence snatching the geometric instrument from the science of building to pass, with its help, from rigorously impersonal science to the exclusively personal feeling of the musicians.

Fig. 140

Symphonic Painting (Rubens)

In the first case, that is to say in Uccello, there is an evident dualism, the picture developing according to two juxtaposed planes—first the plane of sentiment expressed through spirited form and brilliant but somber color, then the plane of reason fastening itself on the other like a parasite. Each makes a visible effort to be absorbed in the other, with perspective trying awkwardly at every instant to enclose between its inflexible lines the powerful, living emotion that constantly escapes it and disrupts it: a touching and painful dualism from which da Vinci, himself, will not escape. In the other case, that is to say in Raphael, perspective

[1] Figs. 41, 68, 139, 140.

enters definitely into the instinctive methods of the poet, who thinks of it no more than a writer thinks of his spelling and having ceased to be a clumsy, half-formed discovery it becomes a mechanical implement. Midway between Uccello and Raphael is Piero della Francesca, who marks the point of supreme, harmonic oscillation and who, after having entirely conquered geometric space, attains the profound solidarity of instinct which one finds between geometry and life in the highest architecture. Henceforth he treats space as if it were an actor—an actor as alive as beings and forms—participating like them and on the same spiritual plane as they, in the drama of creation, and in this game he tastes an intellectual intoxication that we do not find in any of his successors.[1]

In order that the chromatic waves, henceforth free to express the intangible nuances of individual sentiment, should complete their final stage, it would be necessary for the Venetians to perceive the sounds, murmurs, and echoes that are exchanged, by means of the atmosphere, in this definitely conquered geometrical space. One finds also, in the very technique of the architect, the sculptor, and the painter, traces of a mysterious process, moving from our moral skeleton to the flesh that covers it, which pure science reproduces in the same ascending and never closed circle. Architecture precedes sculpture as mathematics preceded the science of anatomy. Sculpture precedes painting as anatomy preceded biology. Biology, in its turn, apparently tends to find mathematical supports so as to return, through them, to the framework of life, as painting passes on to architecture the task of remaking the real space it has gradually quitted in order to discover supra-sensible space with the aid of the musicians.

The spirit of painting floats about it as the air floats

[1] Figs. 141, 142, 143.

about us. This subtle art is the most mysterious and the least known of all those that express us; no doubt because, though barely emerged from definite form and tending toward fluctuating spacial relations, it seems to become fixed without ever attaining the unstable point where the object and the subject reach an equilibrium. It commands means so diverse that they can be diametrically opposed to each other, which has not failed to occur. Drawing describes and states pre-

Fig. 141
Discovery of Perspective (Uccello)

cisely; color evokes and suggests. The one provides the architectural pole of painting, the other its musical pole, while its sculptural nucleus solidifies in the mass in which these two forms of expression fuse when they realize, in a few heroic works, its most intoxicating creations. Truly men like Rubens or Rembrandt or Velasquez seem placed at the center of the mysterious presence of the human mind in the world, bound as they always are by the continuity of the values and

Fig. 142

CONQUEST OF PERSPECTIVE (Piero della Francesca)

relations of tones of which they dispose, to all the sensible points of space, where their harmonic antennæ awaken the sonorous echoes which the musician is to collect; they are bound also, through the continuity and overlapping of the masses they display, to all the points of solid reality, which lead them nearer and nearer to the roots of trees, to the female matrix, to the deepest and most secret geological strata of the soil.

One work, above all others, seems to me to define and to symbolize this impression of a circular world, at once closed on all sides and united to the infinite through invisible tentacles, which painting alone can really create, even if all great things evoke it in a less direct manner—some Egyptian statues, for example, or the *Essays* of Montaigne, or some phrase of Shakespeare's, or some *Oratorios* and *Cantatas* of Bach. The great sketch of "Paradise" by Tintoretto[1] is as far as possible from the "imitation" of natural forms which one finds, nevertheless, everywhere in it, and which are very faithful and exact when one studies it in detail. It is also as close as possible to a vast, concentric ensemble of waves of color, in which, nevertheless, nothing vague or indefinite is to be found. There are, I believe, eight hundred personages and thirty or forty "subjects." Not one is conspicuous though not one conceals itself. There seems to be no "subject" and one does not notice the personages. This miracle is produced by the complex and multiple relations of tones, forms, and contours that interpenetrate one another and reply to one another, of echoes that call to one another and are repelled, of crowded fleecy masses that make one think of heaped-up clouds, or even of the far-away sound of thunder and cannon. It is a pure visual symphony in which nature, closely followed, is only a pretext to build a monument entirely contained

[1] Fig. 144.

Fig. 143

POSSESSION OF PERSPECTIVE (Raphael)

in an imagination determined to attach to its center all the points of the universe.

V

The dance is a neglected art. The cinematograph a naissant art. Both are misunderstood. It seems to me, however, that the cinema and the dance can yield us the secret of the relations of all the plastic arts with space and with the geometrical figures that give us at once the measure and the symbol. The dance in every epoch, like the cinema in ours, is charged with uniting plastic art with music, through the miracle of a rhythm at once visible and audible, that introduces into *time* the three dimensions of space. The living and passionate character of the dance should assure it an eternal pre-eminence over the arts that develop parallel with it and serve it most often as a setting. But on their part these arts have the persistence of the matter that expresses them, they still mingle in our lives, they do not fade from our memories while the sound and the movement of the dance are lost in oblivion with the very existence of the dancer. Who knows whether the cinema, by perpetuating the dance under the eyes of successive generations and especially by finding in its resources the means of prolonging in time the moving drama of form, is not destined to restore to their dignity the most complete of the plastic arts, which incorporate in their rhythm all the expressive elements of the spiritual tragedy which architecture, sculpture, painting, and music have shared hitherto?

The youngest children dance. The animals dance. As a part of the need of the most elementary rhythm, that which urges us to strike the earth in cadence alternately with one foot and the other, I imagine that

Fig. 144

THE VISUAL SYMPHONY (Tintoretto)

the dance preceded music and even architecture. Music, no doubt, was created to accompany the primitive dance and the first rhythm must have been the clapping of hands and the cries of the spectators. Later, when architecture was developing, then later with sculpture, with painting, with music, the dance wound from one to another like a living garland, drawing on their resources in order to increase and diversify the complexity of its figures and the numbers of its executants through costume, ornament, external decoration, and the infinite variety of the movements of the orchestra. It gradually introduced time into the evolution of plastic art, even uniting it to the cultivation of the passions and for a while serving as a bond of flesh among their diverse expressions.

Through its geometry in motion, through its continuous harmony, to which the incessant pursuit of their center of gravity instinctively constrains all those who take part in it, the dance expressed the simplest but the most self-evident among all the victories of the spiritual order over senses that have arrived at the height of Dionysian intoxication. Through its rôle of conserving and exalting the power of rhythm, it has maintained, in all civilizations, an accord between the life of men—now too animal, now too intellectual—and something that perhaps is God but in any case is the gravitation of the heavens.

There cannot be a doubt of this. For gravitation is at the source of the rhythm without which art would not exist. The cadenced sound of our steps and the beating of our hearts certainly prescribe this rhythm for us. But would the rhythm of our steps and of our hearts exist without the circulation of the blood in our arteries and without the weight that attaches us to the soil and necessitates our joints, our muscles, our bony levers? Gravitation regulates them indirectly,

as it acts directly on the flux or reflux of water, on the
rising and setting of the stars, on the periodic returns
of light and the seasons. It is the sole regulator of the
universal rhythmic movement which is the great teacher
of our lyricism and which the dance reproduces mechanically; without which neither architecture, nor sculpture, nor painting, nor music would exist, and which
makes us recognize geometry, the measure of space,
in the order and movement of machines and in the
order and movement of the very universe. The great
mystery is that we felt this rhythm in all superior
works of art as well as in the dance—which is a superior
work of art for the very reason that it is a humble one—
without being able, without knowing how to define it.
It is the mysterious law of repetition, of grouping, of
the play of numbers which, in the building and the
statue, in the picture and the orchestra, assure harmony
of proportions and continuity of movement. It is that
which forces the drama, whatever may be the feelings
that accompany it, grief or joy, despair, enthusiasm,
pleasure or sorrow, to know the delight of a superior
pleasure, which is the intuitive, sudden, complete certitude of possessing and ordering all its elements in the
head and heart.

Thus the dance yesterday and, better, the cinema
tomorrow—because its figures persist—both command
a supplementary dimension, that of time. In it the
play of the body, the arms, the legs, and the counterpoint of combinations group themselves, separate or
mingle on the ground or on the screen; they offer to
the mind, anxious to maintain the sensations that give
it security and strength, a forcible demonstration of the
rôle that plastic art and music play among us, by uniting all their manifestations. Thanks to them, harmonies that have hitherto been cut short, enter into a
state of continuous becoming. I know quite well that

the frieze of the "apsaras" of Angkor[1] already belongs
both to the dance, and to music crystallized in a motionless form but preserving through an almost unique
miracle, the slow, rhythmic, and continuous undulation of movement. Through an irresistible feeling for
the universal solidarity of forms, colors, movements,

FIG. 145
THE DANCE (Egypt)

and sounds, certain works of Tintoretto,[2] Rubens,
Delacroix, certain Dravidian sculptures, had already,
like the frieze—though to a lesser degree—brought us
close to this law of internal and unarrested circulation
which the theory of transmutation has elsewhere introduced into science. But to even explain the confused sentiments which they awaken we must still

[1] Fig. 136.
[2] Fig. 146.

consider the cinema and the dance, which register in machinery and in life itself what these scattered works have only been able to suggest.

I shall not explain why mathematical and musical harmony, whose language is absolutely exact, acts especially on the unconscious; everybody knows the irresist-

Fig. 146

PRESENTIMENT OF THE CINEMATOGRAPH (Tintoretto)

ible effect of music on the senses, and the instantaneous rise of spiritual intoxication caused in certain minds by a sequence of geometrical propositions or of algebraic equations which are automatically right for them. I shall not explain why plastic and biological harmonies, in spite of their uncertain language, act upon the consciousness, (sculpture, painting, and the natural sciences demanding a constant effort of comprehension). Nor why the former harmonies, moving in the abstract, touch our senses primarily, whereas the latter, even when working in the concrete, primarily affects our minds. Perhaps it is purely the effect of the language they speak, impersonal in the one case, personal in the other; thus in one instance we are obliged to communicate with our fellow-creatures, while the other opens all doors for us with a single key.

In any case we always find architecture and painting at the two extremities of the axis, where they reconcile these two distinct forces of the mind in the vast human heart. In one case, to mark the unconscious stage of religions and laws before the appearance of the individual consciousness, we have a maximum of geometrical relations—perceptible but only approximate— and a minimum of frank sensuality, although here matter plays an essential rôle. In the other case, to mark the passage of the individual, surcharged with consciousness, into the unconsciousness of crowds ready to adopt new, universal rhythms, we have a continual sensuous intoxication in mathematical settings that are impossible to grasp although they are strictly exact. I should like to have the dance, and especially the cinema, harmonize all these paradoxical relations in their growing unity.

VI

I have said enough, it seems to me—notably apropos of the "Paradise" of Tintoretto—as to the essential significance of the diverse human interpretations of form in every epoch and in all countries, to be permitted to consider with some skepticism the categories that pretend to relegate painting and sculpture to the rôle of "imitation," while excepting architecture and music on the ground that they are arts of "invention." These are definitions created for the convenience of speech. I know quite well that architecture is a science and should remain a science in which a knowledge of materials and their practical and technical combina-tions has more impor-tance than any ques-tion of sentiment; and that, on the other hand, painting makes use of living forms as a means for displaying its feelings concerning them. But I know, too, that a mysterious unity of style offers to our senses fully as many relationships— here between a Hindu pagoda and the fres-coes of Ajanta,[1] there between a canvas of Vermeer and some Dutch house, elsewhere between the Palazzo Vecchio in Florence and the frescoes of

Fig. 147

ANALOGY (Poussin)

Giotto, elsewhere again between the canvases of Poussin and the palace of Versailles—as exist, on the other hand, between Ajanta and Poussin, between Giotto and Vermeer, between Versailles and the Hindu pagoda, between the Dutch house and the Florentine palace.

Painting, like architecture, does nothing but organize forms if the permanent control over "nature," which

[1] Fig. 45 A.

it seeks, is directed by a mistaken sense of the veritable meaning of this organization. It is not necessary to take literally the crude desire of the crowd demanding the "imitation of nature" from those who seek, under the immediate appearance of the world, relations of continuity and unity which, as a general thing, seem to be contradicted by this appearance. It is such imitation, however, that reveals these laws to them. Nor is it necessary to take literally the architect's pretension of ignoring the accidents and aspects of "nature," of recognizing only its laws. He has been taught them at school, of course, if the instruction was properly given, but he will never apply them in a moving and direct manner if he does not recognize them, fully alive, in the forms around him.

I know quite well that if the Egyptian column visibly imitates the trunk of the palm tree, and its capital the papyrus or lotus leaves, the Greek architect scarcely thought of a tree when he created, in the midst of the little, twisted olive trees, the tall, straight columns that support the architrave of his temples. But I know also that, before marble buildings appeared, the trunks of real trees sustained other trunks of real trees on which rested the weight of the peasant's roof.[1] I know that caves, their openings enlarged or narrowed by men, have sheltered some of these men in the mass of the cliff, providing them thus with a door, a window, a façade, which so many subsequent buildings were to reproduce. And I know that a natural vault arched above them as it arched, later, above Assyrian halls and Roman baths. I am not unaware, indeed, that the architects of the fully developed epochs had entirely forgotten these things. But I am sure that those of them who made best use of the abstract formulas transmitted by traditional teaching, were also those

[1] Fig. 130.

who, when they went through a forest or a defile
between two granite walls, when they contemplated
from the center of the desert or the height of a mountain, the cupola of the sky, the edifices of the clouds,
the succession of peaks, rounded hills, pyramids, recognized, most constantly, the origin of those sensations
from which came the formulas and to which their
meditations on the universal analogy led them back.

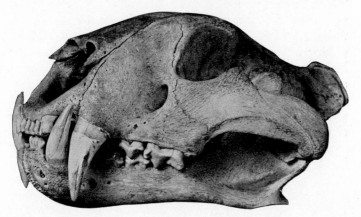

Fig. 148
Natural Sculpture (Skull of a Tiger)

Inversely, a true painter, through hatred of the
recipes taught him in the atelier, may pretend vainly
to see and know nothing but "nature"; he will return
through nature itself and find under these recipes the
living organisms which they expressed at the outset.
The study of architecture will reveal to the architect
the natural splendor of the human groups that form
about a birth or a death. The study of nature will
reveal to a painter their architectonic splendor.[1]

I have spoken of the universal analogy, so dear to
Baudelaire, in which one finds, in fact, the key to the

[1] Figs. 158, 159, 160.

impressive mystery that gives to the work of art, in whatever tongue it speaks, its spiritual value and, if I may say so, its dignity. To surprise this analogy I do not need to explore to their depths the marvelous work of the modern physicists who seek, throughout the three kingdoms, for the lines of force and the correspond-ing molecular equilibrium from which the morphologic formula of the universe will no doubt arise some day.[1] The obviously related analogies suffice, for any one who uses his eyes, to discover in the world of forms a universal architecture that borrows its most forceful poetry from functional logic. Poussin recognized, as had Homer, a palm trunk in the torso of a young woman and compared with this torso the columns of the Maison Carrée at Nimes.[2] Delacroix was absorbed by similar preoccupations in regard to trees, leaves, and the de-signs made by water on sand.

In the *Ecrits* of Carrière there is a very suggestive lecture on this subject dealing with the skeletons of the osteological gallery of the museum, in which the frame-work of the animals appears wholly naked. See the harmonious construction of each of them, the ends of the bones turning in their sockets, the bone levers moved by weight or turned by the play of the muscles, the close overlapping and the hinges of the vertebræ, the amphora of the pelvis to bear the weight of the viscera, the continuity of the bony armature charged with poising and transmitting pressure, and all this apparatus constructed on a monotonous plane, but rendered so living by imperceptible variations of function for walk-ing, for prehension, for mastication, flying, swimming, the profound and elastic play of the heart and the lungs.[3]

[1] Figs. 116, 117, 118.
[2] Fig. 147.
[3] Figs. 119, 148, 149, 150, 151, 152 bis.

Compare all the essential elements of this forest of skeletons, a forest on the march toward a blind destiny, from that of the most gigantic of the saurians before the flood, to that of the puniest reptile or the smallest bird. Surprise the same forms and the proportions in the bony shell that protects this monster, vast as an oak, and this minute insect which a bud could conceal. See the wind from the chase passing into the pointed muzzles, the slender craniums of these ten different animals, see the wake of the water rushing against these bony flukes that extend along these cylindrical bodies, some as big as towers, others small as worms. Note how power is secured to grind bones in combat or the shells of fruits in eating in these twenty wild animals, great or small, whose long

1

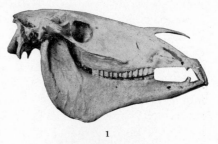

2

Fig. 149
ANALOGIES (Skull of a Horse)

1. Natural Sculpture
2. Prehistoric Sculpture

jaws, adjusted perpendicularly one into the other like pieces of metal, are decorated with fangs, laminæ, grindstones for crushing, tearing, fracturing and foraging. Dig in the earth. Pass through a sieve the humus gathered between the little roots where underground insects swarm. Is this triangle of black stone, smooth with sharp edges, the tooth of a vanished monster or a polished flint from some prehistoric atelier? This canine has the look of a vegetable tubercle. This elephant's molar resembles the ripples dug by water on some alluvial soil. This pot of copper, silver, clay, this bronze or marble bust has been so stamped with the mark of the damp earth, by dark stains and livid lines, that it seems a fragment of it, thrown up from its volcanoes, sleeping under its crust with lava and coal.

Go farther. Extend the comparison. This stag's horn is like a wing or a flame. These roots like greedy fingers that clutch their prey to feed on it. These leaves spread out in search of their fluid nourishment like lungs or fish-gills. The sap of plants, like the blood of animals, circulates through the veins. The hide of elephants, of rhinoceroses, of hippopotami, of crocodiles, resembles the bark of trees, or the rugged and mossy surface of rocks. The skin, the flesh of women, resemble the flesh of fruits, the down of flowers. Certain corollas or shells are like sex organs. These furry coats, variegated, speckled, spotted, striped, these reddish-brown wing-shells, cannot be perceived in the jungle grasses because they blend there with the gold and red, with the velvet of the petals, stalks, and leaves. In the moving pictures these torsos, these breasts, these limbs of negresses seem a black bronze full of motion, of which the resonance is gradually awakened by the gleaming lights. The slow motion gives to these running dogs the appearance of snakes, to these flying birds the air of dancers, to these fighting men the look of swimmers, to these skaters circling about, the appearance of living statues that seek their center of gravity in a sinuous movement of continuous harmony. The egg recalls the giant star, whose rotation about its axis makes a perfect spheroid.

The desert quivers like a sea, and breaks into foam

in the manner of waves. Gulfs, promontories, estuaries, seem embraced by the water, that great plastic matter that wears stone at its pleasure, washes away gravel and sand, slowly changes the profiles of the earth by alluvial deposit or by erosion, and is indefatigably persistent in striking, caressing, falling, or dripping in the same spot. Would you not suppose that water had

Fig. 150

Natural Architecture (Skeleton of a Glyptodon)

taken sixty centuries to model this Egyptian statue with its undulating, moving, smooth planes, balanced like the tide? That for ten thousand years it had rolled under its floods this almost spherical Chaldean or Chinese head? The scratches, as of encounters with the neighboring shingle, the ridges, hollows, and prominences on its surfaces surely seem to have been wrought by water. The movement of painting of which L. B. Alberti asked, "What is painting if it is not seizing the whole surface of a wave?" is like the movement of water which ever-present mist and air reunite at all the points of space. See the line of the earth blending in the distance with the line of the sky and the sweat of the sea, the tree like a mounting mist, fire, a twisting bush which dissolves in smoke and is slowly swept away to blend in the confused flight of the clouds. Follow the clouds themselves, like cupolas, like towers, like domes piled one upon another, sometimes like the ocean, sometimes like mountains, sometimes like fields covered with snow or flowers.

See those glaciers and those lakes glistening like gems. The atmosphere, with its weight, the light, the penumbra, and the reflections that dance, light up and burn out, cause

Fig. 151

Tooth of a Fossilized Elephant

everything that exists to participate in the life of everything else.

The forms of the universe are built upon a single plan. Wherever one looks one finds it. He is poor indeed, who does not know how to see in the skull of a man or an animal, for example, not only an admirably ordered landscape with its valleys and hills, its inner movements, its geological unity and its rhythm, but also a perfect piece of sculpture with its asymmetrical balance, its silent planes, its tapering lines, its expressive reliefs, its sinuous and pure profiles. And when man and his works appear on the earth can it be by chance that his weapon is like a claw, like a horn, like an animal's means of protection, that jewelry entwines the

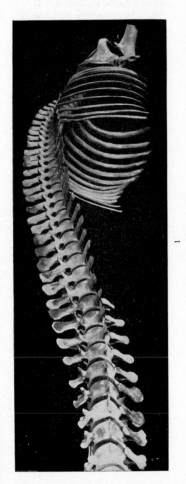

1. Skeleton of Cetacean

2. Body of Hydroplane

FIG. 152

ANALOGIES

neck and arms as a reptile might, that a submarine resembles a fish, an airplane resembles a bird or a gigantic insect, a sail resembles a wing, a boiler or a sewer resembles intestines, and that a motor resembles a beating heart? Is it, then, by chance that religions are constructed on the plane of love, laws on the plane of hunger? Between the mind and the objects on which it dwells and which, for its nourishment and security, attract it and shape it unceasingly, there is a continuous and beneficent interpenetration in which the "imitation" of the object ceases when the intelligence begins and in which "invention" stops when the object is forgotten. The sketch of "Paradise" by Tintoretto[1] in which everything is living form, seems as much a work of the mind as the Parthenon or an automobile in which everything is abstract formula. And if the church of Brou resembles "nature" less than the Parthenon or an automobile does, it is not for want of having multiplied living forms, but because, in so doing, it has disregarded the meaning of the abstract formulas. What gives the abstract edifice its natural appearance, what gives the edifice entirely made of actual things its spiritual significance, is the logical articulation of the elements that constitute both in the fever of discovery and the lucid ardor of creation.

[1] Fig. 144.

Fig. 152A

ANALOGIES (Skull of Cetacean)

Chapter VII. PEDAGOGICAL DIGRESSIONS

I

WE MAY now ask ourselves if the event, the act, the scene—the "subject"—about which the poet discourses to us, is not significant through its peculiar rôle in a comedy that we play with ourselves in order to keep his work on a utilitarian basis. Perhaps we make use of the subject merely to prevent those who cannot participate in the spiritual purpose of the comedy from catching a glimpse of its evident vanity and from ceasing, thus, to place it like a screen between their thirst for illusion and the terror of living. And perhaps we must seek in this, in the last analysis, the secret of the fascination exercised by the religions.

Since they exalt by means of the subject the social virtues they are charged with propagating, no doubt they have for simple souls a sentimental attraction which the harmony of a work of art would not suffice to create. It is their danger, as I am well aware, that the anecdote may take precedence over the great mystic sentiment and lead the multitude, and its interpreter, the artist, to substitute the seduction of the fact for the educative power of relations. And in the periods when this mystical sentiment is weak it is that which leads true creators to deny the virtue of the "subject" and to exalt the virtue of the object, denuded of all its picturesqueness or even of pure metaphysical construction, so that it no longer has any visible bond with reality. When the crowd turns to images like those of the rue St. Sulpice,[1] Courbet turns away from religious subjects to paint a handsome girl sleeping in the hay, Cézanne to study three apples on the corner of a table, others, ere long, to measure hypothetical space in which there is no longer any incident whatever.

The phenomenon is less new than we might suppose. When Hellenistic art runs after the picturesque, the man of power isolates himself to carve a nude woman[2] or demands in vain of the archaic old masters the secret of simplified planes and evident symmetries. When the supports of the cathedral are decked out with the meanderings of sentimental elaboration, when anecdotal sculpture swamps the profiles of the monument, then the portrait delights in its aloofness, and the abstract conception of line for the sake of line, and ornament for the sake of ornament, replaces the concern for function more or less everywhere. One fine day Arab art forgets the intention of the mosque to revel madly in an endless and objectless game of geometrical

[1] Center of the trade in purely commercial church furnishings.
[2] Figs. 189, 200.

formulas.[1] Everywhere the falling in of the keystone
of the social vault gives the misled multitude a taste
for the anecdotal or picturesque "subject" that flatters
its most mediocre instincts, or else it drives the solitary
creator in just the opposite direction, to a rancorous
contempt for the sentimental pretext, that turns now
into brutality and now into pure abstraction, without
any issue, without any regard for the emotional world.
In one case everything becomes disgusting nonsense,
in the other pretentious esotericism.

The subject is, actually, only a pretext, a means of
government, in short a weapon utilized by living mythologies and metaphysics to influence and arouse
popular sentiment, and it has strictly no significance
from the æsthetic point of view, whose one intense
concern is the search for rhythm and harmony. Precisely for this reason the artist becomes truly free
when a strong theocratic or political organization succeeds in imposing the subject on him. During those
periods when importance was attached exclusively to
the subject because it was inseparable from the appearance and spirit of the social edifice, no one spoke of it,
no one thought of it. In periods when men say it has
no importance they speak of nothing else. In regard
to the subject, whatever it may be—pagan myth,
Christian or Buddhist legend, Egyptian or Brahmin
cosmology—the old artists were like soldiers in the
ranks to whom their chief gives real power by relieving
them from any choice as to the end to be attained, while
leaving them free choice of the means to utilize. The
first decorator that arose with a "Mastaba" of the
old empire at Sakkara, the creator of the "Caryatides
of Cnidos" at Delphi, the sculptor of the frieze of the
"Apsaras" at Angkor, the frescoist of the grottos at
Ajanta, the image-maker of Moissac, of Autun, of

[1] Fig. 114.

Fig. 154

COMPOSITION (Daniele da Volterra)

Chartres, Giotto at Padua or Assisi, all enjoyed this advantage, which Michael Angelo began to lose in the Sistine Chapel but which, thanks to his giant's heart, called forth the peculiar harmony of that work, conquered in despair from the mental torture that rent him.

Fig. 155
COMPREHENSION (Chardin)

I refer to that sensation of light-heartedness and victorious peace that obedience gives us when we have neither the means nor the temptation nor even the vaguest idea of contesting the opportunity. Since none of the artists just mentioned was as yet assailed by the political, sentimental, or doctrinaire torment of the search for a "subject," all their united faculties tended to express, with the greatest possible force and simplicity, the form that symbolized in their eyes the subject proposed to them. Obedience means freedom and complete freedom, on condition that he who commands himself obeys the mystic sentiment that entails obedience about and beneath him. As soon as skepticism concerning the ends invoked exists at the top, despair rises from the bottom and disrupts the whole edifice. Neither the beneficence nor the power of art are doubted at that moment, but merely the legitimacy of the subject, and, as to it, first the hesitation and then the ennui of the artisan compromise the power and the beneficence of the art.

It is, then, less puerile but more imprudent to say that the "subject" is without importance, than to imagine that it represents the essence of the work of art of which it is only a pretext, though indeed the main one. The "subject," like money, is only a means of exchange and those who believe in its absolute value recall the misers who believe in that of money. The "subject" of the work of art is, as I have said, its harmony and its rhythm, of which the former no doubt creates unity in space, for our senses, the latter the accord in time with the revolutions of the stars, the cadence of our steps, and the beating of our hearts. The "subject" is only the means of fixing our attention upon appearances and inducing us to penetrate these appearances so as to attain the spirit. But it is this rôle, precisely, that gives the subject its importance and confers upon it perhaps a hierarchical existence which the schools have abased to the point of folly, but which responds, *I think*, to the human value of the illusion that carries us toward it.

It is quite evident that man matters before everything, that the whole work refers first of all to him, always, and to the quality of the emotion that he has been able to transmit to the work of his hands. It is quite evident that two pictures with identical subjects, a Kermess by Rubens and a Kermess by Teniers, derive

their importance—the one capital, the other mediocre—
entirely from the quality peculiar to the man who conceived each and has or has not had the power to project
his emotion at the spectacle into the representation he
has given of it. It is even quite evident that a knife
painted by Chardin, an apple painted by Cézanne, a
flower painted by Renoir, demands a sum of humanity
that reduces to nothingness some Crucifixion composed
by some master belonging to a school[1] though he had
all the learning of a pupil of Michael Angelo or Raphael. Nevertheless, it seems that Rembrandt's "Good
Samaritan," Titian's "Adam and Eve," Greco's "Burial
of the Count d'Orgaz"[2] are capable of arousing in us
a more prolonged echo of humanity than does some still
life painted by the same Rembrandt, the same Titian,
or the same Greco. I say "it seems," not being altogether sure, for the special quality of each work, even
when both are by the same artist, plays the rôle of first
importance.

But perhaps a "subject" in which there mingle a
thousand echoes of our most remote moral or religious
education, of the acts we perform at every moment,
of the sentiments and passions that constantly assail
us, of the permanent instincts that determine the
essential direction of our acts, perhaps such a subject
is most certain to move us, even if our æsthetic culture is
very advanced and if we are aware that the "subject"
is never actually an *event* but rather the *order* which
the mind is able to establish between events. Where
ability and emotion are equal, perhaps it is a work's
degree of complexity that assures its hierarchic rank.

But here again I might be answered that Rembrandt,
Titian, or Greco painted a still life with the same complexity of thought or sentiment which they brought

[1] Figs. 95, 154, 155.
[2] Fig. 210.

into telling us how a warrior, clothed in iron, is carried
from the tomb, in the presence of angels, by ascetics
whose livid faces are drawn by suffering and prayer,
how a wounded man found by the edge of the road is
picked up and his wound dressed by a charitable passer-
by, and into depicting the splendor of man and woman
in the first dawn of the first garden. Unquestionably.
Nevertheless, the force and importance of generous
sentiments common to all men remain, it seems to me,
more essential in the latter case than in the former.
Even with the whole weight of their creative force,
Michael Angelo or Rembrandt could not modify the
inner currents provoked in us, as in themselves, by the
centuries of spiritual exaltation which morality, religions, successive philosophies have accumulated about
certain sentiments that concern the development and
the fate of the whole species. I know very well that a
tuft of grass by the edge of a pool has as much plastic
value as a Crucifixion, when both have been painted
by Rembrandt. But as it has less sentimental value,
perhaps there is less chance that we shall succeed in
seizing its plastic value by means of sentiment.

II

It is this sentimental value, unhappily, that drives
creative minds away from the "grand subject," when
the reign of the anecdote succeeds the reign of faith,
and that impels them to seek the law of continuity and
constancy in the relations of color and form—which
is the true subject of the work of art—by painting a
knife and a glass on a kitchen sink. There any uncertainty is impossible. There can be no question of
anything but a plastic structure, raised by its own
exaltation beyond good and evil. This spectacle of
humility—or of pride, if you will—possesses so great

an educative power that, if one knows and wishes to understand it, it can lead to lyrical effusions supremely charged with humanity. A cake decorated with a sprig of laurel, by Chardin, more surely satisfies a mind anxious to taste the emotion of birth or death, than does some canvas by Guido or Barocci that strives to represent one of these events with all possible elo-quence.[1] These means which are, I repeat, those of

Fig. 156

Massacre (Goya)

harmony and rhythm, lead such a mind to seek in the first sentimental emotion which it will experience on its way, an impression analogous to that which the canvas by Chardin gives it, and it must necessarily find it, eventually.

The most human spectacle does not remain human, does not even really acquire its human value unless it is transmitted to us by methods free from the anecdote that makes us laugh or weep. If indeed the painter

[1] Figs. 154, 155.

and the sculptor are deeply moved by the death of a friend, for instance, or the apparition of a child, or by some famous execution, they reveal it only by a pitiless following out, through purely plastic processes, of the significant prominences that render the scene perceptible, the profiles that define it in space, the receding planes that make this space participate in it, everything that makes it a block of closely united elements, and the secret rhythm that gives it unity in movement. The reward of such an attitude is that any one who gradually reaches this impartial view of the world enters an absolutely pessimistic spiritual region where he only considers death and pain—unless they touch him personally—from the æsthetic point of view. This forces him to regard the image with an intellectual delight that leaves no room for pity.

I once surprised myself wishing that a certain spectacle of war might continue, because of its beauty. And I have realized in this connection why the "Massacre of the Innocents," by Brueghel or Poussin, the "May Second" or the "Massacre" by Goya, the "Massacre of Scio" or the "Medea" by Delacroix, the terrible equestrian effigy that Titian made of "Charles the Fifth," the "Horrors of War," by Rubens, all the Crucifixions by Rembrandt or by the Primitives of Flanders, France, or Italy, the sanguinary idols of the Aztecs, the Hindus, the negroes, the Assyrian bas-reliefs of the chase or of war, so many other works in which carnage or violence are displayed or described, leave only an impression of certitude, calm, light-heartedness, security.[1] The sentimental anecdote is completely effaced and the creator and the spectator breathe an atmosphere of indifference concerning the optimistic ends that man attributes to life, and of definite acceptance of the cruelty of God. I have read,

[1] Figs. 55, 69, 80, 156, 157, 163, 193.

I do not know where, that Michael Angelo one day pierced with a lance a street-porter in order to study his agony. It is useless to point out the absurdity of the anecdote, if one attempts to make history of it, but if one is willing to consider it as a legend it is useful to emphasize its symbolic truth.

It was while watching, one day, a surgical operation[1] that I surprised the secret of "composition" which confers nobility upon any "subject" and that can assure to the "great subject" its manifest pre-eminence over all others. The group formed by the patient, the surgeon, his aides, and the spectators, appeared to me like a single organism in action. I saw at once that it was impossible it should not be so, since each was at his own task and all united about the same center where the event was taking place, some through their profession, others through their passionate interest in the spectacle, this other because he constituted the chief reason for the event. It was the event itself, the very nature of the event, that determined in every dimension and aspect of the group the positions of the bodies, arms, hands, shoulders, heads, none of which avoided or could avoid its all-powerful influence without weakening, thereby, the harmony and rhythm of this group. The light fell where it was necessary for it to fall for each of the actors to see what he had to do. The disposition of surfaces, the arrangement of planes, the succession of masses, the height or lowness of reliefs was determined by function. An inner functional logic rigorously established a visible structural logic, of which nothing could be modified without the functional logic itself ceasing at once to move toward its end. If a painter had been present, if he had asked the different actors of the drama not to stir so that he could copy the scene, the ensemble would have been disrupted,

[1] Fig. 159.

F IG. 157

P LASTIC D RAMA (Delacroix)

the organism would have ceased to exist, the emotion would have disappeared with the function itself. The mistake of all schools is to "pose" the scene. Now, even a portrait is not "posed." It is made in the intervals between sittings, when the painter dines, talks, walks with his model, or does not even see him. All the more reason for not "posing" an event that is capable of revealing its plastic unity through the multitude of elements that animate it. Every composition that is not organic has the rigidity, the coldness, the emptiness of death. I am wrong, for death is living. Man, by means of art, has succeeded, as a general rule, in being more dead than death.

In short, the scene has an inner arabesque, of which very few hitherto have suspected the actual existence and of which the "composition" is hardly anything but an unconscious and too merely approximate symbol. It is a complex organism, composed of habitually independent elements, which only a moral force can unite, which only an æsthetic force can render. It can be expressed only with difficulty and, as it were, theoretically, by sculpture. It can merely be evoked by line. Only great symphonic painting which plays as it likes with forms, values, colors, reflections, passages, lights, and shadows, expressing the universe in all its dimensions, can catch for all time its ephemeral but essential life. The room where a woman is giving birth, the care of the infant, his first steps, accident, death, reading, or music enjoyed in common, certain works of industry, agriculture, or war that group men and women about a concentric and profoundly absorbing action, reveal in this way the plastic drama to anyone who knows how to watch them.

The Egyptians had the intuition of the thing, certainly, but they had at their command scarcely anything but the linear convention, cadenced by a social

and religious hieratism too severe for them to be able
to evoke from its depths and animate with its inner
circulation the complex organism that alone can reveal
the law of the great composition, in which sentiment
and plastic art necessarily fuse. The Greeks, with their
concern for anatomical perfection, could scarcely have
suspected its existence, as the pediment of Olympia
and the *Fates* of Phidias seem to testify clearly.[1] It is

Fig. 158

ORGANIC COMPOSITION (Melody: Giotto)

not until we reach Giotto,[2] in whom the end of the
Mediterranean effort coincided with the blossoming of
Christian tenderness, that we see this main and fundamental sentiment being formulated for the first time in
a decisive fashion by the intelligence, which unfortunately commanded, as yet, only rudimentary methods
and could merely project, unfalteringly, its shadowy
outl'ne upon the wall.

[1] Figs. 1, 14.
[2] Figs. 81, 158.

Beyond this the slow labor of clearing away by Masaccio and da Vinci, by Michael Angelo, Raphael, Titian, Tintoretto, and Rubens was necessary so that Rembrandt and Rembrandt alone in painting up to this period, might make the maximum and the totality of his methods converge toward the end to be attained.[1] In him the "subject" is found exactly at the point of

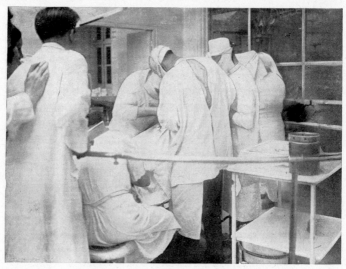

FIG. 159

NATURAL ORGANIC COMPOSITION (Operation)

equilibrium between the human emotion and the plastic impression, and he grasps this fugitive moment with such power that the whole world—at that instant amalgamated by light and present through all its elements in a few bent shoulders, a few bowed foreheads, a few hands held out toward a tomb or a cradle—seems a single organism operating in the space occupied by this tomb or this cradle. It is the event itself that

[1] Fig. 160.

composes the groups and delegates to the plastic symbol its power of sentiment.

In the instinct of the image-makers of the French cathedral and the Buddhist sculptors of India, especially of Cambodia and Java, there was already appearing an irresistible impulsion toward an organic order analogous to that of Rembrandt.[1] I remarked, apropos of Giotto, that this new and most fruitful conception of a whole is quite evidently a sign of the meeting of the

Fig. 160

Organic Composition (Symphony: Rembrandt)

ancient principles of architectonic construction and of Christian sentiment at its height. We know the analogies of Christianity and Buddhism. They were to pursue one another, for the sake of our spiritual unity, as far as the form which visual emotion assumes in the secret heart.

All this is very simple at bottom. It is never our business to invent episodes but to combine with sobriety and express with power the order according to which

[1] Figs. 15, 97, 136.

every event appears to us. This is done I feel sure, by all born creators. Rembrandt takes most of his "subjects" from scripture. Michael Angelo also. Villon, Pascal, Baudelaire seem almost incapable of inventing episodes, a privilege belonging almost always to the inferior Romanesque or dramatic literature. Shakespeare, himself, has recourse to history, like the Greek or French tragic poets, like the Jewish lyricists. Can we say that all these lacked imagination? Except for Rembrandt and Rubens, do we know a painter endowed with an imagination more grandiose than Tintoretto's? Yet he borrowed from Titian or Michael Angelo most of his "subjects." On the basis of his immediate emotions, the genuine creator combines the episodes which his traditional deity or habit celebrate more simply. Nor is the event the real point of departure. It is the immediate emotion aroused by the nude woman, by birth, death, man at his work, and the relations of all these things to light, space, and the agitation of man's heart. Does it suffice, then, to copy? No doubt. But it is necessary to know how to copy. To know how to copy is to know how to summarize, simplify, choose, accentuate. To copy is to disengage from a chaos of confused sensations the significant points to which emotion is attached and which are united by thought through passages subtle enough to allow only these peaks to emerge, while clearly showing their lasting relationships.

III

We cannot really judge of these questions save in the hours when some great common sentiment sweeps an entire crowd, already prepared by collective, secular education, toward the material symbols of the image to be realized. If this sentiment and this education are

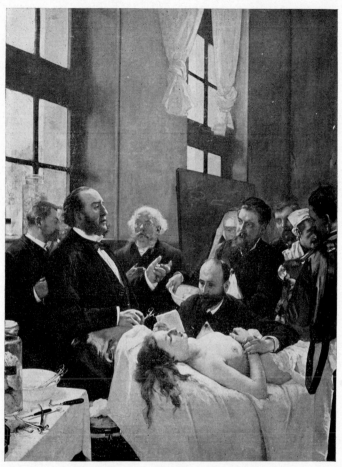

Fig. 161

NATURALISTIC COMPOSITION (Gervex)

lacking, it is necessary for the individual—by a sort of miracle, as if he had been divinely chosen—to possess them himself and, while tracing them to their natural sources, to have sufficient cruelty toward himself to keep watch over his sentimental emotions through his æsthetic emotions, and his æsthetic emotions through his sentimental emotions in a reciprocal and continuous exchange. The artistic education is the most arduous of all, for it consists neither in registering nor classifying nor expounding facts. The only means toward such an education, the only authority as to its value lies in the sensibility of master and pupil, and sensibility— since it admits no instrument of measurement—will not suffer any standard of choice to be imposed upon it.

Plastic art is, of all arts, the least understood and the least easy to understand. Through the ear we receive the opinions of others, which demands virtually no personal effort. Through the eye we are forced to form one for ourselves. Which is why we do not choose to believe in the education of the eye but recoil from it instinctively, because it demands a personal effort of which few of us are capable. We willingly admit that algebra or music necessitate a preliminary initiation, because they express themselves with the aid of rigidly conventional symbolic signs and present an infinity of possible combinations. But as soon as we are able to distinguish an elephant from an umbrella we regard the education of the eye as completed. From that moment we plunge headlong into uncontrolled sentiment, which the painting or the statue is henceforth reduced to the servile rôle of exalting, and which the most puerile symbolism—precisely that which is content with distinguishing an elephant from an umbrella— suffices to express.

Everybody, or almost everybody, knows that the word, or in any case the sound, only indirectly repre-

sents the object, which gives the poet and especially the
musician unbounded liberty.   Everybody, or almost
everybody, believes that the image is the object and
declares himself satisfied if the object is recognizable.
No one, or almost no one suspects that the permanent

FIG. 162

THE CONQUEST OF YOUTH (Titian, at 95 years of age)

need of checking up the world of imagery by the real
world demands an incessant effort that permits no
faltering; almost no one suspects that sculpture, and
especially painting, stand at a particularly unstable
point of equilibrium between the subject and the object.
Those who would be incapable of learning this language

—the most intellectual of all—decide at once that it is unintelligible. Those who would be capable of learning, decide that it is the least intellectual of tongues and reserved for a few persons whose visual endowment is no doubt estimable but insufficient to educate and ripen the mind. No one has asked himself why, for example, the period of finest production is so different in the different arts. For the musician and especially for the writer it almost always lies between the fortieth and fiftieth years; the education of the brain by the eye being slow, arduous, unceasing, and indebted to nothing outside itself, almost all the great masters of painting have produced their finest works after their fiftieth year and, when they have lived to be very old, have not ceased to reveal their steady rise in freedom and strength up to the end. I am thinking, in the matter of the great painters, of Veronese, Rubens, Rembrandt, Velasquez, Poussin, Delacroix, Cézanne and, in the matter of those who have lived to be very old, of Cranach, Frans Hals, Goya, Hokusai, and of the sublime examples of Titian[1] and Renoir.[2] The plastic education, more than any other, appeals only to those

[1] When I wished to choose a picture from the old age of Titian to bear out this text, I found myself confronted by a singular difficulty. Having resolved to give here only such illustrations as had not appeared in the four preceding volumes of this *History of Art*, I discovered that the paintings of Titian which illustrate them and which I had assembled at that time without taking into consideration their chronological order and relying solely on my preferences, had all been painted after the master's sixtieth year: the Doge "Gritti" at 64, "Paul III" at 69, "Salome" at 74, "Diana at the Bath" at 83, the "Education of Aurora" towards 90, the "Nymph and the Shepherd" and "Original Sin" toward 92, the portrait of "Titian" between 90 and 95, the "Christ Insulted" toward 94. It is one of the nudes mentioned above that I should have liked to reproduce to show what radiant spiritual youth the master possessed at the approach of his hundredth year. In default of them I have chosen the resplendent canvas at the Prado which he began to paint toward the age of 90 and did not finish, perhaps, until he was 98.

[2] Figs. 105 A, 162, 212.

Fig. 163

SUBORDINATION OF DETAIL TO MOVEMENT (Delacroix)

who wish to acquire it not as the result of fashion or pedantry, but through passion.

Everything changes after we have pondered the words of Spinoza: "The ideas that we have of exterior bodies indicate rather the constitution of our own body than the nature of exterior bodies," and when, on the other hand, we realize that painting, almost to the same degree as algebra or musical notation, is a language the conventional elements of which can group themselves according to infinite combinations that have no other object than to display a formal and colored harmony tending to recreate the unity of space, and of a formal and colored rhythm tending to recreate the continuity of movement. Innate and universal competence then seems laughable, esotericism irritating, humility necessary. I remember the time when I regarded Egyptian work as that of infants, the Chinese as monkeys, the Dravidians as madmen. The period is not so far away when I considered the Toltecs as monsters, and the negro artists as gorillas. Yet among them were forms, evolved long before, which I could view from a wide and distant perspective and which, by means of education and atavism, might have formed part of the normal necessity of my usual vision.

It is all a matter of convention, not even of universal convention, and one must know the signs of it according to the period and the place. How should a man without culture conceive the forms to be born, how should he understand even the forms that were being born, when ancient forms escape so often the understanding of the most cultivated man? I have heard it said that the Chinese, who belong to a superior civilization, have absolutely no understanding of what a European painting represents—a portrait, for instance—and are quite ready to look at it upside down. And I imagine that the day when Paolo Uccello introduced perspective into his works, although devised by him to approach reality as closely as possible, the spectators, accustomed to the conventions of the school of Giotto, found his works wholly unintelligible.[1]

It is necessary to learn. Even, perhaps especially, to learn that the same language can express different periods, different ideas, different characters, independently moreover, of its own nature. Not only Racine and Baudelaire, but Racine and Vaugelas, Baudelaire and my coal-dealer use the same words. People consider Michelet and Victor Duruy as historians because they make use of similar materials. Nevertheless, Jean-Paul Laurens, although he speaks the same language as Delacroix, is closer to Victor Duruy than to Delacroix, and Delacroix would agree better with Michelet, though speaking another language, than Michelet would agree with Victor Duruy.

"Painting is a matter of the mind," said da Vinci. We must realize this if we wish to restore its dignity by wresting it from the Bœotians. But we must also realize that it is a matter of poetry as well, and not suppose that two men who express themselves by painting are both painters because of that. There are grammarians of painting who are no more painters than the grammarians of language are writers. My coal-dealer speaks French, but Baudelaire is a poet in French. Cabanel expresses himself in painting, but Renoir is a poet in painting. We move "through forests of symbols," certainly. Here, again, we must realize that some of these symbols, alike at first sight, conceal a different spirit, and that some others, dissimilar at first sight, mask the same spirit. There is less distance between Homer and Corot, who are separated by nearly three thousand years, and who express themselves through signs that have no analogy, than between

[1] Fig. 141.

Corot and some illustrious professor of painting who lives in the same epoch and uses similar signs.

Granting this, and that we are familiar with the convention that pretends to enclose the world, whether in the rigid or sinuous play of lines on a plane, or in the animated reliefs of volumes on an irregular surface, or in an entirely detached form imitating the real form, whether one accepts Egyptian symbolism, Hindu symbolism, Greek symbolism, whether one consents to more conventional representation still, in which the linear arabesque, the flat tone, the introduction of values and half-tones reproduce at will all the preceding effects augmented by the immense melodic and symphonic resource of color, it remains for us to penetrate the very spirit of the work, that is to say its quality. This is a less arduous task than the first, since all language bears in itself a secret harmony that is proper to it and that is not clearly evident unless it unites with the spiritual harmony of man by passages so subtle that both fuse in an irresistible unity. But for that very reason this quality is less easy to define; and, in the last analysis, it need render account to nothing save to the sentiment of the individual.

Anatomical rendering is only one more convention, and perhaps more dangerous than any other since Occidental art, thanks to it, has almost been engulfed in the search for physical perfection, while Oriental art, which gave no thought to it, penetrated as a matter of course, through its constant symbolism, into the empire of ideas. Without discussing anatomical rendering any further, therefore, we may say that line, mass, and color derive their accepted meaning from the mind alone and that none of them has the right to pretend to be closer to reality than the others, even if we admit that art endeavors to render reality. Neither line nor mass nor color exists by itself. Once their form of ex-

Fig. 164

Subordination of Detail to Form (Java)

pression is fixed, all are functions of that inner force which springs from the enthusiasm of an artistic multitude at work or from a solitary poet. None of the methods created to symbolize form have reality save through their spiritual relations with the expression of an idea, the ensemble of which lies entirely in the intention of the creator.

It is this ensemble that we must first seek to understand. The surgical operation, mentioned above, revealed to me in a flash the supremely important and almost unique rôle which this ensemble plays, and at the same time the means we must use to succeed in expressing it. Not a detail, no matter how insignificant in appearance, but depends upon it and is determined by its essential function, as the form of the humblest organ is determined by the function of an organism of which it is only a part. Detail does harm if it is not indispensable to the radiance of the ensemble. The ensemble does not radiate unless it forms a whole from which nothing can be taken away. The narrow gleam of the knife in the "Medea"[1] of Delacroix assumes a tragic significance because the entire movement of the drama, the terrible face that looks back, the flying hair, the torso swollen with anger, the arms clasped about the limp children, all converge in the gleam of the knife through the play of the lines. The woods would seem less deep in the Fête Champêtre,[2] and the green shadow that floats between the black trunks less mysterious if Watteau had not accentuated the silence and the peaceful seclusion by this rose in the ivy, this crimson ribbon against the gray satin of a corsage.

I remember, in a certain "Emtombment" by Rembrandt, an almost imperceptible blue stripe that runs across Christ's shroud. What is the meaning of this

[1] Fig. 163.
[2] Fig. 57.

almost gay note in the greatest drama of history? One
does not see it unless one analyzes the picture: only
the ensemble appears at first, the weight of the corpse
in the arms of friends, the sorrow of the women, the
bleeding wounds, and the inertia of the god. It does
not force itself upon one. But the moment one sees it
one knows why the flesh of Christ is so livid, why this
odor of the sepulcher floats over all these suspicious

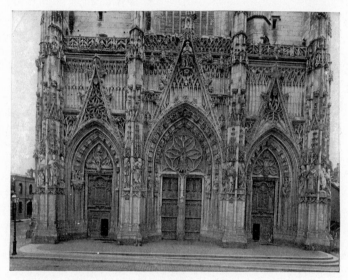

Fig. 165
Tyranny of Detail (Abbeville)

whitenesses, why this almost inaudible cry of the flute
introduces into the wail of the oboes and the violoncellos
as it were a faint recollection of the joys of the world
that renders everything more hopeless. In a portrait
of a woman by Goya it is impossible to see anything but
a mouth where the blood beats above glistening teeth,
nothing but flaming eyes, warm arms, a few flowers or
sparkling jewels here and there, because there is nothing

else and all this is necessary to express and suffices to express the image of her vicious beauty. I know a Javanese Buddha,[1] smooth and naked, in which the surfaces slide into one another like pure, unrippled water, a sort of block of uniform light, the whole of whose single wave ends in two mannered and charming hands, well cared-for, pulpy, full of creases and hiding-places like flowers. The curve of a hand, caught by chance in the *apsaras* of Angkor, is prolonged,[2] through the serpentine quality of the torso down to the foot of the dancer because nothing superfluous intervenes, neither a misplaced trinket nor an excessive muscular protuberance, to break the continuous wave that unites them and is repeated the whole length of the frieze in invisible echoes.

We should look at a picture or a statue as we look at a monument, not in regard to some carved leaf but in regard to the structural logic that determines its posture and indicates its functions. This logic itself will lead the eyes back over the carved leaf so that we can admire its very veinings. The absence of this logic would explain why the leaf, lost in the enormous edifice, would be enough in itself to arouse our distaste. An error does not shock in a harmonious ensemble. In an inharmonious ensemble we see only errors, even if not everything is error. Suppose a man stood at Chantilly, between the modern château and the outbuildings of the old château. I should ask him to look first at one building and then at the other. If he did not yet understand I should ask that after having taken a long look at the church of Brou, or even at the church of Abbeville, or even the Cathedral of Rheims, in which there are so many splendidly attractive details, he should turn to the Palace of the Popes at Avignon.[3]

---

[1] Fig. 164.   [2] Fig. 136.
[3] Figs. 125, 165.

IV

The ornamental profusion of architectures in a state
of degeneration corresponds, in the picture, to sacri-
ficing an ensemble which its painter shows himself, by
this very fact, incapable of conceiving, to useless anecdotal or picturesque
details. Neverthe-
less, this profusion
acquires a singular
savor in the Primi-
tives who employ it
—I mean especially
the Primitives of Ger-
many or Flanders,
for the Italian mani-
fests an admirable
plastic intelligence
from the outset of
painting. It is because
in the German or
Flemish Primitive
this profusion does
not rise from a desire
to dazzle the spectator
by a false science, a
servile virtuosity, the

Fig. 166
Assimilation (Poussin)

display of an erudition as inordinate as it is hollow, but
from a candid scrupulousness not to forget anything he
knows or feels. What saves him is the freshness of what
he feels and the naïveté with which he recounts what he
knows. The ensemble, which has, in him as in most fully
developed masters, a profound spiritual existence, is not
given its unique value, as in the case of the latter, through
plastic processes that subordinate the emotion experi-

enced to the consciousness of this emotion and to the means of expressing it provided by the intelligence. The emotion experienced, which has been aroused by sentiment, is expressed precisely by the accumulation of everything that can help to render the fervor of this sentiment. If detail dominates here, it never harms the ensemble, which is itself nothing but an accumulation of details arranged as well as possible about a single emotion that confusedly floods them with its power.

So, while in him who attains the peaks of painting the equilibrium is realized between instinct and reason, it is broken in the decadent, who does not even suspect it and gropes his way blindly, with the tip of his Academic sword, in an anarchic universe. In the Primitive this equilibrium strives to be realized, and the work derives its touching character from the very passion of this striving. At first the beginning of love, then its full possession, finally its dissolution in the disgust and lassitude of the act. Compare from this point of view Gentile da Fabriano, Raphael and Barocci, or, to choose three names in a single school, Carpaccio, Titian, Bassano. And you will appreciate what distinguishes detail envisaged as a logical function of the whole. In one case the detail and the whole both subordinate themselves to their function as regards sentiment, in the other the detail and the whole are both deprived of logic and sentiment.

In the latter case you will get a perfect example of academic procedure, which the young Rembrandt still utilized in the "Lesson in Anatomy" at the Hague,[1] and which he suddenly renounced, having achieved success and fortune, to watch men toiling, agonizing, dying in the dwellings of the poor quarters, women toiling, weeping, giving birth to children, and to watch children being born or playing. The School substitutes

[1] Fig. 102.

THE CAGE

for the organic conception of the masters, which it is incapable of comprehending, what it calls "composition," a collection of recipes borrowed from the exterior aspect of their works, from the grouping of objects and figures whose concentric arrangement it seizes but of which the human source is absolutely inaccessible to it. It is, however, simple to grasp it; simpler, indeed, than to discover rhythmic formulas. It is simpler to contemplate a living spectacle from the standpoint of one's own personality than to attempt to render this spectacle from the standpoint of the so-called arrangement shown by a canvas of Raphael, Titian, Rubens, or Poussin. It is a matter of suffering, feeling, loving, of comparing one's love, one's sensations, and one's suffering with the impressions one receives of the visible world and binding them together with lines of force that compel the form and the heart to agree. The mysterious thing is that this ability should be granted to very few men. Almost all serve up again in their "Model Resting" the polygons and pyramids that they have taken bodily, with a tracing, from the "Mass of Bolsena" or the "Transfiguration."

Does this mean that tradition does not exist in forms of art springing from the same people, that technique cannot be transmitted, perfecting itself from age to age, that the craft of the architect, the sculptor, or the painter cannot be taught? It is so far from meaning this that I believe, quite on the contrary, the tradition of the great artistic civilizations is strictly bound to the progressive discovery and the joyous conquest of the organic character of art. The tradition is born, grows, gathers strength, ripens, wanes, and dies at the same time that the spiritual life of a people is born, grows, gathers strength, ripens, wanes, and dies. Men of the same craft, speaking the same tongue, working in the same shop, the same atelier under the orders of the same master, use the same tools, grind the same colors, handle the same substances, spread over the same stones the same layer of plaster to fix the painting there by the same processes, jointing the same scaffolding made with the same wood according to the same principles with the same ropes and the same nails.

The instrument plays a human rôle in the formation of the artist. It shapes his hand. It attacks the material, different according to the place and the period, with an iron more or less strong, more or less sharp, more or less hard. Geological shapes and the quality of the light intervene every instant, during several generations to orient the master and his disciples

Fig. 168

THE BIRD

toward a fashion of seeing that gradually modifies their fashion of feeling and being. This is well known in the case of language itself which fashions little by little the form of reasoning. A man, no matter how great, does not run away from his craft, his guild, his race, and the impulsions which they give him without running away, at the same time, from the universality of mankind which this craft, this guild, this race have helped to model; it is they which transmit to men the secrets, sentiments, and ideas that have come down from other times. And this is so true that the greatest return to the real traditions that are disregarded or falsified by the School most of the time.

This was the rôle of Rubens, restoring the painting

of his country to its Flemish sources against the Romanizers of Flanders, after having, according to the counsels of those same Romanizers, studied the Italians but understood them better than they. It is the rôle of Poussin, accomplishing in Italy the same task for France. It is that of Delacroix re-establishing, amid the outcries of the Academy professors, the great animated form of an organic movement against a tradition that had been led astray by the pupils of David. It is that of Cézanne leading Impressionism back to the monumental approach to a three-dimensional world when the painters had lost themselves in the dance of atoms and of floating reflections. The appearance of the heroic individual has always marked the break with an old, worn rhythm that is out of breath, out of touch with its sources, and the introduction of a young rhythm in the traditional settings. These consist, everywhere, of the national character, the teachings of the historical and geographical surroundings, the social and ideological evolution that has circulated subterraneously in the soul of the last generations, and the will to maintain the mind at the level of the rising flood of life so as to understand it and, in case of need, master it. It is these things that a master worthy of his name teaches his pupils.

The strictness of the tradition, which enslaves and perverts the weak, will never prevent the strong from revivifying its spirit from time to time through the revolutionary intervention of the very power that animates them and which they add to the age-old edifice like a spire or a tower. What always revolts the herd is that, since the organ changes its function before changing its form, it is never aware that the function has been changed and that the new form, which is the poet himself, is precisely the announcer of the new function. The traditional creator, the poet, is not the

Fig. 169

Life (Greece)

professor who employs his most skillful recipes in constructing a Greco-Renaissance palace to the glory of all the arts; he is the engineer who exhibits an airplane in the hall of that palace.

The palace has no style, the airplane has. That is the whole matter. Tradition, even if it appears in the form of revolution, has for its object to maintain and

re-establish style in the expressive forms of an epoch, a people, a function, or a man. That is to say that it is a structure taken from life and returning to life after passing through the mind; it is a structure whose unity in space and continuity in time restore to the man, to the function, to the people, to the epoch in question their universal appearance and significance. He who wishes to defend the School can furnish

FIG. 170
STYLE (Persia)

only one argument of any value. The task of the School is, perhaps, to outline faintly in time the arabesque which the masters traced yesterday or will trace tomorrow in space. In this way it may manifest, according to its modest means, the continuity of our effort between the great moments of our spiritual life, since they are separated by critical periods in which all rhythms are lost. For example, perhaps without the school of

[1] Figs. 167, 168.

of T'ang in China, a prodigious hour of the human soul
strikes in which its power of love, reaching an apogee,
arrange themselves spontaneously according to its maximum of will-power.   When style preponderates the
reign of dogma comes quickly, giving the illusion of
capturing life, impressive at first but speedily tyrannical,
sterile, and soon deadly.   When life is in the ascendant

Fig. 172

Panathenaic Procession (Byzantine Art)

and gives the illusion that it will not burn out, there
comes a state of chaos that is intoxicating for those who
feel it, but anarchic and exhausting if it does not lead
to a new equilibrium, thanks to the action of some great
individual or some ardent group of individuals.

There are a hundred examples of these alternative
rhythms; for example: the Egyptian style of the new
empire that ended in a monotonous academicism from

which, at the *Saïte* epoch, the artists of the Nile tore
themselves away to recover, though indeed in frailer
forms, the musical undulation of surfaces that had
characterized the works of their ancestors ten centuries
before;[1] the Greek style, from which the life of the
Hellenistic world escaped in an increasing disorder to
end, through the assimilation of a thousand foreign
contributions, in the Byzantine style where one finds
again the essential elements of the eurythmic preoccupations that prevailed among the forerunners of Phidias;[2] the Buddhist style, born of a moral reaction
against Brahmanism and recovering the sensual orgy
of Brahmanism at the end of its road, through the
artists of Cambodia and Java, whose carving makes
us sense the very perfume of flowers, the murmur of
trees, the ripple of water;[3] the French ogival style,
definitely shattered by the formidable upheaval caused
in the fifteenth and sixteenth centuries by their fierce
conquest of liberty of sensation and of criticism, but
reappearing—for those who have eyes and according
to its own essential rhythms that date from the period
of the primitive cathedrals—in the symmetrical arrangement of the chateau of Hardouin Mansart.

One could go much farther in the demonstration of
this constancy of the same style through ages agitated
by political institutions and by the successive erection
and destruction of the national power in the material
and moral order. In some French factory of today we
see again the general appearance of the palaces of
Louis XIV. In some Italian automobile or ship we
recognize the trenchant manner of the architects of
Siena[4] or Florence five or six hundred years ago. The

[1] Figs. 32, 173.
[2] Figs. 171, 172.
[3] Figs. 91, 97, 136, 188, 202.
[4] Figs. 71, 79.

megalomania of the Roman style has not varied, from the Cyclopean works of the Etruscans to those of the engineers of our day, including the builders of the Coliseum, including Michael Angelo and the palace architects during the two centuries that preceded the revolution. We can go even farther back and compare, for example, the style of the English and French cathedrals of the thirteenth century with the style of the immemorial raised stones of insular Britain and continental Brittany; in the latter case we have animation and delightful irregularity of surfaces and profiles, and in the former their straight lines, their coldness, their rigidity.

Style can only be defined through the constancy of its

FIG. 173

PERSISTENCE OF THE ARCHITECTONIC
RHYTHM

(Egypt, Saïte Period)

relations with the country and the race, the age-old effort of which goes occasionally so far as to create forms so remote from their living original that it is scarcely recognizable and remains unknown to the creator himself, or rather to the executant, to the tapestry-worker, potter, cabinet maker, or decorator. Stylization is nothing but the schematic systemization of a style. It is repugnant to Europe in general—if one excepts furniture, pottery, jewelry, and architecture which is after all the most noble form of stylization— but Egyptian antiquity and Asia have extended it to all manifestations of art, from the humblest to the most grandiose. It is the anonymous, obscure work of ten, twenty, a hundred generations of workmen bent upon their task of conserving every member which makes up the symbolic framework of the initial emotion. We find it in the ensemble of the monument as well as in its slightest details. Sometimes, as with the Arab decorators, it reaches pure geometry, but more often, fortunately, it turns to the motionless rhythmic dance of ornamental motifs tending to symmetry, such as we find in Byzantine or Romanesque, Peruvian or Polynesian decoration, or again it attains that inexhaustible freedom in the arrangement of the schematized form in which Japanese artisans are past masters. In their case, everything is dominated by the race-factor which leads, in religion and politics, to obedience to a law that has been accepted once for all, because it is recognized as favorable to the development of the social type.

What gives Europe its special characteristic, in the lyrical as well as in the moral field, is that the individual appears to rescue it from that somnolence into which the monotonous repetition of the same rhythm invincibly bears it. Between life that rebels at being dammed in and the dam itself, giving to life its peculiar

Fig. 174

Occidental Objectivism (Vermeer)

Fig. 175
EQUILIBRIUM (Egypt)

expression, a singular contradiction exists which will never be solved. It seems that the longer the rock of style holds, against the flowing torrent of life, the more chance there is for the survival, intact, of the conception of life which that style represents, but also the more it runs the risk of impeding the course of the flood. Egypt and China offer us the most illustrious examples of these complete civilizations, stylized from one end to the other, which prefer death upon the spot to renewal. Style which is an instrument of enfranchisement for him or for those who conceive it, is an instrument of enslavement for him or for those who revere it. This is the source and the secret of that permanent tragedy which the soul of man will always harbor; it is through mastering his spiritual life that he creates his own liberty, but he only creates his liberty to the detriment of those who have not the power to discipline their own. Obedience is the law of moral liberation. Grandeur and slavery reciprocally condition each other. A civilization is the more durable the more

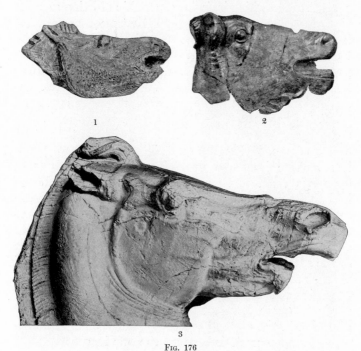

FIG. 176

PERMANENT OBJECTIVISM

1. Head of a Horse, Prehistoric Art.   2. Head of a Bull, Ægean Art.
3. Head of a Horse, Greek Art

it knows how to maintain the reciprocal dependence with the more constancy, rigor, and, if you will, cruelty.

V

The resolutely symbolistic civilizations alone can offer this long resistance to the incessant encroachment of the images that other civilizations bring in from outside and to the curiosity fired by powerful individualities within the civilization itself.   Singular mystery that opens between the Oriental and the Occidental soul an abyss which is, indeed, capable of being crossed, since they have never ceased to react upon each other, but which is very difficult to close.   The one tends to remain within itself and to see in the world of phenomena nothing but an inexhaustible symbolic treasury destined to represent its vast but obscure aspirations.   The other tends constantly to emerge from itself, to keep account of its aspirations toward positive conquest by the never complete definition of the nature of those phenomena, upon which it strives to model itself.   The language in which the Occidental soul expresses itself is symbolic also, no doubt, like all human language, but it aims unceasingly to trace the symbol from the object itself.   Whereas once the essential aspects of the object have been caught, the Oriental soul aims only at absorbing it in the fluctuating life of the symbol.   The latter pursues *its* truth, the former pursues *the* truth.[1]   If both, in their great hours, resist the fixity of their nature it is because, according to the needs of those hours, there is a constant change of direction in the truths that we pursue both in and outside of ourselves; it is because the one in grasping the object perceives his own mystery, as the other, wishing to utter the mystery, is forced to grasp the object.

It is none the less true that an Occidental will not understand the art of the Orient, that an Oriental will not understand the art of the Occident if they refuse to explore the two borders of the abyss where flourish two illusions of equal fecundity, that which defines the world by what passes in man and that which defines man by what passes in the world.   If

[1] Figs. 174, 177.

the Egyptians seem to me to have realized a miraculous accord of these two grandiose illusions[1] it is perhaps because the geographic, ethnic, cultural elements of the Orient and the Occident fused in them with an equal depth, an equal power. This harmony has never occurred again, save perhaps in music. Who knows if, one day or another, thanks to the initiative of music, it will not recur?

The strange thing is that no matter how far back one goes into the past of Asia or Europe one finds these two attitudes of mind, even before the influence of Egypt, through the instrumentality of Greece, had spread over these two slopes of the Old World and transmitted to them the principles by which each of them was to determine its aptitudes and develop them so logically as to be characterized by them. Assyrian art, which aspires only to expression, already shows monsters contrived to express some central idea, the character of which—in this case violence and cruelty— is only emphasized by natural shapes. Mycenæan art, on the contrary, ignores composite monsters and aims at the truth. What am I saying? A hundred centuries, perhaps two hundred centuries before, the troglodytes of Perigord and the Pyrenees thought only of reproducing, with as much energy but also as much exactitude as possible, the images of animals and men in their everyday occupations.[2]

The rôle of Greece was to confirm the entire Occident in this primitive attitude by educating directly or indirectly, one after another, sixty generations of architects, painters, and sculptors. Meanwhile it had also reawakened Asiatic sculpture, which was henceforth to pursue its road alone, everywhere fabricating unheard-of beings with the bodies of men and the heads of

[1] Fig. 175.
[2] Fig. 176.

beasts, with the bodies of beasts and the heads of men, creatures furnished with twenty arms, looking out from seven faces,[1] endowed with infinitely combined attitudes of strength, tenderness, death, and love.

The above is, to be sure, a summary statement of the rôle of Greece, one ceaselessly contradicted by sudden interpenetrations, by the Arab conquest, the Mongol invasions, the Crusades, the navigation of the fifteenth and sixteenth centuries, the incessant flux and reflux of two worlds engaged in material or spiritual warfare. It is a statement corresponding to the general reality, however, pointing, with European art, to a plastic universe peopled with natural forms, always close to man and life, depicting man and life, even in the most mystical works of religious symbolism, with fidelity, insight, unfaltering exactitude, and refusing to abdicate its interested optimism. On the other hand it shows Asia forcing man and life, even in such familiar objects as house and clothing, to assume the aspect of its boundless dream, distorting rocks with fantastic figures, giving tangible shape to its grandiose nightmares, and refusing to abdicate its hopeless pessimism. When Occidental art is abandoned by faith, at the periodic visitations of criticism and negation, it falls a victim to its incapacity to see and seek the spirit beyond or outside the form; and again when the faith of the Orient slumbers, or is poisoned by too many miasmas or enervating pleasures, its art is undone by its refusal to interrogate this form in itself, and by its consent to lie passive before the pretended immateriality of the mind.

This obstinate refusal of the Orient to emerge from the symbol is found even in its architecture which, we must admit, suffers from it and nowhere, save in a few civil or military buildings of China or Northern India,

[1] Fig. 177.

Fig. 177

ORIENTAL SUBJECTIVISM

presents that nudity of surface, that density of mass,
that simplicity of proportions and of rhythms which,
through France, Italy, and Greece, have made the
grandeur of Occidental architecture and to which it
was fortunately led, in its great periods, through its
concern with the purpose to be achieved. In China, in
Japan, in Indo-China, in the East Indies, in the whole

FIG. 178

ANALOGIES OCCIDENTAL OBJECTIVISM (France)

FIG. 179

ORIENTAL SUBJECTIVISM (India)

of Dravidian India, an evident symbolism prevails from
the top to the bottom of the edifice and determines its
least details, now accumulating, one after another,
forests of bas-reliefs and statues that rise tier upon tier
in cones, pyramids, or spheres, in a fever of ornamentation that recalls the unwholesome bloating of succulent
plants bristling with poisonous darts,[1] and now super-

[1] Fig. 131.

posing, on a complicated framework, cornices and roofs that are useless from the functional point of view.

On the contrary, even in the periods when religious symbolism takes possession of Occidental architecture, it remains faithful to its great lines, to a simplicity of conception and structure that places the entire edifice in equilibrium about a definite function, such as a crowd to shelter, heavy bronze bells to raise over the towns, as defense against surprise or assault, definition of the organism, even the spiritual organism, through the agency of utility, the rational distribution of masses in view of solid construction, and a harmony of the ensemble that satisfies at once the practical and logical needs that characterize the mind.[1] It is true that Occidental painting and sculpture are reproached for these very qualities, or rather for a too constant concern with them, and that they often give it an indescribable air of bureaucratic propriety, limited on all sides by the fear of ridicule, of the unusual, of the excessive. And our art does this just in the way that the monstrous architectural faults of Asia can, when her painting or her decorative sculpture is considered, assume a lyrical grandeur, capable of modeling or hollowing out mountains and almost unknown to the Occident.

Almost unknown, although from the eleventh to the twelfth century, especially in France, the Occident did pass through a period quite analogous[2] to that which we have described. A less intoxicated period, unquestionably, since, as we have seen, architecture resists to the very edge of decadence the measureless swarming of forms which only succeed after three hundred years in bending, and finally in breaking its osseous framework, under their weight. Like Asia, the Occident was firmly

[1] Figs. 30, 53, 88, 124, 125, 195, 206, 217.
[2] Figs. 178, 179.

resolved to consider the material universe only as a thought of God. I am aware that this is the theological idea, I know that Christianity cannot make its symbols penetrate the soul of the people save by invoking precisely the testimony of this material universe. I am aware that the image-maker brings his most candid application to copying the scenes and the beings that are the constant source of his everyday emotions, if indeed philosophy sees here the representation of the spiritual drama that determines its concepts.

Fig. 180
ALLEGORICAL ORTHOPEDICS (Rome)

Nevertheless, Christian symbolism lives in the heart of the image-maker as it does in the mind of the philosopher; it is merely a prolonged echo of a remote perturbation of the soul that has become common to virtually the whole Christian world. As in Asia, all the scenes of life are henceforth obscure symbols and the emotion which the image-maker experiences is his "subject." When long study of these scenes substitutes in the image-maker—as indeed it does in the philosopher—the need to express this reality more and more accurately, for the need to use it to express a moral emotion, then the forms, though stripped of their symbolic meaning for the multitude, will acquire a new symbolic sense through the conquering thought of a few great individuals. Then we shall see in the Occident, as in Greece after the third century, and in almost the whole of Roman sculpture, allegory[1] trying to replace the lost symbolic emotion to suit the needs of mean souls. Instead of emerging from within the form itself, blossoming out of it, so to speak, uniting with light itself through imperceptible passages from plane to plane, from profile to profile, from mass to mass, the allegory will plaster itself upon the form, like a moral orthopædics designed to sustain the inner architecture which it has forgotten as well as the mystic emotion that once drew attention to it. I know no one in painting but Rubens who has had a sufficiently powerful feeling for life to be able to introduce allegorical figures into the general movement of his work, and Giotto who has had a soul pure enough and an intelligence supple enough to give such figures soul and intelligence.

VI

First after Phidias, again after Giotto and the French cathedrals, has the Occident been deprived of the universal symbolism according to which it conceived the world of appearances. And I believe that it is partly the fault of allegory that it has been driven to seek the elements of an individual symbolism in this naturalistic conception of form which has led it furthest from the Orient. The Greco-Roman need for truth which has been expressed twice, first thanks to Greece and Rome, next thanks to the Italian Renaissance

[1] Fig. 180.

through the pursuit of anatomical expression, has determined everywhere this naturalistic conception which
has saved European architecture, and by introducing
modeling into its painting, has conferred upon it, in
the last analysis, the sometimes grandiose but more
often commonplace privilege of transferring the illusion
of life, through values and perspective, to a two-
dimensional space.

Greek art, and with it a great part of European art
after the fourteenth century, is in truth more monstrous
than these very Egyptian, Chinese, Hindu, Aztec monsters that, in a horrible or tender mystical communion,
combine human forms with animal forms, animal forms
with plant forms, the forms of life with the forms of
death.   Monstrous because it does not dare, like them,
to carry the spiritual life into a form resolutely and
fully symbolic, which enthrones it on a mystic plane,
outside the real.   Therefore it chains us to a determined
perfectionism that forbids us lyrical rapture.   The great
divisions—idealism and realism—that have been forced
upon all Occidental art, and from which Oriental art
escapes almost completely, go back, finally, to this
exclusive care for descriptive perfection which has so
often been fatal to the art they affect, even though it
has caused the emergence of a few great individuals.
Caused, I say emphatically.   We should have but a
poor explanation of Rembrandt or Michael Angelo, for
example, if the Occidental need of truth had not weighed
upon them for more than twenty centuries—what am
I saying?—for the twenty thousand years that separate
them from the reindeer-hunters, no doubt—and had
not imposed on the incessant conquest of their moral
equilibrium the pathetic air of a soul that wishes to
shatter its matrix while modeling itself on the form of
this matrix, now with fervor, now with humility.

Each of these divisions responds, it is true, to some

Fig. 182

Contemporaries (Botticelli)

Fig. 181

Contemporaries (Ghirlandajo)

precise thing. They are both the complementary expressions of European naturalism. They have not
ceased to penetrate each other, as in Rubens and the
French romanticists, to spring from each other, as when
the Bolognese school was grafted on that of Rome and
Venice, for example, or when Praxiteles and Lysippus
succeeded Phidias, to alternate, one with the other, as
in France when we go from the Clouets to Poussin,
from Poussin to Chardin, from Chardin to David, from
David to Corot, from Corot to Courbet. They even
exist side by side if one will compare, in the same country and at the same period, the Clouets with Jean
Goujon, the brothers Le Nain with Le Brun, Ghirlandajo
with Botticelli,[1] Carpaccio with Giorgione, Tiepolo with
Guardi.

Nevertheless, the two currents that bear them are
easily discovered if here, also, we will steep ourselves
in the customs of the country and the race, in their
spiritual history and their particular reaction to events.
European naturalism almost certainly leads to plastic
"idealism," its southern peoples who tend to define the
race; and almost certainly to realism, its northern
peoples who tend to define the individual.[2]   Let us remember that in both cases it is a task accepted by
virtually the whole of humanity, and that in one place
it is expressed socially by Protestantism and political
liberty, in the other place by Catholicism and the
tendency to trust to autocracy or even convulsive
Cæsarism in matters of social organization.   For in one
case it is necessary to stimulate, develop, and warm
the inner life that tends to stifle the duller instincts, the
less burning passions, the less mobile imagination, and
then seek the real man, and describe and characterize
the forms seen close at hand, in the dwellings where

[1] Figs. 181, 182.
[2] Figs. 183, 184.

Fig. 184

Realism (Rembrandt)

Fig. 183

Idealism (Raphael)

the winter is spent, or out of doors where, drowned in fog, the relations of the forms to one another are uncertain, confused, broken—more sentimental than plastic.

In the other case it is necessary to simplify the inner life that has been ravaged by more precocious instincts, less restrained passions, and a more richly nourished imagination, and subsequently to define man as a genus, man as a function of the social interest, to establish the unity of forms as they appear in light and revealed by light, plunged in a space where everything solidifies, having for each other relations of contiguity and continuity that tend persistently to plastic generalization.

It has been said of Hellenic art, the father of European naturalism—using singular expressions, for that matter—that it mingles the ideal with the real, as if the ideal and the real were two sauces of almost equal consistency which could be mixed together in a pot. And yet that art did possess an exact feeling for equilibrium which resulted in the impossible and perfect monster we have already met with. Is it the direct ruggedness and descriptive power of the Doric, that had come down from the North, or the sublety and generalizing memory of the Ionic, that had sifted in from Asia, through the islands, that explains the mystery? The fact remains that the never forgotten elements of form, unceasingly and constantly scrutinized, impress on Hellenic generalizations a character of direct, intuitive exactitude that make us feel that we just passed an actual example of them a few minutes earlier, when we turned the corner of the street that leads to the museum, or climbed the path that leads to the Acropolis, and that its most searching and faithful descriptions have something universal and typical which, the moment we leave the Acropolis or the Museum, show us a monument of architecture in almost all the passers-by.

The savage realism that characterizes Spain, Southern and Catholic, constitutes a singular exception to that naturalism, with its two complementary faces, which in the last analysis, distinguishes the Occident, when one thinks of Asiatic symbolism sweeping both the individual and the species away together in a torrent of spiritual excitement, in which the universe itself is a factor. A sort of fury drives Spanish realism to pursue form to its most frightful abnormalities, even to its leprosies, and to enthrone in art not only the individual, under the appearance which is proper to him and the aspect he wears amid his everyday acts—a task in which the Fleming,

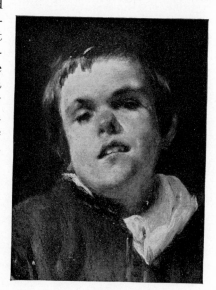

Fig. 185
SPANISH MONSTER (Velasquez)

the German, the Dutchman, the Northern French excel —but also the abnormal individual, the blind, the idiot, the lame, and to open to rags, rubbish, and filth the gateway to the illusions which the idealists say were created to make us forget filth, rubbish, and rags, as well as the existence of the blind, the idiot, and the lame.

No doubt to explain this striking contradiction it

would be necessary to search for the mingled ethnic and geographical causes, to investigate, perhaps, the chaotic aspect of a soil that is broken, wild, rugged, degraded, lacking in harmony of shape, or perhaps the old Iberian heredity of which we know so little; and, almost surely, Arab fatalism impressing on Catholic discipline the fierce resolution to transplant the supernatural into life and, precisely because of this fanatically to accept this life, even to its worst horrors. In any case here, as in Holland and in Germany, the idealism of form is unknown to artists, who never alter a shape for the sake of more attraction or surer charm, but for the sake of more emphasis and better characterization. They cannot escape from this implacable realism save by introducing into it a harmonic unity which is also reality—but which only a few exceptional men have been able to discover in this cruel landscape with its subtle harmonies of silver, trembling in space, in the black of hair and cloaks, the pearly tone of jewels, the pink of roses, the red of pomegranates, carnations, and hair-ribbons.[1]

Rather than the Florentine or Greek ideal of form, then, it is symphonic painting which, by way of Spain and Venice, Flanders and Holland and France, has opened up the road of the musicians and has saved the Occident from its need of realistic truth, though we must admit that architecture, system, science, and industry have progressively arisen from that truth. Around anatomical sculpture, projected on a plane by the visual imagination, it has created an artificial space that binds it to all the points of space and mind. Thus truth, urged to the limit of its powers, leads fatally to a new illusion which is the mystic sentiment of the continuity of the universe. It is Asiatic mysticism that leads the Occident to the love of truth. Why

[1] Figs. 33, 185, 186.

Fig. 186

Spanish Harmony (Goya)

should not truth lead the Occident, which conquered it, back to the mysticism of Asia? This would be a sufficient justification of the universal symbolism from which art cannot emerge save through the emancipation of a few choice souls who bring it back, inevitably, to universal symbolism.

FIG. 187

BRANTÔME, FRANCE

Chapter VIII. THE POWER OF THE IDOL

I

A RELIGION, or rather a somewhat formless mass of beliefs which had accumulated, ranging themselves side by side, and often fusing, endured for fifty centuries. It peopled the valley of an African river with temples, tombs, avenues of colossi, pylons, pyramids, and obelisks, as if life and death had had no other function than that of demonstrating the truth and the constructive power of those beliefs, around which all social and domestic and political and military life was arranged. An art as categorical as it was subtle, in which the spirit of fineness and the geometrical spirit are merged, fills the vast space of the oasis and of the desert and five thousand years of history, which is practically unknown to us save for the testi-

391

mony left by this art; it fills this space and time with a
species of musical rhythm which is uninterrupted and
which bears, on the surface of its wave, an inexhaustible
freshness of impressions, of sensations, and of sentiments as vibrant as the life in the murmur of the dawn,
as firm as the logic in the still voice of the mind. The
soul of man circulates in the combining forms of the
gods, aside from whom men cannot conceive the labors
of the fields and the river, the universal symbolism
which sets the hawks soaring in the formidable light,
which builds a monstrous temple in order to lay within
its darkest center the mummy of a crocodile, and causes
to arise, stone by stone, a mountain of granite, fixing
the unanimous movement of the heavens.

Another religion, during five centuries, covered the
reddish promontories which enter the waves like the
prow of a ship, with small, harmonious temples that
seem to be constructed both upon the scale of the visible
universe and that of pure intelligence, and, without
effort, to reconcile in an eternal balance all the contradictions of the moral and the social life, antagonistic
divinities, warring interests, and struggling factions.
Here, in the whole monument as in its slightest detail,
in the statue of the god as in the frieze and the metope
where the adventure of the city is spread forth, there
was discovered a harmony—which seems to have been
immediately accepted and defined for all time—between
the real elements of the most concrete world and the
idealistic and generalizing tendencies of the mind, between the least dissimulated sensuality, on one hand,
and reason on the other—the type of reason most stub-
born in defending its conquests, between the most fleet-
ing shudders of the moving surface of the forms and
the most permanent laws of their inner structure, which
little by little determines our spiritual edifice. The flanks
and the arms of the gods were exposed to the swords of
men, the breasts and thighs of the goddesses plunged,

Fig. 188

BRAHMAN IDOL (Cambodia)

side by side with those of the women, into the clear streams bordered by laurel woods.

Another religion, one that is immemorial and that still lives, and that might rather be called a confused mingling of a hundred profounds myths thrown up together by a tide, as the sea when it ebbs leaves upon the beach dead fish, jellyfish still alive, flowers of the sea, and a coating of salt—this religion hollowed out, sculptured and modeled mountains; sometimes for a century or more it led four or five generations to penetrate a mass of granite in order that they might live there, love, be born, and die there, and each day cause innumerable forms to blossom there, where scenes of copulation and of the lives of the apostles are found beside each other. Another religion, issuing from this one like a glowing child from a delirium of passion, covered all of eastern Asia and the islands in the dazzling seas of the Orient with prodigious edifices which the wild beasts, the birds, and the reptiles invaded from top to bottom as if in the trunks, the branches, the leaves, the corollas, and the pollen which grow there and fly as in a whirlwind, they recognized the odors and the green darkness of their native forest. The Brahmans pushed forth from within the stones haunches in movement, the thousand divine arms bearing the lotus or the axe, calmed breasts, and eyelids made heavy by sleep, and the incessant rise of the animal instincts in man. Likewise the Buddhists sculptured flight, sculptured the dance, sculptured the swaying and the very coolness of the palm, and the very murmurs, the spasms, the sighs, and the perfumes.[1] And if Brahma,[2] the inexhaustible matrix, welcomes, in his four flat faces, the deep flood of material life which rushes in from every side to participate in modeling his forehead, in causing

[1] Fig. 202.
[2] Fig. 188.

his nostrils to beat, his mouth to tremble, and his eyes
to be bathed with somnolent voluptuousness, the robe
of Buddha, between his knees, seems a chiseled cup
where the light comes to sleep. The confused universe
is present wherever man is, even if the form of man is
alone upon the rock. Man is present wherever the confused universe is, even if the carved vegetations and
waters represent no more than the feverish bogs and
forests which he could not traverse.

And though that other religion, proscribing the image
of every living and moving thing, the better to isolate
itself in the contemplation of the invisible, covered the
deserts with light cupolas, and with minarets shooting
up like cries of ecstasy, its whole spiritual movement
turning and expanding, and sweeping along in its whirl
something of the odor of roses, something of the colored
palpitation seen on the breast of doves;[1] and although
still another religion, on the contrary, piled up in the
disorder of a single tottering mass all possible forms,
especially those of death—claws and fangs, empty eye-
sockets, and the teeth and tongues of snakes[2]—in one
case as in the other the idea of a divinity active and
present everywhere governing the agreement of man
with religion, in an exaltation which the multitude feels
and which it translates into a language which stirs us
by its unanimity.   It is the same spectacle in the Occident and in the Orient, when Christian Europe, between
the sixth and the fifteenth centuries, suddenly acquires
consciousness of this spiritual unity which it has conquered from the chaos of sensation and from the tragedy
of history, through some chosen race which seems destined to propose its moral image to the future, under
the splendid appearances of a material image in which
man, even when most heavily bound down by animality,

[1] Fig. 70.
[2] Fig. 55.

and his divine vision of life are to recognize each other
for an hour. Is there any need to evoke, under the
overlapping vaults and the sturdy pillars which amass
the orb of the spheres above a golden shadow, the gleaming mosaics in which slender forms are elongated, where
immense eyes open, concealing in their depths a complicated and sensual mysticism around which are lights
that seem to tell of danger, blue flies and green flies
over sleeping waters, putrefaction, and poisons hidden
under the luxuriance of flowers?[1] Is there any need,
above all, to recall the vast efflorescence which carried
upward, over the pavement itself and from the sur-
rounding countryside, clear forests, murmuring waters,
the produce of the kitchen garden, grapevines on the
slope of the hills,[2] so many beasts, so many vegetables,
so many leafy vines, and so many familiar countenances
which, as a fervent crowd, form the escort for the pillars
in their swift ascent, and for soaring vaults which cradle
in heaven the courage of man as they render his works
divine?

If, from the Andes to the Himalayas, from the Pacific
to the oases of Africa, and from the Nile to the North
Sea, one tries to seize at a single glance the universal
plastic poem in those manifestations of man through
which he has most constantly and magnificently defined
himself, one finds it connected almost everywhere with
a mystical support which is the more impressive because it translates almost everywhere a unanimous sentiment. Art seems never to have attained summits
comparable to those which it has mounted, almost always at a single bound, in concert with religion, which
then mingles with it in so close and familiar a manner
that it is impossible to separate one from the other without annihilating both by the same stroke.

[1] Figs. 89, 172, 204.
[2] Fig. 191

II

And yet, if one penetrates more deeply into this mystery of æsthetics which is so poignant—as poignant as the birth, the hesitations, and the decline of love—how many facts leap forth suddenly before the anxious investigator and oppose themselves to that too-simplifying conception which connects the development of art with the development of faith, and which affirms without hesitation that art does not develop, or languishes, or falls as soon as faith is lacking, or oscillates or weakens! Hellenic art at its decline, and Hellenistic art almost in its entirety, even and perhaps especially in their most arresting manifestations—beautiful goddesses wholly nude who are no longer any more than women,[1] from whom all the heroic fervor has disappeared, innumerable statuettes of courtesans and of women of the world, tormented portraits of poets or thinkers, and dances upon the vintage are only a passage (sensual, familiar, and full of regrets and of promises) between the unity of Paganism in its death-struggle and the presentiment of a new mysticism which is nowhere formulated. During three or four centuries, in this nervous, restless, and often erotic art which flowers on all the shores of the European, African, and the Asiatic Mediterranean, it is practically impossible to find any trace whatsoever of religious sentiment. The same phenomenon, at the moment of the second Renaissance, when Italy, with da Vinci and the Roman school, conquered the Platonist evasion which attempted, in the fifteenth century, to hold Christianity to an enervated and morbid form which its mystico-sensual character was, on the contrary, to sweep forth beyond the borders of Christianity, in order to launch

[1] Figs. 189, 200

the modern world upon unexplored paths: Venice peoples the palaces and churches alike with the most

Fig. 189

PROFANE STATUE (Hellenistic Art)

magnificent forms that painting has realized in the reciprocal, close, and continuing exchange of colorations and reflections —the waters, the lands, the skies, and their animal and vegetable multitude contributing the most powerful of their voices to the choir of the senses, which mounts from all the races to affirm their taking possession of the poetic universe. All religious sentiment had disappeared from these forms, to such an extent that nude goddesses were to be seen in the sanctuaries and that, in banquet halls, swarms of angels and holy families covered the walls.

In Italy as in Greece, the religion, which adored images and was visual before all else, scarcely perceived the progressive

substitution of one idol for another idol.   The idol
retained the same name, and its apparent forms
changed only insensibly from one generation to the other
in the proportion that its inner life matured and rose,
like the juice of a fruit, from its depths toward its surface, to burst forth and spread over it in full expansion.
In other places, in the East of Europe, and especially
in the North, the process was quite a different one.   At
Byzantium, in the eighth and in the ninth centuries,
the Church and the Emperor tried to break the idol and
to push Christianity back into the invisible interior of
abstract mystical sentiment, as, in the same periods,
Islam was covering the conquered lands with edifices,
where no human figure, no silhouette of an animal, and
no leaf of a tree ornamented the capitals and the altars.
And it is precisely at the hour when poor and stiff
forms,[1] enveloped at every point in the matrix of the
most fixed dogma, are appearing timidly upon the profiles of the temples, which had been practically bare
until then, that St. Bernard, in the following terms,
anathematizes the still lean and quite confused budding
of the popular belief which is to submerge the edifice and
at the same time lift it up: ". . . So manifold and so
astounding does the variety of the forms appear everywhere, that the monk is tempted to study the marbles
far more than the books and to meditate upon these
figures far more than upon the law of God."   The monk
was, moreover, to lose his unique privilege of building
and decorating the church; he was to leave to the corporations which were being formed so strongly within
the frame of the commune the business of erecting and
ornamenting the religious monument, under the same
conditions and according to the same principles as the
civic monument.

It seems therefore that the æsthetic apogee of West-

[1] Fig. 190

ern Christianity, between the end of the eleventh and the end of the thirteenth centuries, in its ensemble, and despite the symbolic meaning of the ritualistic formulas for architecture and for the images, was a kind of confused protest of the instincts of a devout people against the original commands of a mysticism which the concilia and the bishops were maintaining as well as they could. Christianity, by its incessant appeal to love, had

Fig. 190

CHRISTIAN IDOLS (Autun)

amassed so much sap in the imaginations which, at the same time, it was compressing by its multiplied prohibitions, that the unanimous desire to spread forth this sap in the immensely varied and nuanced form of the hundred thousand living or inert objects which make up our universe was to spout forth with the power of a flame held in by the volcanic crust. We must not forget that the founders of the Church, St. Paul the Jew

and St. Augustine,[1] were explicitly and fiercely icono-
phobes, and that Jesus himself, a Jew, with all his
universal tenderness, had never appealed to the image
in order to stir the hearts of men. The immense concentration upon themselves which, in the earliest consciences, had marked the birth of the new religion,
necessarily implied the misunderstanding of natural
forms or even disgust for them. They could not reap-
pear, first at Byzantium, then in Italy, and finally in
France, save as concrete symbols of the life, of the feelings and of the expansive imagination seeking, outside
of their contact with the forgotten universe, to express
in the tumult and the fever of enthusiasm, the healthi-
est, the most animal, and the most fecund of all the instincts. The Christian paradise and the Christian myth
were so real and so beautiful in the candor of the people
that it had to appeal to the innumerable forms and the
marvelous colors of the world to glorify them.   The
grapes of the vine and the salads of the market, the spar-
kle of the seas, the purpled gold of the skies in the
autumn forest, and all the occupations which, in the
fields, bring forth bread from the earth and, in cities,
manufacture wood into troughs and iron into tools, invaded the monument to carry the whole of man nearer
to the work of God. It is the fault neither of St. Paul
nor of St. Augustine nor of St. Bernard, but perhaps a
little bit that of Jesus, if man, thanks to this very orgy
of the senses, was, while studying God's work, to forget
God himself. For the cathedral, dying of the excess
which had brought it to birth, but at the same time
awakening the objective curiosity of certain minds in
the multitude, crushed full-blown Christianity in its
fall.

At all events, a miraculous equilibrium had here, for

---

[1] Perhaps a Semite. He was of northern Africa, which had, in the past,
been colonized by the Phœnicians.

a century, been able to maintain—between the abstract
religion due to the brain of the Prophets modeled by the
desert, and the love of the charming forms which
characterize the soil in Western Europe—the powerful
idea of a universal symbolism expressing the unity of
the soul by the multiplicity of the aspects of this soil.
It maintained itself, in the heart of a people which is as
distant as the land on which it dwells both from Catholic paganism (forgetful of the Christian law in order to
imagine the poem of form as an expression complete in

Fig. 131
Profane Idols (Amiens)

itself—independent of the pretexts which inspire it) and
from Protestant puritanism, forgetful, in order to
return to that law, of the immense variety and the immense charm of the forms in which the theater of England, and Germanic painting and engraving, and the
Nibelungen had, however, found their nourishment.
Here, consequently, there occurred a phenomenon the
reverse of that which in Italy wrested form from religion. Puritanism wrested religion from form. It has
been believed, it has been said, that Rembrandt and
German music express the Protestantism of the North.

The whole of Dutch painting, and before all and above all the whole of Rembrandt's painting, are an instinctive and probably unconscious protest against the iconoclasm of the Beggars. They are the pious transporting of the image from the church into the house. The whole of German music, with that of Beethoven in the front rank, appears, after two centuries of frightful religious carnage, as a secret revenge of the spirit—protected by the hermeticism of musical language—against puritanical fury, and the return to the abstractions and to the original prohibitions condemned in advance in the North by Shakespeare, by Dürer, by the chorale of Luther himself, fed with meat and beer, joyous and barbaric, as, with song, he led the crowd forth to battle. Protestantism and Catholicism are more or less happy means of governing, more or less durable and more or less suited to the peoples who adopt them, and the one did not will German music any more than the other willed the ogival church of the provinces of Northern France. As to Christianity in its primitive purity, there was needed its profound and prolonged contact with the souls of peoples formed by their soil and their mysterious atavism, their joys, their food, and their misfortune, for it to be transformed in the intimacy of those souls, to the point of expressing them by means whose use and abuse, precisely, had, by reaction, caused its birth.

III

But there is more to be said. Very much is lacking before we can find the highest and purest tension of the religious spirit coinciding everywhere with the highest and purest expression of the æsthetic sentiment of one people. The examples of this are innumerable, from Egyptian polytheism to the modern monotheisms, from .

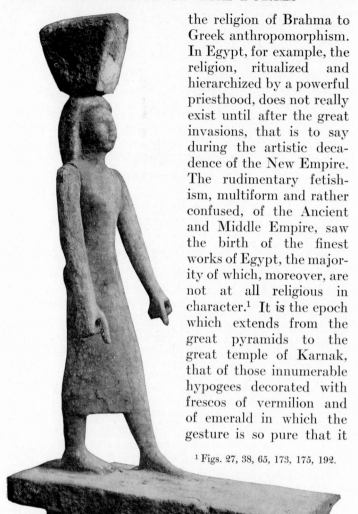

the religion of Brahma to Greek anthropomorphism. In Egypt, for example, the religion, ritualized and hierarchized by a powerful priesthood, does not really exist until after the great invasions, that is to say during the artistic decadence of the New Empire. The rudimentary fetishism, multiform and rather confused, of the Ancient and Middle Empire, saw the birth of the finest works of Egypt, the majority of which, moreover, are not at all religious in character.[1] It is the epoch which extends from the great pyramids to the great temple of Karnak, that of those innumerable hypogees decorated with frescos of vermilion and of emerald in which the gesture is so pure that it

[1] Figs. 27, 38, 65, 173, 175, 192.

FIG. 192
PROFANE STATUE (Egypt, v Dynasty)

seems to express the silence; it is the epoch of those seated scribes and of those marching statues of wood, around which everything seems dead. In Greece, before the eighth century, at a time when the Doric order has not yet plunged its powerful roots into the ground, and when a few formless wooden dolls and a few poor earthen vases express the beliefs and the primitive needs, religion is much more firm than at the times when the Peloponnesus and Sicily are covering themselves with sturdy temples which seem like squatting beasts. Nearly a thousand years before the first mountains of India receive into their entrails a people of painters and of sculptors, Brahmanism exists; and Brahmanism is still active, as living as ever in the depth of men's souls, when four or five centuries have passed since Hindu art lost that vast mobility full of searchings and murmurings, which make one think of the sea. The petty practices of Chinese fetishism, surviving the mystic crisis of Buddhism and floating upon a great depth of tolerance and of moderation in religious sentiment, did not prevent the sculptors from erecting on the desert, avenues of warriors and of monsters so majestic that they seem contemporaries of the most ancient solitude. Islam, which is as robust as ever in the faith of the people—or which was so, at all events, less than a century ago—has, for five hundred years, been without the secret of the mysterious life which the geometrical formulas chilled in the arabesque, and the secret of the fantastic lightness of the construction. Moreover the Arab, its creator and its propagator, has himself constructed nothing. He delegated that task to the conquered peoples, who were artists and producers already in their past, and who contributed, in serving him, their natural genius, perhaps their desire to please the master, and the freshness of a sentiment renewed upon contact with an unknown myth. Hindus, Egyptians, Persians, and

Berbers made of Islam their faith. And the Turk, despite his faith, has not known how to build.

These eclipses, these hesitations, and these silences are perhaps more striking in Christianity than elsewhere. Outside of Italy and especially of France— outside of Flanders and of Spain at times, of Germany to a small extent, I dare not say of England—this religion which persists for eighteen hundred years has not produced a truly specific efflorescence, of a living and multiform style, innovating and conquering each day and in all places, save during four centuries at most. Christian art disappeared from Italy even before the fall of the free city, and from France when the Commune gave way. In the most fervent periods, the fifteenth century for example, when the drama of the time was sweeping into all souls like a torrent, when it was without trace of bewildered mysticism, when the religion of Jesus was less discussed than at the period when it was joyously mounting everywhere above the countryside and the cities by means of a thousand towers and spires trembling in the sound of the bells, it was no longer, in its imagery, any more than a tormented and complicated thing whose supports were falling away, whose inner structure was becoming dislocated, and whose profiles were disappearing under the profusion of the ornament.[1] In Spain, during the most Catholic centuries, when the Reformation had caused fanaticism to arise, and when the soldiers, their rosaries on their wrists, carried the cross and torture into the whole of the West, and later, when, to prevent the touching of a poor idol in the niche of an old pillar, a whole city let itself be slaughtered, man after man, woman after woman, and let house after house be burned or torn down, the great forms of art—Velasquez and Goya—are almost completely secular, by no means

[1] Fig. 165.

mystical, in any event. The only mystic, the only man who gives that sensation of supernatural realism which is Spanish Christianity—living cadavers dressed in purple and in iron under the sepulchral lamp, cold ashes, livid lips, and the narrow idea arising to a great height—is not a Spaniard, but a semi-pagan from the Orient whom the people calls "el Greco."[1]

Certain forms of Christianity itself, some issuing from the Catholicism of Rome, others from Byzantine orthodoxy, and others again, it is true, from iconoclastic puritanism, have had no more than an insignificant plastic expression, a nonexistent one at times. Polish or Prussian or Hungarian or Austrian or Russian or Jugo-Slav art has not really passed the popular stage, Hispano-Americanism has not

Fig. 193
COMPOSITE IDOL (Assyria)

even attained it, the Eastern rite has not renounced the Byzantine icon indefinitely repeated, and American Quakerism and, in its train, the multitude of religious sects of that vigorous people have, for long, preserved silence, a silence which their attempts at Europeanizing have broken with unfortunate effect. It is no new phenomenon, moreover, which we see in this. Old reli-

[1] Fig. 210.

gions have remained silent. That of Iran, for example, so pure from the moral point of view and upon which there was grafted without being penetrated by it, a hybrid, heraldic and monarchical art,[1] which drew all of its elements from Assyria, from Egypt, from Greece, and from India—and which never took root in the soil. That of a neighboring region, Chaldea, and Assyria especially, whose direct and terrible art[2] developed almost entirely outside the religious spirit, the myth inspiring only certain composite monsters whose cruel character emphasizes the violence of the habitual sources of inspiration—hunting, war, tortures, executioners, victims, vultures upon carrion, and men and lions in combat. That of Rome, while very sincere and vigorous, but of which the plastic expression is only imitation and repetition of older forms, whereas an admirable civic architecture—of circuses, theaters, roads, and aqueducts[3]—affirms the grandeur and the permanence of an intention in which there appears no trace, however fugitive, of a religious sentiment. This architecture, moreover, develops when the mythology has reached a completely anarchical stage, at the moment when paganism is at its death-struggle, when Christianity is stammering, and when the new cults of Asia, tottering and jostling one another, are confusedly invading the Latin world, which lets them do their will: an admirable maintenance of the unity and of the majesty of the mind advancing alone—for utilitarian purposes, to be sure—like a ship upon the waves.

However, let us state the fact. Something is lacking in that art, as also in Greek art especially after Phidias, in Japanese art[4] which develops almost exclusively

[1] Fig. 170.
[2] Figs. 69, 193.
[3] Figs. 34, 127, 213.
[4] Fig. 194.

outside of religion, and in European art since the
sixteenth century, if one sets to one side the heroic
souls who have possessed a sufficient constancy and
continuity of effort to hold up the columns of the temple
and to maintain in themselves a religion surviving the
forms of the confessional—Michael Angelo, da Vinci,
the symphonists of Venice, Rubens, Poussin, Rembrandt, Velasquez,
Watteau, Goya,
Delacroix, and some
others. But even then
an immense sadness
hovers over their
solitude. In reality,
at the hour when for
once—for once only
in the historical de-
velopment of a group
—the sudden matur-
ing of the religious
sentiment coincides
with the loftiest
moment of energy in
this group, something
supernatural appears,
not falling from God
upon man, but arising
from man to God.

Fig. 194
PROFANE ART (Hokusai)

Faith has always been
equal to itself, doubtless, since the time when formulated
and ritualized religion collected all hearts into a common
belief. But something unforeseen has taken place.
Historical forces have acted for centuries, by chance
most often, designating one people rather than another,
because its geographical position is favorable to its
fecundation, because the drama of war or of politics

is more terrible here than elsewhere and more valiantly accepted, and because, above all, a particular genius which it gets from its soil and from its secret atavisms has formed it for this rôle, and because, suddenly, in a great broad current of enthusiasm, it has hurled its belief, like a virile seed, into the womb of the universe. Such is the crisis of love in the great races, such their organic virility; and during its hour their mystic strength, multiplied by this same virility, seeks and finds its nourishment. It is from the greatest moment of energy, not from the greatest moment of faith, that there issues forth the greatest moment of creation of the species. From the eleventh to the fifteenth century in France, the civil or military edifice is equal in value to the religious edifice. The most beautiful cathedral of the North is not superior in quality, from the point of view of structure, to the Valentré Bridge at Cahors or to the Palace of the Popes at Avignon.[1] Whether the species reaches its faith before its apogee of power or after it, if spiritual energy has departed, art, the expression of that spiritual energy, will depart likewise from the species, to disperse itself amongst chosen individuals and to concentrate itself wholly in certain superior brains.

That which creates art, in a word, is the meeting of virility and of love. It is natural that, up to now, the great religions should have been the pretext for this creation. But they have not always furnished it, and there is no reason whatever why new mysticisms, free from dogma, should not come, in the future, to favor that meeting. The Italian Renaissance, wedding with nature for a second time in the enthusiasm of consciousness, offers the admirable spectacle of a crisis of love analogous with the one I speak of. Perhaps the first

[1] Fig. 195.

Fig. 195

Dry Surroundings; Civil Edifice (Cahors xiv Century)

contact of Egyptian energy with the prodigious and still unexplored world of forms at a time when the Egyptian religion was yet stammering, perhaps the monumental statuary of the Chinese after the disappearance of Buddhism, and perhaps the ferocious art of Assyria are in themselves, despite their secular character, miracles which one may compare with the fecundation of a great religious sentiment by an exceptional energy of a national or specific order. However, it is not doubtful that up to now the most powerful unity of that sudden sweep toward the spiritual conquest of the very body of the universe, that burst of energy which carries along together the mystic enthusiasm and the virility of a people or of a race—the one element, moreover, animated by the other—it is not doubtful, I say, that up to now this has almost always and almost everywhere manifested itself under the visible and sensible appearances of religion.

IV

I have said enough to show that I do not absolutely accept the saying of Nietzsche: "Art raises its head when religion loses ground," unless he meant that art often exists before religion and survives it and replaces it when it deserts the hearts of men, and assumes the rôle of a religion in certain cases, often magnifying this rôle when the heart beats in the breast of a hero. Idolatry, fortunately, survives the idol, because it leads mind to mind across appearances, and because it is the only thing that leads in this way. Outside of idolatry —and science is at present the predominant form of idolatry, the most unanimously and candidly accepted, the most cherished, and therefore the cruelest—outside the matter of the world which men interrogate in order to discover what gives it form and movement, there is no longer anything but arid abstraction, the play of the unstable, a circle leading to death.

The idol as a fetish everywhere precedes ritualized religion. It is everywhere reborn, when religion declines. It is everywhere loved and studied, even outside the religion. It is not true that it is born by grace of the religion alone and as a matter of religion. Totemism is not the origin, but one of the origins, of art. There is also—and doubtless it comes first— utility, which creates ceramics, the weapon, the garment, and the tool. There is the obscure sense of rhythm and the need to express it, which create music and the dance—one sees this clearly with the child. There is love, which creates tatooing, adornment, the dressing of the hair, and the jewel.

Fig. 196

Mundane Painting (Persia)

There are hunting and fishing, which call forth recital and description, recital and description which gain from being illustrated. There is the need for shelter, from which there came forth architecture. The immense solicitation of forms, colors, and movements

414   THE SPIRIT OF THE FORMS

awakens anxious curiosity in primitive man, and he
cannot deliver himself of it save by imagining an
approximate equivalent which shall prove to him his
power of re-creating, for his joy and also in his interest,
a universe endowed with forms, colors, and movements.

Neither the cult of the spirit nor objective knowledge
destroys idolatry. They change its place or renew it,
and that is all. We saw this clearly in the case of the
iconoclastic Jewish idea, which reached the heart of
the Occident only by means of the cathedral with its
wealth of form. We saw it in the case of Eastern
Christianity when it decorated the Pan-Athenaic processions with new names, and when it called Orpheus
David in order to maintain the lyre among us. We
see it in the bosom of Islam itself which cannot prevent
the Persian illuminator from replacing the religious
idols with the most charming painting of the city and
of the world that exists.[1] We saw it in the Italian
Renaissance laying its nude Venus in the bed that is
still warm from the presence of Mary when she gave
birth to the god. We saw it in the sonorous idol that
was being born in the heart of the musicians, where
puritan prohibitions had trampled down the images.
The symbol changes, to be sure, and therefore the idol,
so that the pure cult of the spirit or objective knowledge
may find a mooring not yet filled up by an illusion
which had existed for too long. It is by renewing the
idol that man regains his footing on solid ground,
whether that idol is called Isis or Brahma, Osiris or
Buddha, Athene or the Virgin Mother, Aphrodite or
Huitzilopoctli, Dionysos or Jesus.[2] Each is separated
from the other by abysses of blood. And yet, when one
of them falls into the abyss, the succeeding one, which
caused it to fall, gathers to itself the love of mankind.

[1] Figs. 68, 196.
[2] Figs. 11, 15, 55, 164, 188, 197, 200, 201.

Fig. 197

Egyptian Idol

The greatest moments of the spirit are those of idolatry, because from each we get one of the aspects of the definitive idol which we shall never carve. For this aspect, which the spirit created by eagerly studying the object and its own relationships with that object, comes to be neglected by the spirit, little by little, as soon as the latter has moved completely around the aspect, has traversed it in all directions, and found out that, now, the aspect has become an empty one. Thereupon the spirit seeks elsewhere, it reaches some spot where there is no longer any visible form, and finally adores itself in its immaterial essence until the day when, turning to emptiness, consumed by its passion, it seizes from the hot ashes of itself certain hard nuclei, veined with fire, in which it gradually perceives new appearances. The soul of mankind does not increase itself, or at least does not find itself again, unless the matter of mankind transmit to it, through the contact of the senses with the matter of the universe, the soul of that matter, in which man's soul recognizes itself. What man adores in the idol is in no wise outside himself, neither is it in any wise outside the world of the senses, which is so made as to reveal to him his own sensibility. It incarnates his spiritual life in its ever-fleeting form. In it he seizes his power of renewing his qualities.

The invisible idol of the Jews, of the Puritans, of the Arabs, and of the Rationalism of the scientists has not been able to impose itself upon the multitudes by any means other than that of a grand literature or music, of an architecture storing up coolness, repose, and shadow at the limit of the waterless deserts where the flaming sun makes life impossible, or by means of a utilitarian system capable, at least provisionally, of satisfying the needs for well-being of the body and for conquest by the mind—idols, idols yet, not less disappointing, in the long run, than the visible idol; and they are less honest ones, I fear, since they promise definitive moral solutions which they cannot give. What incredible poverty on the part of the moralistic abstractors who, for centuries, impose by the sword the verbal idol of the Bible or the Koran to the exclusion of the others, and imagine themselves the possessors of the spirit in its purity! Iconoclasm reveals its strange misunderstanding of the conditions and of the means and even of the essence of the higher cult of the spirit. It annihilates a language whose letter alone strikes it, and which it does not understand. It is ignorant of the fact that form is an instrument from which are drawn spiritual harmonies as pure as those that one asks of the lyre, of the printed book, of the silence of a great soul, or of the liberating activity of a hero. And perhaps indeed it thus betrays its hatred of consciousness, as if it had an intuition that the idol which, as soon as it is really formed, represents the highest human peak of religious sentiment, is also, because it situates and describes that peak, the very point where consciousness (which is the first dawn of an idol in formation) will take its flight. The spirit, in order to increase and communicate its strength, has everywhere sought for material symbols wherewith to render it more accessible to the senses. When it has bound them one to another, and its new symbolic language is absolutely organized, this very language brings it to the revelation of a universe of phenomena which wrests it from its solitude. Iconoclasm, in this sense, is perhaps necessary, since it attempts to protect for the longest time possible the tabernacle of the spirit from contacts with the senses which enervate it and at first dissolve it. But iconoclasm does not know that the spirit has been created by the idol and that the idol alone can re-create it. It is when the idol ceases to be beautiful that it may fittingly be broken.

An Aymara legend—the most beautiful of legends— has it that the creator peopled the world with statues and animated them in order to civilize the world. Is it really a legend? Being carried everywhere, from city to city, from shore to shore, across mountains and deserts, the idol everywhere insinuated the spirit. It is civilization itself. It is the most universal and the most veracious of languages. Into an immediately concrete form, living, existent, insistent, and having a reality of its own, independent of the conventions which preside over articulate language, it translates the abstractions and the relationships which reveal the solidarity of things among themselves and of these things with us. A fetishism, continuing even to our days, was perhaps the one which fertilized Egypt and thereby the whole human race of the later time. The idol of the negroes entered, with the caravans, into the upper valley of the Nile, the rough idol, crudely carved from wood, sensual,

Fig. 198

RELATIONSHIPS (Negro Art)

terrible, daubed with red and blue and showing the attributes of sex, the ingenuous and bestial idol whose profiles were to become calm, whose planes were to become firm, whose surfaces would be made to undulate like limpid water, and which was to mount in the thought of a charming race like flower in the morning.[1] If Egypt, now a dried-out bough, really issued from this, and, through Egypt, Greece and India, Asia and Europe, what do we not owe to it? What should we not have owed some day to its Polynesian sister, advancing from island to island on the prow of the painted canoes, peopling Easter island with solitary colossi and awaking America doubtless, if the Spanish idol, colliding with the Toltec idol, had not crushed the new world to dust and compelled it to accept the Occident? There are idols which die, certainly, and for ever. But sooner or later they are dug up, and sooner or later, in some civili-

Fig. 199

Relationships

(Egyptian Art)

zation centuries old, they are the determining cause of a more or less deep-seated disturbance whose echoes are heard in the most distant future.

Observe now the course that is followed by those which encountered virgin races which were ingenuously awaiting love. See the Phœnician mariner landing on

[1] Figs. 198, 199.

all the sandy shores of Africa and of Asia, at all the rocky coves of Europe, and displaying his gewgaws at the water's edge. See the circle, at first hostile or timid, of natives armed with flint, naked or dressed in skins of beasts, and approaching step by step, beguiled by the smile of the fat, curly-bearded face that is lit up by the red lips and the white teeth of the strange man dressed in purple whose arm, encircled with golden bracelets, turns this way and that a little figurine painted with ochre, vermilion, and azure. There are women in that circle, as you must not forget, who caress and beg, and also some exceptional beings, less noisy than the others, who wonder how that robe could have been dyed, that statuette could have been colored, and that jewel melted and carved. Follow the Ionian fisherman also, prudently advancing in his little bark from island to island toward the shores of the Peloponnesus where the blond invader has burned and razed the cities, slaughtered the men, carried off the women, and smashed the old idols, and who is now astonished by this little dark man who had made him laugh at first and who now captivates him by reciting wonderful fables which agree with those which his shepherds bring back from the mountains and which are illustrated by painted images carved in olive wood, by potteries on which tentacles are twisted, where girls begin their dance and musicians begin to play. Give attention to the growth of their harmony as it reaches out to the temples covered with statues and with frescos, where the philosophers, bit by bit, surprise permanent relationships and equilibriums, the gliding of the spirit from surface to surface, and the articulation from form to form of logic and of calculation. Follow the peddler who crosses the Apennines and descends into Etruria to display, to tribes enervated by a mysticism which does not nourish them, vases on whose background of flaming red there is the quick movement of black forms; see how the tribes bury those vases in their funerary vaults, after having silhouetted on their walls the shadows of those forms. Accompany the architect or the statue-maker from Attica when he is seized by some centurion who takes him by the collar and throws him into the military trireme, with his plans and his models which will thereafter furnish him his task of explaining them to the Roman engineer and marble-worker. Install yourself behind the Macedonian pha-lanx, in the chariots which transport, with the baggage of the army, admirable women of tinted marble whose hair is of a reddish color and whose nipples are brown, going to the bank of the Indus where multitudes, pos-sessing no art, but intoxicated by sensual legends, await them in order to make them fecund, and with their children people the immense peninsula, and spread their genius, by the Buddhistic missionaries who think they are bringing nothing but their gentleness and their god, into Indo-China where gigantic temples will arise, into China where the cavern will take on movement, and even to the islands of Japan, where their trace will remain visible for centuries after the time of Jesus. Follow their course upon the other slope of the world, first to Byzantium, where they conceive the idea of clothing themselves in order to become more troubling, as they concentrate their terrible sexuality, mingled and kneaded with mind, in their fathomless eyes, their pal-lor, their painted mouths, and the jewels which clank on their arms and glow in their hair. You will see them reaching out thus to the two shores of the Adriatic, and around Florence and Siena, encountering and ardently embracing other images descended from the Gauls, and bearing in the folds of their robes, in their ingenuous smiles, in their direct and human gestures, and their discreet colors, a reflection of the stained glass left in

the cathedral, so that they might there replace the
carpets of which men had caught a glimpse at the time

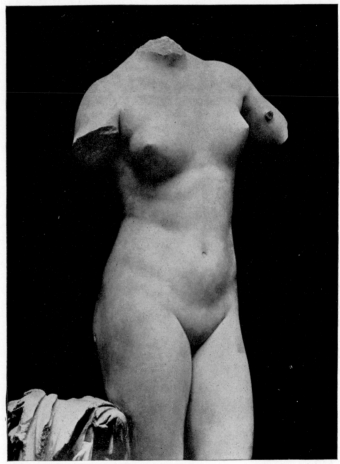

Fig. 200
Pagan Idol (Greece)

of the Crusades, the far-away carpets of Iran on which
the flowers of Persia and the gems of India are crushed

together in the depths of the weave. After that, you will see them confronting their thin colors and their ripe forms with the thin forms stamped on strips of paper which are sold for a few coppers to the Patricians of Venice by German soldiers of fortune who are coming down from the Alps every day; and their colors are confronted with the ripe colors spread out on little canvases which Florentine bankers order in Bruges or in Ghent. I should never come to an end in following their Odyssey. Today, through the sudden invasion of the immemorial idols of Africa, of Asia and of America, the spiritual skeleton which the Helleno-Latin ancestor had bequeathed to us almost intact lets itself be broken or dislocated in order to permit all the rivers of the spirit to deposit their alluvions in our weakening energies.

V

Thus the idol pursues its march, always reborn, always integral, silent moreover, and affirming nothing but itself, among those contradictory or even antagonistic systems which die, one after the other, in their explicit claim to be the holders of the Truth. One religion is iconolatrous, another iconoclastic; this one is materialistic or realistic, that one is idealistic or devoted to the spirit; here is one that is sensual or indeed bestial, here is one that is moral or indeed ascetic; now love is exalted by one, now flouted by another; they condemn or glorify war, and are eager for the blood of victims or rebel at the shedding of blood. But all, at their great moment, even when they break an image, do so upon the authority of another image, verbal or musical, or plastic, most often, and by means of this image they plunge into the heart of men the definitive form which history recognizes in them. The idol is not alone the vehicle—it is also the governing test of the myth. What am I saying? The idol is, in reality, what creates the myth, or at least what renders it living and enthusiastic in our hearts. One of these myths— and doubtless the most human one—succeeded really in establishing the conviction that their god was more than spirit only with those among its faithful who devoted to it their finest moments of energy and tenderness, only by making of each one of them an accomplished idolater. The birth of music, taking possession of the torrent of dull images which were circulating deep down in men's hearts, and spreading that torrent forth in all the directions of its rebounding waves, re-created Asiatic pantheism in the North. Mediterranean polytheism reappeared in Italy by impressing wonderful visages upon all the morose passions whose mystic exploitation had smashed the ancient world. At the halfway point, in the French cathedral, the two met to encircle Christianity with such a murmur of life that its idols, which thought to lock up religion in the temple, plunged it back into the universe.

There, indeed, is the key to the mystery. Only the polytheistic or pantheistic religions create the idols and are created by the idols in a passionate and continuing exchange of ideas, of sensations, and of sentiments. The monotheistic religions, on the contrary, being hostile to the idol, either triumph with the help of the idol or else die where they have grown up, unable to renew themselves. For monotheism cuts the world into two irreconcilable forms, thus ending in a terrible duality which, in the oscillations of the spirit in search of its sources, can lift it up for an hour and prevent it from perishing through the exercise over it of a kind of dictatorship, but which is quite incapable of achieving by itself the creation of one of those poetic edifices through which man, becoming conscious of his harmony

with the world, is consoled. When God remains outside
the forms, he is perforce the born enemy of the forms,
which ceaselessly baffle his activity and which he tends
to annihilate. To be sure, there exist everywhere, or
at least there seem to exist everywhere, two essential
forms facing each other which are called, according to
the times and according to the places, according to the
circumstances or the needs, god and nature, spirit and
matter, body and soul, good and evil, reason and passion, intelligence and instinct, movement and form,
male and female, or life and style. But dualism has
always attempted to wrest them one from the other and
to subordinate them one to the other for eternity.
Whereas art, and that activity which is the art of living,
conceive both of them as all-powerful and make them
genuinely divine at the exceptional moments when,
in the heart of the poet, of the hero, or sometimes of
the crowd itself, the state of love multiplies them one
by the other in a miraculous agreement. It is precisely
the ethical religions (spoken of as so essential, so profound because they condemn appearances) that live
according to the appearances of two antagonistic forces,
whereas art, through appearances, which it loves, goes
straight to unity.

Since this very unity is the highest and also the most
consoling form of the religious sentiment, it is art,
therefore and definitively, which gives to religion its
most moving aspect. Religion is only the frame and
the pretext for the creative energy of man as it reaches
its summit and as it lends to him the enthusiasm which
it draws up from the consciousness of itself. There is
no "religious art." Any art is religious in its essence;
and, with love doubtless—of which it is the spiritual
flower—it is the sole creator and also the sole reliable
evidence of that grand intoxication which moves
mountains and which is called religion. It affirms the

eternity of that religious spirit which precedes, includes, and buries the forms which it assumes in the sects, and

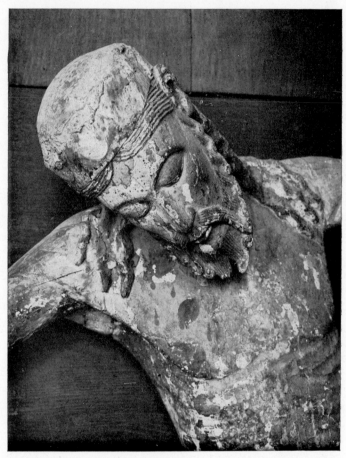

FIG. 201
CHRISTIAN IDOL (France)

it shows that they are masks placed upon its true countenance by the temporary needs of the instincts to be developed and the directions to be taken.   Art plays

with the religions, tenderly, but with fury. It plays
with the religions like that divine monster, the only one
beloved, the only one knowing how to love, who sees
in all women nothing but successive incarnations of
love, and who leaves each one of them broken, bruised,
and sometimes dead, but carried by his mere embrace
to the summit of her true power, during the time that
she belonged to him. Art, like that monster, is immoral, being indivisible and realizing in itself, by the
mere fact that it is living, the cruel unity of life. It is
the hard idol which persists upon the desert and upon
the tombs because it did not place the arid idea of moral
perfection at the threshold of the knowledge of form;
and, residing at the center of the passions, of the antagonistic systems, and of the pathetic drama of action and
of movement, it has sought its food within those struggling forces and shaped its bronze or its stone from their
accepted contrasts.

Fig. 201A

Fig. 202

Chapter IX. THE POWERLESSNESS OF THE POLICEMAN

I

IN FACT, since the artistic ability of man left its first traces upon split flints and the walls of caves, we do not know of a single one of its great moments that coincides with the appearance or the development of what we call "morality"—according to Saint Paul, or Socrates, or even the Zend Avesta. At first, everywhere, at all epochs, these great moments declare themselves against a social background terrible in its violence, its conflicts of passion, its debauchery, and duplicity. Art may be ferocious, like that of Assyria or Mexico, sensual, musical, and charming, like that of Egypt; it may express warlike or amorous customs and range from the cult of the phallus to the cult of the eagle-headed man or of the monster with the empty orbits, clothed in serpents, upon which priests cause human blood to flow. But not once does it offer even a veiled protest against the power of women, the injustice of men, or the indifference of the gods.

Here and there negro or Indian blood circulates, burning and black, leaving its dark trace, like a clot, on the surface of the idols or tinging with rose and carmine their straining breasts and proffered lips. The art of the Hindu peninsula is merely one immense coupling in which all forms marry one another, that decay is close to birth, asceticism to vice, famine to orgy. It is the painful lifting of the mind above religious animalism into which it continually falls back and which cradles it with its warm limbs. The hero, Rama, will indeed conquer the powers of evil, but naked dancing girls encourage him to do so, and the forests he crosses rain on his steps the empurpled snow of their flowers. There rises from this whole art the odor of rut and carnage. When it passes into China it is aired, no doubt, and its sensuality purified. But there is no question, in its monumental forms, of imposing a unilateral meaning upon the laws of life, and if the scribes and monks take possession of art it will be neither to reform it nor to curse it, but to penetrate it with sweetness, to make women walk there, children laugh and play, birds fly, gardens blossom, murmuring waters flow.[1] Whether he bears witness to all this or whether he withdraws into meditation, the sage leaves morality to fight the monsters without which wisdom would not exist.

Nowhere in these countries, to speak truly, is there any question of morality, save perhaps among the Chinese to whom Confucius, some two centuries before Socrates, some six centuries before Saint Paul, brought the essentials of the discipline that was to constitute the basis of Occidental ethics. Neither was there any question of it in Greece up to the time of Socrates.

[1] Fig. 41.

The unity of Greek art appeared unshakable. The human poem was deified in the rigorous sense of physical beauty, which the sexual instinct surely defined for us. In cities devastated by the vilest intrigues, by the most bloody dramas, when triremes filled with soldiers were incessantly putting forth for battle and pillage, plastic idealism set up the naked man and the naked woman as a pious offering to the security of the world, maintained by the warlike and amorous energy of the race above the horrors that wracked it.

Fig. 203

Wisdom (Chartres, XIII Century)

We know the aftermath of Greek art in Egypt, Sicily, Ravenna, and Byzantium, the frightful fermentation of vices in the later Roman Empire. The gold-laden idols, with their great elongated forms, their asymmetrical faces emphasized by rouge and marked by deceit and lust,[1] seem to distill a sort of poison at the same time that they dispense the love necessary to maintain the curiosity and restlessness of the mind. We know the license of manners in the age of the cathedrals, the concubinage of the priests, the permanent scandal of the convents and the monasteries, the license of the fabliaux, and the mystery plays, the throngs in the

[1] Figs. 89, 172, 204.

Court of Miracles, the making of counterfeit money by kings, the frightful cruelty of wars and executions, the forgetfulness of morals in the scholastic battles and the metaphysical enthusiasms of the theologians. All this rose in piles of stone to invade architecture from top to bottom. On the other hand there was sly wisdom, amused tenderness, goodness, joy, often broad jesting, sometimes anger, but never maledictions, anathema, or a sculptural sermon.

We can find no similar contrast save again in connection with Christianity, at the moment when the English theater, cradling the soul of Shakespeare amid the smoky lamps and the uproar of the crowds, put three dramas a day upon the boards while the streets were clamorous with furious revels, when drunken or murdered men rolled in the gutters, while decapitated heads adorned the battlements of the Tower, and when a septuagenarian queen had her twenty-year-old lovers butchered if they wearied of her. For it appears that the so-called ethical religions have, even more than the others, offered this surprising contrast between the explosive character of the savage instincts of man and their own pretended moralizing intentions, which have been unable to express themselves save by seizing, with a kind of fury, upon the means of satisfying these instincts. Mussulmans from India to Morocco and from Egypt to Spain avoided appealing to forms of flesh to decorate their sanctuaries to be sure, but this was because the rich were able to secure them at home and the poor believed they would attain them in Heaven.

The adventure of the Italian people is the best illustration of what I have just said. Far more than in the case of the Greeks, the first transport of sentimental Christianity accentuated in them the uncompromising antagonism between morality and the poem inaugurated

by the contact of the soul of Francis of Assisi with the
wonderful universe.   The Italians like the Greeks dem-

FIG. 204
DOUBLE MEANING (Byzantine Art)

onstrated that this poem could and no doubt should
develop on the social terrain that was most ravaged by
unbounded passions and most bloodstained by warring

interests. Unwittingly, and contrary to the ancient paganism animating the Christian idol, Italian art transformed this poem by introducing Christian love with all its frenzy into the dazzling pagan idol, through which Venetian painters, completing the effort of their race, increased the spiritual wealth of humanity.

II

As for those partial or total eclipses which art undergoes everywhere, even when religion continues, they coincide almost everywhere with the appearance of morality. To tell the truth, I do not believe that morality provoked them. Art, in fact, so far as it is really art, is stronger than morality and also more innocent, being so independent of it that it goes to the point of ignoring it, while morality lies in wait in the shadow and knows very well what it does. . . . Whenever art has, for a time, extinguished its love of form by possessing it, morality has attacked it like those parasites that suck the agony of the eagle or the lion: "All her virtue returned," says Stendhal, "because love left her."

If morality were, as people imagine it, the highest emanation of religion, why should the harmony so frequently noticed between religions and the artistic emotions disappear, or even turn to a complete antagonism when morality divests itself of religion? For it is a fact, and so constant a fact that it appears over long periods of history, precisely, indeed, over those in which the ethical religions, shattering the conquering unity of the great civilizations, cast aside one of the two poles of the soul, instantly chilling it. The hatred of form has no relation to spirituality save in the primitive monotheism of the Semites—Jews or Arabs— which affirms that the spirit lies outside the idol and should dispense with images and symbols in order to conquer and preserve its purity. Later, it forms part of morality, especially of Christian morality, of that of Saint Paul, for example, which is typically Christian, of the Reformation, of the *Gueux*, and finally and especially that of the Puritans of England and America. The terrible dogma of original sin ends by breaking the idol which is flesh, and therefore unwholesome. Every time it comes to life, for the needs or the interests of the moment, the cord and the hammer depopulate lintels, capitals, and niches. Theaters die down, the dance flees, music is cast out, harmonious speech turns to ice and expires on the lips of poetry. The sadness of virtue spreads like a black veil.

Must we continue? We have already met with those wells of shadow which only the reappearing idol has succeeded in crossing, or which the wave of music, born in the still meditation of some solitary heart, has suddenly filled with sound. Art has, no doubt, sometimes dispensed with religion in order to conquer, in a great collective effort, this anonymous and fervent universality which assures its most moving accent. But never, when morality prevails, has it been able to survive save by demanding that the solitary hero protect its wandering steps. We see this after the Reformation when individualism, born in the North, an offspring of the Reformation itself, protects the lyric flight of the heart against the Reformation; it does so through Rembrandt and the Dutch painters, through the English poets and the musicians of Germany.

This result had been anticipated in the sudden importance of the individual in the ancient world when, after Socrates, there appeared the concern for morality which was to end first in stoicism and later in Christianity. Of the swarm of artists who were snatched from architecture and scattered over all the roads of thought and sensation, a few turned directly to sensual researches, that were charming but every day a little more enervated, and so caused color and light to play over the feminine body. The less talented brought to the help of the fashionable ideas of the time such devices as flying draperies, flowing locks, imploring eyes, eloquence in marble and honesty in bronze,[1] until these same ideas, through hatred of the amorous art that persisted amid all this artifice, shattered them both and, seizing upon the hearts of women and the poor, demanded a new mythology with new delusions.

We have seen the destinies of Christianity bound so strictly to the idol that today the idol defines it for us in its most living expression and its largest humanity. But the idol draws back every time that morality advances, and every time that the idol draws back Christianity, if it gains some ground in the hypocrisy of the law, loses an equal extent in the candor of the heart. The response to the sensual and spiritual orgy of the sixteenth century in England, is the other orgy of furious Puritanism, morality closing the theater in which King Lear had raved and Lady Macbeth had washed her blood-stained hands, where Coriolanus affirmed his pride, where Cleopatra and Desdemona had filled so many hearts with despair and love, where Hamlet had pierced so many minds with the fearful intoxication of doubt. We are familiar with the first effect of the Reformation in Germany, arresting point-blank the development of painting and the trades. And as for France, we see there a continuous effort of the mind to gain time over morality and turn aside its severity by secularizing the idol (under guidance of Italy), and to harass this morality with the sharp arrows of Rabelais and Montaigne, up to the day when the combined efforts of thinkers and artists should

[1] Fig. 205.

have reorganized an intellectual architecture sufficiently
imposing to forbid their enemy to tread the waxed par-

Fig. 205
ELOQUENCE

quets, the beautiful straight alleys, the groves and glades
approached by statues and pools symmetrically arranged.

This fashion of escaping from the yoke of morality was besides, whether one wished it or not, a phenomenon similar to morality itself, but carried from the social plane to the intellectual plane. Jansenism had a part in it. A collective discipline could never be in France what it was in Anglo-Saxon countries. Christianity in France, in the seventeenth century as much as in the thirteenth, always responded to æsthetic rather than to moral ends. The contrary was true where the Puritan ruled severely. But the superiority of the French on this terrain was dearly bought: academism corresponds to Puritanism and attempts to lead back to the common rule, by force if necessary, those who fall out of line. Colbert and Cromwell, Descartes and Hobbes, Boileau and Milton are not so far from one another: the art of poetry drives out of the Parnassian paradise those who do not obey the rules of its administration. The subordination of religion to the state does not accord ill with the subordination of the passions to the intelligence, and if in France we do not go so far as to cut off the head of a king who reads the Bible in another language than ours, we find it natural to ban an artist who has spoken with irreverence of the orthodoxy of Le Brun.

In art as in psychology, the codifying of certain illusive accents presented through the hero entails the misunderstanding of certain other accents without which the hero would not exist. Jesus is no more a moral man than Michael Angelo is an æsthetic man. Each is a creator, therefore a monster, upon whom it is impossible, without betraying him as well as ourselves, to model ourselves, even approximately. Morality arises, then Puritanism, classicism, and academism, according to the tendencies and special aptitudes of such and such a people, when this people no longer has the strength to support the great weight of life and its atrocious or sublime actions, which it performs with equal enthusiasm.

This means that these codifications are sometimes indispensable to the salvation of the multitude. They are a halt in the confusion of retreat which allows us to breathe and to hold fast to energy and love that are ready to slide into the abyss. If art appears to us as a conquering sword which enlarges indefinitely the territories of life, morality is a shield that tries to oppose the advance of death. But this shield also stifles the remnants of life covered by it and runs the risk of hiding the seeds of new life which appear here and there. The Anglo-Saxon Reformation and classicism in France had no other aim than to substitute for the organism broken by the Renaissance a rule of life and thought destined to give the world for a few moments the illusion that this organism had not ceased to exist. It thus temporarily snatches the individual from the ruins of this organism. When a great social or religious body is in its full power of creation and expansion, it has only to make rules in order to create the "good" and the "beautiful." It represents an equilibrium of forces in which antagonisms enter with the same necessity, the same ease, and also the same intoxication as the arms, legs, torso, and head of the dancer enter the harmony of the dance.

In order to live, in order to come to life again, art, like conscience, conditions an eternal becoming. Morality, like æsthetics, appeals to eternal verity. In the former there is movement and discovery through risk, in the latter a fixed certainty in the will to obey. The former springs from ourselves. The latter descend from others. The latter alone really touch men because they pass from heart to heart. Such "moral" works as have succeeded in moving us, the Gospels, for instance, or the *Pensées* of Pascal, would pass unnoticed if an ir-

resistible artistic force did not animate them. But are
these truly "moral" works? I do not think so.

III

It would be imprudent, moreover, to confuse "morality," which is merely the transposition to the social
terrain of a sexual metaphysics based on original sin,
with the prohibitive disciplines generally attached to
religion, disciplines from which no society has been
able or, we fear, will in the future be able to escape.
These disciplines, all of which deal with actions that
are permitted or forbidden without transcendental reasons and which do not raise hermetically sealed walls
between two regions of the spiritual world, shutting
them henceforth and forever away from each other,
have never embarrassed the artistic development of
man. On the contrary they have usually exerted a
beneficent influence upon it by freeing its activities
from those hesitations and indecisions that bewilder it
on a terrain where it no longer knows its way, and that
weaken or destroy its energy: "Behold thy God . . . ,"
"Do not take this field, it is your master's or your
neighbor's . . . ," "Do not take this woman, she is
your brother's," "Remain in the condition to which
you were born, you are made for it."

The man who desires to carve the image of a young
girl from some olive tree, or the head of a hawk from
some block of lava, is not prevented by this from realizing his desire. But to make his salvation in this world
or the next depend upon his denial of these very powers
of love is what frustrates him. It is true that sometimes,
when the interdiction has lasted for centuries, we witness
a sort of irrepressible eruption of the poems that have
accumulated during the silence of our ancestors. Which
might lead us to believe that the goodness and grandeur

of the majority of men is quite indifferent to God, since he often sacrifices ten or twenty generations to produce one of those miraculous vivid moments in which one generation suddenly seems in harmony with him.

From that loftier viewpoint which sees our universal adventure as a phenomenon, not isolated in time but moving, evolving, sometimes regressing throughout an indefinite period, like a living being, it is very hard to determine what may have been the effect of this or that form of social discipline upon the creative powers of the mind. Looked at externally, it all seems quite evident. It is entirely natural that the Assyrian *Sar* should construct palaces dominating the desert from afar and into which he might crowd the multitude of slaves, women, and soldiers that were destined to serve, gratify, or protect his passions. It is quite natural that the priests of Chaldea should raise high above the driving sandstorms terraces from which they might watch the circular movement of the heavenly bodies through the pure emptiness of space, and that the Hellenes, assembled for the festivals that were expressly authorized by all the constitutions of their cities, should watch with passionate interest the play of muscles under the sun-tanned skin of the athletes and their harmony of movement in running and jumping. We have no difficulty understanding why the image-maker of the thirteenth century introduces the gestures of French workmen and the forms of French flowers, into the setting, now charming, now ferocious, of the Judeo-Christian mythology that had gradually been imposed upon them by councils and bishops. Or why the Roman autocrat raised up aqueducts and paved the roads that brought wealth and life to the heart of his empire from all his scattered provinces. Why a château surrounded by gardens symbolizes a sort of political system of the intellect surrounding the French autocrat. And why scenes of household labor and landscapes in which sky and water blend, epitomize in painting the effort of the Dutch burgher to establish himself comfortably on the land which he has conquered.

But it is impossible to pretend that such or such a method of governing men will imprint such or such an accent upon this or that way they have of expressing

Fig. 206
ARID SURROUNDINGS, CONTRASTS (Albi)

themselves. Any enquiry on this terrain leads to widely varying results. So variable, in fact, that we wonder if our habits of mind allow us to understand the spiritual structure that has been imposed upon men by the modes of grouping and government that we call autocratic, theocratic, aristocratic, democratic; these are only labels that we apply to forms that probably correspond to nothing more than the meaning we give these words at a given time.

A few things, however, may be stated definitely.

Tyranny does not necessarily prevent the blossoming of the poem. Liberty does not necessarily favor it. It sprang up far more vigorously in the blood-stained England of Elizabeth, than in the England that lay crushed with liberty and wealth under the trident of Victoria; more vigorously in the Spain of Philip II, where the Inquisition burned, tortured and broke upon the wheel than in parliamentary Spain where book and press were free to criticize; in the France of Louis XIV rather than that of the Directory, in feudal Japan more than in liberal Japan. On the other hand the free German cities of the thirteenth century, the small, peaceful principalities of the eighteenth bestowed lavishly upon Germany what its military strength could not give it, causing it to blossom with trades and swarm with ideas. And the Albigensian liberties did not prevent Southern France from raising its magnificent epopee of stone,[1] which, on the other hand, Ottoman despotism rendered weak in Moslem countries and obliterated entirely in the Christian lands which it occupied. If the reign of Napoleon is barren, that of Louis-Philippe shows an amazing flowering, and if from autocratic Russia, from its cities where every house bore the seal of the police, from its fields cultivated by human animals, from its ruins, from its convict prisons there rose the sound of great music together with the roar of the deepest moral abyss that literature has ever illumined, free Holland, at least for two centuries, has said nothing.

One thing only seems probable, at least from this point of view: that systems of government in which authority dominates—theocracy, autocracy, aristocracy —almost everywhere favor the rise of architecture and subordinate all other arts to it that is to a central and primitive edifice about which the crowds assemble and upon

[1] Fig. 206.

which all eyes are fixed. For example, observe the old the-
ocracies or monarchies of the Orient, of Islam; notice
the encounter, in the tenth century, of the Catholic
theocracy and of the rising monarchies of the Occident
in the categorical Romanesque temple which seemed to
clamp to the soil a pitiless vault extended over the labor
of men; see the classical age of the French. On the

Fig. 207

CONTRADICTION, CONCILIATIONS (India)

other hand, in all systems in which liberty dominates
or tends to appear and which are generally called
democratic, domestic sculpture and especially painting
first invade, then stifle, then ignore architecture, because the individual finds in the play of forms, lights,
shadows, and movements a medium better suited to
follow step by step the infinite meanderings of feeling
and ideas aroused in him by his desires and sensations.
  These so-called democracies, by the way, often as-

sume an aristocratic or corporative form, as for instance
Greece after Pericles, the French Commune, the Italian
Republics, the Low Countries after their liberation and
France for the last hundred years. Democracy does not
hinder the development of the artist, whom liberty
ceaselessly goads, solicits, disturbs, leads, and launches
on unexplored roads. But it hinders unity of style,
which equality destroys in the monument as well, by
destroying from top to bottom the hierarchical principle in all its functions and aptitudes. Perhaps we
should see in the art of India a sort of tragic oscillation
between these opposed poles. The régime of castes
reigns there, rigid as iron; but the free play of instinct
which it permits the multitudes that flood its social
strata in a muddy, foaming torrent, imprints a hybrid
form upon its entire art. The processes of contrasts,
illumination, passages, and values proper to painting
force the very stone, in its monumental setting, to
obey the slightest sensual impulses of all the individuals.[1]

IV

If the political and moral order can be the occasion
of a work of art, it is never, in any case, its determining
cause. It is, like it, the effect of anterior forces that
flow over and through them both only to outlast them
and take shape, later, in fresh poems. The idea of
attaining perfection, which animated all Greek art on
the physical plane[2] and which Christianity seized upon
and transferred to the moral plane, has no doubt a
decisive influence upon the orientation of crowds and
the effort which it demands of them. But if it was able
to give—at one time to Greek art, at another to Puritan energy—a unique accent, one that was appropriate,

---

[1] Figs. 39, 131, 132, 177, 178, 207, 216.
[2] Figs. 85, 208.

for an hour, to the race or the epoch, it has the most disastrous effect conceivable if we pretend to extend its too limited rôle to all civilizations, to "civilization" itself. It cuts off half of our spiritual universe, condemns anthropomorphism to define an image that is indeed splendid but destined to quickly encounter, on all sides, limits that cannot be surpassed, and forces morality to deny the fecundity of the passions in order to attain a negative virtue which is speedily deserted by curiosity and imagination.

The idea of indefinite progress which attaches to it is, moreover, contradictory to it, since nothing exists beyond perfect beauty and perfect virtue. And the one is just as powerless as the other to justify or even explain the historic rôle of the grandiose civilizations— of Egypt, Chaldea, China, India, Islam, Mexico, Peru, or even the mediæval Christianity of the Occident— all of which have loaned to them or borrowed from them necessary elements, but which have developed and spread independently of them and have exercised a universal influence at least as profound and durable as theirs. What am I saying? Between those forms of art and association that have arisen from typical Oriental civilizations, dominated by the idea of fatalism, and those that have sprung from typical Occidental civilizations, haunted by the ideas of perfection and progress, there exists a contradiction that would be irreconcilable if both held rigorously to the structure of their systems and did not succeed, unwittingly, in breaking them at every instant. Oriental fatalism, denying the necessity of effort, should logically end in abolishing the civilizing idol that necessitates much labor when it comes to giving a gigantic rock the form of this idol. Occidental progress, denying the necessity of mystical imagination, should logically end by raising to the rank of idols the office chair of the bureaucrat, the palm of the academician, the black coat of the preacher and the furnace of the engineer. For mystical imagination, alone, surpasses visible form and rigid morality and so ceaselessly widens the association of spiritual symbolism with the infinite world of forms that stirs in our desires.

Happily, in both cases, there exists the amorous force of races, and it is this which resists the idea of perfection or which conquers the fatalistic idea in order to realize its poem through any means whatever. It is this which has created each of those successive epic poems that constitute the history of great peoples and the ensemble of which constitute history itself. It has found expression in spite of the metaphysics that would condemn it to inertia, in spite of moralities that would lead it to the absolute. These epic poems bear in themselves their past and their future. Not only are they never re-lived but they are never even continued. When some brutal event, some war of extermination, for instance, does not cut down their roots or tear off their blossoms they grow and disappear, leaving their task finished. Nor can any other epopee replace them by beginning where they ceased, but only by reassembling the scattered elements of the world and imposing a new order upon them.

Of course every form of art can and should sooner or later penetrate the neighboring form, or the following form, or some other form which will appear in the more distant future. But it is fulfilled in itself, with its powers and its defeats, quite as if it were a living being. It is born, it expresses itself, it dies. That is all. It is not, in any case, an advance over the preceding form, and if it is sometimes more beautiful, that is because the race that imposes it has been more favored. It can also be less beautiful, less expressive, rather. We should once for all renounce this idea of the beautiful,

Fig. 208

Borderland of Perfection (Athenian Art, v Century)

bound up with the idea of the perfect, which limits the sensations of man and emasculates the power of the creator. The child, also, may be superior to his father or to his more distant ancestor, but he finds in heredity, chance, circumstances, many excellent reasons for remaining inferior to them.

Progress, in short, reduces itself to differences. Dutch art, as a whole, and in spite of its vivid and truculent flavor, is certainly less moving than Egyptian art as a whole. Japanese art, the child of Chinese art, is slender and caricaturish compared to it. The art of the conquering Britain is meager—aside from the poets—if we compare it with that of the Hindu slave. Italian art since Michael Angelo is not so great as it was before his time, and the once powerful Christian art is now no more than a sick hireling accomplishing its labor without pleasure. "Progress," if it does actually exist outside man's stock of tools, has nothing in common with art. Art can indeed acquire from age to age a larger complexity and can use the perfection of the stock of tools to explore new sensations and live new dramas, but every collective or individual manifestation of it is self-sufficient and erects on the road of the nations the only really visible and expressive milestones of their task that we can recognize.

In fact, if art endures it is because it, alone, unites, while morality on the contrary divides. All true civilization is a lyric phenomenon where knowledge and becoming rise and reign together. Art is civilization's highest peak which life does not succeed in scaling unless it accepts fearlessly the elements of energy and love which all our instincts impose upon it. The successive moralities, morality itself, only exist as functions of this poem which they betray when they pretend to lead and inspire it. If we are willing to include among the poets those who express themselves masterfully in ideas and actions then we can truly say that it is the poet, alone, who finds analogies, classifies values, and discovers passages leading to unity. He is nothing unless lyricism harmonizes and rises with him. And, if he so wishes, morality itself, which he subdues even while enjoying it. Outside of lyricism there is nothing but servitude. He who obeys only reason knows nothing of wisdom. He who obeys only sensual impulses knows nothing of liberty. Lyricism is the ascendent life in which the passional powers and the spiritual powers, affirming and fortifying themselves through one another, deliver the flame from the altar to the poet. It is he whose task is to abolish contradictions by discovering their point of equilibrium about which he oscillates tragically during the whole conquering life of the race, and which he attains and determines only for the space of a lightning-flash.

V

It follows that art which is nourished on the passions so that it incorporates them alive in the harmony of its substance, conditions tragedy. We have seen, in connection with morality, that the foundations of every one of its great edifices sink deep into an abyss of horrors. But this fact becomes still more impressive when we take up the matter chronologically and discover that the birth and youth of the most representative artists of the race coincide, almost everywhere, with the most sanguinary convulsions which this race has undergone. We know that Hellenic art, which at all times sprang up on a terrain furrowed by the fury of politics and war, attained its most stable point of equilibrium when the generation that was present at the Medic wars ripened. It was these wars that gave his first childhood impressions to the great sculptor of the Olympia, inasmuch as the "Combat of the Centaurs and the Lapithae" was raised to the pediment of the temple some twenty-five years after them.

We know that Phidias was born the year of Marathon, where Æschylus fought and where Pindar might have fought, and when Pericles and Sophocles were four and five years old. We know that Euripides and Democritus were born the year of Salamis, when Herodotus was four years old. We know that Thucydides, Socrates, Hippocrates, Alcibiades, and Aristophanes were the sons of those who saw the burning of Athens and who drove Persia back into the sea. We know that the most fruitful part of their lives took place during the horrible Peloponnesian War, when Plato, Xenophon, Parrhasius, Zeuxis, Scopas appeared, and from the ruins of which rose Aristotle and Demosthenes.

We know that, much nearer to our own times, from the fourteenth to the sixteenth centuries, the astonishing multitude of Italian artists was born, grew up, worked and died among the furious quarrels of the Republican cities and while Venice was extending her victorious sway over the seas. We know that the art of Spain, which lasted a hundred and fifty years, had the explosive character of its military and colonial expansion and appeared suddenly, at the same time. We know that the "golden age" of English literature is also the most atrocious age of English history, war without, war within, the brutal rise of the Reformation, and that the cradle of Shakespeare floated on a river of blood. We know that all the painters of Holland, silent before and since, were born between the extreme dates of the frightful insurrection of the Low Countries and in the twenty years that followed the re-conquest and the possession of their homes by the conquerors. We know that the great romantic generation, without a single exception: Stendhal, Ingres, Rude, Géricault,

Corot, Barye, Balzac, Delacroix, Hugo, Berlioz, Dumas, Michelet, Comte, Daumier in France, and elsewhere, in countries that suffered from the same storm, Weber, Schopenhauer, Schubert, Mendelssohn, Schumann, Richard Wagner, Chopin, Byron, Shelley, Carlyle, were born and grew up between the outset and the end of the military expansion of the Revolution and of the French Empire. These are facts, of which I cite only the most impressive.[1] It seems as if each of the poignant crises in which the existence of a group of men, its needs, customs, and modes of association, is brought into play suddenly by the political drama or by the drama of war, were followed by an explosion of spiritual energy that absorbs its fury and anxiety so as to create and nourish great imaginations.

This is natural. Danger, terror, anguish, moral and material suffering are everywhere. In the midst of all this the child appears, testimony of violent raptures and unexpected deaths, of the daily tragedy that includes his mother's tears and his father's cowardice or bravery, in which his brother is handed over to the executioner, his sister to the soldiers. The child grows up wild, secretive, obliged to dissimulate what he knows and what he feels, and learns to accept ecstasy or disaster as the ordinary ailment of his imagination, learns to choose alone a burning road at an age when an easy road or a blind alley is usually chosen for him, learns to welcome responsibility and risk as his companions in play. Very young he has acquired, along with a sovereign indifference in the face of events, the most terrible of which are the most normal for him, a habit of meditation that makes him stand silent and motionless before a flower on the edge of the road, and that opens

---

[1] I refer those who would study this phenomenon more closely to my book, *The Dance Over Fire and Water*, and, more especially, to the chapter "Tragedy, Mother of the Arts."

strange depths in him as soon as he meets with love.
And how can we describe the subtlety and power of the

FIG. 209
TRAGEDY (Michael Angelo)

ferment that can rise in the flanks of man and woman
in the sometimes unique embrace in which both, after
being borne in despair and tears, to the supreme exalta-

tion of amorous delirium, are torn from each other by the tocsin or the drum?

It is true that one objection is possible. Do not the apogee of art and the apogee of violence both depend upon the same anterior causes, on the irresistible rise in the race of energy and love which bursts forth at the same moment and expresses its supreme unity in two ways at once, that of instinctive forces obeying their frenzy and that of spiritual forces obeying their lyric essence? It is possible, but they seem to condition each other, and if the spirit of war and the spirit of revolution should disappear one day from the city of men I can imagine, dimly, some sort of collective drama that would fulfill in us the task which the spirit of war and of revolt have hitherto assumed, so cruelly but so magnificently. Such a drama might, indeed, avoid bloodshed, but it would overwhelm all human beings with rapture, anguish, anger, or pain; it would be a passional drama in which the entire race participated. Love even—perhaps especially—when it does not shed blood plays best this rôle in the individual, through its furious lyric exaltation, its poignant alternations of despair and intoxication, the immense void which it leaves when it passes and which art and action rush to fill. But this sort of love is not known to every one. Far from it! And it cannot replace in the entire species the universal tragedy that bears man and woman, through their acts, through their thoughts, through their sensations, through their sentiments, through their generative power into regions of spiritual energy and anxiety the existence of which had not been even suspected, previously, by most of them.

The drama, of course, still exists in times of peace in the conflicts of passions and interests, but it is diffused, sullen, deadened, and makes no deep impression on the receptive soul of a child, who grasps it not much better than the unreceptive souls of almost all men grasp the silent drama of the courses of the stars, for example. Yet the latter is a terrible drama, the most terrible of all—an interminable and aimless course in the void, the cold, the night that has no dawn. And even if the poet suffers, even if he knows perfectly that every stroke of the chisel, every strophe, every harmony of his is won from the silent drama represented by the conflict between his thought and the solicitations of things, the torments of love, the feeling of annihilation—even so, does he realize that every stroke of the chisel, every strophe, every harmony also introduces a new drama into the world? Sensibilities awakened by him, understanding that has been bewildered, enthusiasms newly roused, communions suddenly created, the meetings of minds, the meetings of hearts, discussions, theories, systems, a whirlwind of youthful forces rises at his steps! Conflicts are born. Strong currents of ideas appear and flow from the æsthetic plane to the sentimental plane, from the sentimental plane to the social or political plane, and multitudes are roused because a single man has spoken. It is easy, of course, to see that the word of Jesus has released torrents of blood that are ever growing larger. But how can we avoid seeing that Michael Angelo, also, has made innumerable victims, not only by giving rise to imitators and plagiarists, but by laying on the threshold of the modern world, which dates from himself, the fundamental tragedy of the spirit,[1] which is to destroy mysticism through knowledge and then, having reached the limits of knowledge, to have no choice save between mysticism and death?

[1] Fig. 209.

Fig. 210

Greco

Chapter X. UTILIZATION OF DEATH

I

W E FIND ourselves, then, on the verge of the abyss of fundamental pessimism. Art does not bear witness to the truth of religions which, quite on the contrary, are nourished on its substance and grow anæmic or die when it abandons them to bestow its love elsewhere. It has nothing to do with any social finality whatever since, high as it ascends, it has never been able to maintain at this height that political equilibrium of which it constitutes, no doubt, only an ideal image, impossible even to determine, and since the pretended instrument of this equilibrium, "morality," reigns only over the ruins of art and flees the moment it reappears.

Even if its material realization may be favored during one or two generations, by peace, and the general well-being, art sinks its roots into the drama of history and does not appear even conceivable unless man lives constantly in a state of inner war against the excessive violence of his instincts of conquest or the excessive calm of his needs for security. It is antisocial from the optimistic point of view that is taken by society—at least by Occidental society—that of the pursuit of an indefinite perfection of universal happiness, which is troubled by its imaginative constructions, and of universal repose, which is disturbed by its perpetual evolution. It is often immoral and especially through its inexorable exaltation of love. It is always unmoral since it seeks to draw from events and objects harmonies that are quite independent of the sentimental quality which moralists see in these objects and these events. It is cruel, even when it is tender, and indeed this is most often the case, cruel like the civilization which it represents and symbolizes; since in order to realize its proper equilibrium it accepts, like it, to explore unreservedly the redoubtable domain of the passions. It is constantly preoccupied with death,[1] before which it alone dances, while everything except itself trembles, recoils, dissimulates, or drops its tools at the sight of it. If feeds on its own rapture in catching for a second the semblance of things, and on its despair that this semblance dissolves the second after.

When its mysticism is exhausted it turns to knowledge and quickly runs over its rigorously closed circle, beyond which the empire of mysticism and of annihilation begin again. It is helpless before this state of affairs. It alone knows that it is thus helpless since it is content to exist on condition that it wanders neither to one side nor to the other of its own path. It is great only in the

[1] Fig. 211.

measure of its lyric fervor and in its power of describing and expressing. It is when the general energy and faith

Fig. 211
THE GAME WITH DEATH (Chartres)

in one's own strength ebb that art defines and demonstrates, and it is then that the hero, whose energy and faith have persisted, appears as the one who accepts unconditionally. Art is the only thing that expects nothing of life but life itself, and seeks no recompense save in its own free functioning or, as the last extreme, in death.

Nor does it find anything but a derisive consolation in the hypothetical sanctions life offers and that can be

FIG. 212

THE GAME WITH LOVE (Painting by Renoir at the age of 78 years)

accepted only at its great universal moments of fervor and expansion by simple souls who meet with some religion on their road. When art inhabits a truly heroic heart then the vision of annihilation rises from this heart together with the vision of terrestrial and spiritual magnificence and mingles with them in a confused rapture of admiration and horror. Even the idea of the indefinite survival of his poem can only, at very brief instants, console a great soul. He knows that a few centuries or a few millenniums will be enough to efface it, if humanity continues to grow in power and possibilities. He knows that museums are funereal places where the crowd does not enter, that frescos only five centuries old crumble to dust from minute to minute on the walls of the Campo Santo, that at every hour and throughout the world the stone of a temple falls, that every day ivy and grass entomb a god. He knows that an idiom changes, then dies, and that the spirit of literature evaporates in passing from one language to another. He knows that even music demands interpreters whose future associations will inperceptibly change the symphony by reason of the gradual modification of individual or collective needs. He knows that of most living works there will remain, some day, only the biography of their author in some encyclopædia, and that since encyclopædias overflow with material, eventually the name alone will survive. And even should this name survive as long as there were men, though frozen in a sonorousness that had never an echo, he knows that one day there will no longer be a single man to be nourished on it, when the dead earth swings about the dead sun.

In short the whole of art is a symbolic representation, in the life of the species, of the drama of love that transfigures and overwhelms the life of the individual. Its poignant illusion endures as long, in regard to the life of the species, as endures, in regard to the life of the individual, the formidable flood of sensations, sentiments, and power that are brought him by love. And this flood appears, renews itself, or fails according to the quality of the imagination or the amorous strength that heredity, circumstances, and chance have imposed on the species as well as upon the individual. Art has love's atrocious cruelty, disdaining today the form it has most worshiped and toiled over so that it may love another tomorrow. It has love's faculty of becoming incarnate in many successive forms. Sometimes, like love, it meets no beloved form on its way or—monstrous phenomenon!—does not seek to meet one. For certain peoples in regard to art, like certain individuals in regard to love, live out their lives in the most gloomy silence. Like love, finally, it seeks out and transfigures the most dissimilar forms, which by turns obey and resemble only its own intrinsic nature.

Art assumes in the face of death the same attitude as love. It has love's terrible uselessness and importance, and that accent of mingled ecstasy and terror with which it speaks in the loftiest hearts. Ecstasy that arouses in us the power to create life, together with all its wandering energies, but which endures in the senses only for the space of an hour, in the soul only for the space of a few years and which saturates the consciousness of its end with terror. As with the growth of love, the growth of art is perhaps more intoxicating than its fugitive but total possession. As with the decline of love, the decline of art is perhaps sadder than its total but fugitive possession is painful. The act of creation, in the flesh as in the spirit, is the most lyrical, perhaps the only truly lyrical of our acts. Nevertheless this act, in the last analysis, serves only to foster death.

II

Art is therefore a game, as the philosophers have called it. It is a matter of dancing on the edge of the abyss or hiding it with flowers. It is a game which, apart from the quality of its result, gives to men as great as Michael Angelo, Shakespeare, Rembrandt, or Beethoven an impulse as irresistible as that which leads the young child, like the young animal, to frisk, leap, and squeal in the sunny meadows, the little boy to play at bases, the little girl with dolls, the statesman to flatter the passions of the people so that he may begin or end a war, the professional soldiers to make war well or ill, the judge to demand men's heads, and the lawyer to dispute them with him, the doctor to watch over the recovery of health, or the rupture of the functional balances that make and unmake health, the broker to force market values up or down, the astronomer to foresee the date of eclipses, the drunkard to become intoxicated, the citizen to vote, the lover of adventure to launch himself into the air or to plunge under the waves, the idler to join the idler about a green table where little rakes heap up the black and red chips and the clicking of the ivory dice mingles with the crackling of paper.

It has been given to some men of my generation to know an old man, entirely ossified in his joints, who could not get up, sit down, or lie down alone and who with a brush tied to his stiffened hand created ceaselessly roses, anemones, red fruits, the flesh of women and children, whose contours seemed to be kneaded and caressed by blood mingled with light. This petrified old man, who had never expected anything of death, who no longer expected anything of life, played, simply played, and as it was impossible for him to cultivate any other game one would have said that the more complete became his physical ruin the more increased from hour to hour the dance, leaps, and caprices of his mind, its irrepressible youth and ardent search for egoistical pleasures. Now, an old dog never plays. But Renoir demonstrated, merely by his endless playing, that his game alone places and defines the inner man in the face of death.[1]

But this game is not disinterested. Even if we con-

[1] Fig. 105 A, 212.

fined ourselves to this singular example we should see at once that man, merely because he thinks, has acquired the particular faculty of being bored, that in order to avoid boredom he invented the game—well before the seventh day, probably on the first!—and that at certain moments when the ennui was too difficult to overcome he had even gone so far as to accept morality, which is also, perhaps, only a game. Indeed the game is not always directly useless. Sometimes, with apologies to Kant, it has its aims. There is architecture from which all the arts have emerged, as the leaves, twigs, and branches spring from the trunk sunk in the soil. There is the crude shelter of the first men, perfected from age to age, there is the venerable house, cradle of fire, cradle of the family, cradle of the trades, cradle of the city, cradle of the race, cradle of the mind. There is the art of the Roman engineer,[1] which is beautiful only as it is useful, in which the road, the bridge, the aqueduct, the circus, the theater dispose their naked planes and their categorical masses in tiers, as if to subdue space to the domination of the most imperious needs of man. Yet this art becomes ugly and almost ridiculous the moment it is disinterested, for example in the temple which in Roman art, does not respond either to a deep popular sentiment or to a social system that was nevertheless very definite.

Placed the whole length of the human adventure by the urgent need to endure, to communicate, to resist, to conquer are man's enduring milestones—harsh Italian palaces, making their native towns bristle with towers, the military walls of Vauban, the bridges and roads of France, lighthouses revolving above shimmering waters, tunnels piercing enormous masses of rock. And in our own day we have those American factories that raise their salient profiles and their giant cupo-

[1] Figs. 34, 127, 213,

Fig. 213

Utilitarian Architecture (Orange)

las over the plains and cities, their flesh cement, their
bones and muscles of iron, their joints exact, their
work performed in a humming, mechanical silence.
There is that mute flight of belts and pulleys, the
coming and going of the pistons and cranks, sure of
their unconscious and interlaced harmony—such music
and dancing as should indeed take place under the
ogival vaults, the stony nerves and the light co-ordi-

Fig. 214

Utilitarian Architecture (Vauban)

nates that sustain and cradle the structure in space.
There is that new architecture, the only living one
today, of machines that possess and express both the
violent life of animal organisms and the cold calculation
of science. Locomotives, ships, airplanes, launched
amid crackling electric sparks and fantastic flashes of
light, throw out their chests to cleave the atmosphere,
spread their wings to overcome weight and hide in

their secret bellies, under their iron skins, fire that circulates through their viscera.[1]

Science? No doubt. But arousing emotions that compare with those we get from some prelude of Bach, or from an Egyptian or Greek temple when the drowsy dynamism suddenly comes to life and sends a quiver over its surfaces. Architecture is science first of all,

Fig. 215
UTILITARIAN ARCHITECTURE
(Limousine & Cie., Freyssinet, Engineer; Orly, France)

nothing but science, and all the arts, in detaching themselves from it, lose their power of expression in the measure that the spirit of artifice triumphs over the spirit of geometry, gradually destroying it, causing it to sink in its turn, stifled in fripperies, and in the last analysis destroying architecture with it.

It seems that architecture and the machine—like

[1] Figs. 35, 71, 168, 215, 218.

furniture (which is architecture also), like pots and all the objects of the household and the home—draw the impression of harmony which they give from an adaptation of function as perfect as possible; it seems that, in architecture and the machine, there springs from the marriage of biology and geometrical theory an intermediate being that partakes of both. But it would be dangerous to attempt to include entirely in these somewhat rigid definitions all the later developments that have sprung from construction. Strictly speaking, Greek sculpture at its highest point fulfills, almost alone, the complete requirements of function. Its anatomical perfection undoubtedly does this, but only to strike against limits that it has never been able to surpass, from which comes both its beauty and its weakness.

All the rest, Egyptian statuary whose long rhythmic waves incorporate all the spirituality of the block in light, Chinese painting, in which immensity gathers about a bird ruffling its feathers at dawn, Hindu bas-reliefs, stirring eternally, the great symphonic painting that introduces in the Occident the sense of the universal communion of movements and forms, the whole of music and poetry—all the rest rise and sink in imaginary regions much more complex and confused. At the most we can find the principle of adaptation in the intoxication they arouse in the intelligence and the sensibilities to which they offer a sudden intuitive view of the universal conditions of life. Every great work, in fact, gives a feeling of enthusiastic security which affirms the accord of man's developing mind with some fugitive appearance that has been caught for all eternity. The mind and the appearance change, but the artist has caught a point of meeting so stable that thirty centuries after, or the day after, man has the vivid impression that he possessed the universe in the second when he reached this point.

III

We can then affirm that art, the theater of which is the love of life and the instinct of its vanity, is at once the most tragic and the most useful of our games, more tragic than hunger, which only wrings our entrails, more useful than bread which feeds the flame that lights the road that leads to where bread grows. Even when the Egyptian painter works in the shadows, decorating with brilliant pictures walls that will never see daylight, even when the carver of images buries figurines and urns in funeral caves, even when an architect borders a gigantic river with two lines of tombs—even then they are at play, and the more paradoxical their play is, the more built over an abyss, the more determinedly bent on its preoccupation with death, then the more necessary it is to maintain and increase man's spirituality. Even the pyramids are useful, not only because they undoubtedly served as a cosmographical instrument for the Egyptian priests, but through the very quality of their harmonic proportions, through the effort of science and patience that their building represents, and because they represent the reign of intelligence over original disorder.

It is not the object of art to conquer the passions—that is the affair of morality—but rather to order them, through the deep need of the will to power, that is itself a passion. Amid broken and chaotic appearances, amid broken and chaotic impulses, art intervenes to create a spiritual order and make a coherent structure of our entire moral and social life, from the primitive dance up to great poetry, by means of all the peaceful or violent games of the individual or of the collective body, through sculpture and painting, architecture and music, war itself and government.

Greek polytheism may invent, through tragedy and plastic art, a system of relations that gives universal life the appearance of a world built up like an argument.

Hindu pantheism[1] may cause forces to be born of one another or die of one another in the ceaseless movement of forms that rise up out of immense confusion, only to immediately sink back into it. The transformism of the Venetians and of Rubens may find in each of the thousand harmonies of an immense painting an echo of all the others, which Rembrandt may unite and blend in the single glance of a man, mingling the flesh, bones, and blood with the flame of the spirit. The fact remains that where there was anarchy there is now order, where there was sensation there is intelligence, where there was uncertainty there is security. It scarcely matters, after all, that the unity and the continuity of style which an artist, a generation of artists or a whole race imposes upon life should be only an illusion introduced by us into the world for our personal use, for it is of this illusion that our power is built. This illusion which constitutes the object of our love and what we believe to be its aim, is only a phantom indeed, a pretext if you will, but it is certainly the most necessary of all. This illusion leads us to the sole reality, I mean the energy that drives us to seek love, so as to experience it to its depths.

The sole reality! Our power is a living thing. It, alone, is not a snare; it makes us what we are and what we become. But its pretended ends are chimerical. At the very moment when we deify it by building temples to it, by dedicating statues to it, by drawing symphonies and paintings from it, we believe this god that we are creating to be external to it. It is in us,

[1] Fig. 216.

entirely in us. The forms which our desire gives it only
exteriorize for an hour the exaltation with which its

FIG. 216

PLASTIC TRANSMIGRATION; PANTHEISTIC SURROUNDINGS
(India)

presence fills us. Art is only the symbol of a fugitive
image that we shall never reach but the desire for which
maintains our heart at the summit of a universal life

that rises unceasingly. Thanks to it our effort is probably immortal. It suffers eclipses, of course, but it springs up elsewhere when it fails here, it increases suddenly here when it doubts or hesitates elsewhere, and through its vital necessity it assures to the lyric illusion the rôle that art plays daily in the world of the imagination. Man must persist on his tragic road, merely in order to live, for it matters little that death awaits him at the end of the road, him and all those to come, if only he has the strength to follow it with bloodstained feet and his two eyes raised toward the spring on the height. He sees the blood on his feet only when he no longer sees the spring, and the truth that destroys the mirage is so insupportable that he draws from it and from it alone the new mirage that will uphold him. The wounds of Christ are the wounds of the ancient world, and yet the Christian world has built upon them its monumental fairyland and drawn from them its prodigious poetry of love, as the Buddhist world has raised its gentle power on the breast of Brahma ravaged by carnage, as the future world will create its unknown poem on the pitiless truths revealed by the monuments sprung from the Renaissance and carried by science, industry, and war to their paroxysm of cruelty.

The conquest of an equilibrium is much more moving than its full possession. The life of Michael Angelo, for example, or of Beethoven, is an admirable symbol of this desperate pursuit which forbids man to halt in his path under pain of immediate decay and death, surrounded by ennui. Never for more than a second did they attain that superior harmony in which the peace of the heart begins and from which spring the rivers of delight. Every moment some force in them surpassed and destroyed some other, and it was only amid tremblings and occasional crashes that the for-

midable edifice reared its spiritual towers and its banners
ever fluttered by the storm, in which the dramatic
destiny of humanity rises and quivers with the pride
of knowing itself without hope and yet necessary to its
own consolation. The grandeur of man lies precisely
in this unconquerable pride which drives him toward a
summit, fortunately inaccessible, and gives him the
rapture of the soul assured of conquering but whose
victory has not brought with it the weariness of combat.

IV

Man, nevertheless, is not cruel. But he only reaches
the height of his noblest powers by obeying the obscure
forces that ceaselessly compel him to use inexorable
control when faced with his natural indolence and the
false security felt by his fellows who remain in the old
road hollowed by those who have lived. Love, art,
science, the idea, action, civilization, it is these idols,
and not man himself, that tear and torment man.
The cruelty of the gods appears in the perpetual necessity of effort which they inflict on his spirit. The fact
that the blacks begin to die off the moment the whites
appear, does not mean that the whites are systematically
trying to kill the blacks. It means that one mode of
civilization has lost the power to resist another, its
customs, its works, its morality, its poisons, because
all its powers of struggle, resistance, and expansion
have been turned in another direction and employed
in other circumstances. When a Hindu poet accuses
the brutality of the European, his fury for war and
external destruction, has he sufficiently meditated on
the fury of war and inner destruction of his own race—
that frightful indifference to every useful end from which
spring fanaticism, epidemics, famine, the unmeasured
and devastating fecundity of life and death? Is it the

fault of changing Europe that China does not change? And if Japan snatches its arms from Europe in order to strike it, is that the fault of Japan? Which is the more guilty, ancient Mexico watering its idols with its own blood, or Spain watering its idols with Mexican blood? And which should we praise, republican Rome imposing peace and order through war, or imperial Rome provoking disorder and war through peace? Must we invoke liberty in order to justify revolution which practices terrorization in the name of liberty? Should we not, when we condemn the terror, think of those autocracies that threaten with terror in order to protect liberty?

Forces oppose forces, and that is all. If one of them prevails, the other destroys its vices. But if it had not had those vices would it have exercised its virtues? And if the virtues of the other had equaled its own would it have conquered? The cruelty of the gods is holy. And we know it well, all of us, since we invent the gods. The Greek idol succeeds to the African idol, the Asiatic and European succeed to the Greek idol. The European and Asiatic idol influence each other by turns so as to reawaken the flame of illusion in those who are beginning to lose the heroism needed for living. Man can only choose between suicide and effort; the high function of art is to give this effort the accent of enthusiasm of which morality deprives it, and to tirelessly replace a living heart in the breast of death.

Wagner who, as I believe, had arrived half way between the fundamental pessimism of Schopenhauer and the tragic optimism of Nietzsche, left religion and morality to the masses and gave art to those strong souls who reject happiness as unworthy of them and forge for their use a system of illusion built upon despair. It is only suitable for times similar to those in which he lived himself, times when all values are

questioned, and rare, clairvoyant men are faced with
the somber truth. Nevertheless there are hours in the
life of a people when, reaching the peak of creative
energy, they possess at once an incomparable intoxication of æsthetic activity and the illusion that exercise
of this activity assures them happiness beyond the
tomb. These universal miracles correspond, we have
seen, to the crises of love that transform the life of
individuals, and cause cathedrals, mosques, and pagodas
to rise from plains, from wooded slopes, from deserts,
and from swampy forests. They express the highest
power to which a multitude can attain. It is no doubt
to attain them that whole generations remain station-
ary, stupefied into an abject obedience that preserves
mirages of the grossest felicity or of the most dismal
sadness, while a few ardent hearts consent to suffer
hopelessly in order to gather the scattered forms and the
wandering sounds with which they prepare the return
of one of these miracles. It is the creators of myths,
the poets, who play the rôle of the greatest importance
in the moral universe, since they bind the universal dead
illusion to the universal illusion that is being born
through a chain of personal illusions to which they consent to sacrifice their rest.

It is impossible to consider without delight to what
paradoxical testimonies of confidence in man and life
the pessimistic sentiment of the world has always and
everywhere led. What if men have had to fear and
despair before a potter could turn his pot, and, having
passed it through the fire, place fresh flowers in it,
before a tapestry-weaver could crush into the depths
of his tissues the fruity flesh of the atmosphere and the
fields, singing with a light, free heart in the unconsciousness of annihilation! From the brilliant light of the
Nile which sculptures in bold profiles a thousand colossi
of porphyry, to the ruddy atmosphere, pricked by

Fig. 217

STONE CONSTRUCTION (Chartres)

smoky candles, in which the English theater made the murderers of kings converse with the winds and the stars, from the Saronic Gulf bordered with little regular temples to the gardens that interlace their geometrical basins of water, their alleys of clipped trees, and their walls of falling water like figures in a dance, from the avenues of monsters that lead through the yellow desert to the tombs of Manchu princes to the vast harmonies

Fig. 218
STEEL CONSTRUCTION (Eiffel Tower)

of German music, from the caves of the Dekkan that swarm with innumerable figures of lust, carnage, and tenderness to bulbs and spindles turning like a sigh in the warm, quivering air, from the great naves of France swung on their limbs of stone to the factories of America swung on their limbs of iron[1] all the voices of men reply and agree, affirming their continuous and unanimous aspiration toward an imaginary god who grants them in return only the incomparable power of facing their frightful destiny with a firm heart. The

[1] Figs. 217, 218.

aim of art is, in the last analysis, to wring from us our consent to life, since the rapture we get through art out of life is conditioned by its horror.

Let the drama, sorrow, and death persist implacably. Christianity, which has clearly seen their necessity is mistaken, I believe, as to their true meaning. The drama is not a punishment. Sorrow does not signify the fall of man nor death his accession to life. These elements, one and all, proclaim and arouse in him an inexhaustible imagination; it creates power, the power to surmount them, and goes on to the point of fertilizing the ashes of his passions. Terrible as life may be, the existence of the creative activity without any other end than itself is enough to justify it. The game evidently appears, at first sight, the least useful of our deeds but it becomes the most useful when we discover that it increases our enthusiasm for life and makes us forget death.

THE END

INDEX

Abélard, Pierre, controversies of, 34
  philosophy of, 229
Absolute, approach to numerical, 286
  no circular, 274
  no verticle, 274
  of poets, 208
  searchers for, 209 *et seq.*
  search for, 204 *et seq.*
Academism, semblance of order
  under, 80 *et seq.*
Accent, analogies of, xiii
Acrobat, image of God, 171 *et seq.*
  more than plastic expression, 175
"Adam and Eve," Titian, 334
Aedes, rôle of, 52
Æschylus, 6, 450
  dramas of, 15, 229
  Prometheus of, 83
Æsthetics, mystery of, 397
Ajanta, sculptor, work of, 317
Alberti, L. B., on movement in
  painting, 324
  on perspective, 248
Alcibiades, 450
Alexander the Great, infusion of
  Greek culture by, 85
Alexandrine, three unities in, 59
Allegory, effect on universal symbol-
  ism, 381
Altdorfer, Albrecht, harmony in
  landscapes of, 164
Amiens, statues of, 32
Analysis, alternate rhythms, 251
  beginning, 79
  engendered, 2
  Greek, 255 *et seq.*
  intellectual, 5
  Occidental, 5, 256
  suppression by science, 256
Anaxagoras, influence on Phidias,
  228

Angelico, Fra, 48
  no identity with Rubens, 303 *et
  seq.*
  place in evolution of art, 298
  resources of form in movement, 79
Angkor, palace of, 70
Antithesis, between morality and
  custom, 198 *et seq.*
Antonines, conditions under, 54
Apelles, work of, 42
Aqueducts, æsthetic appeal, 282
  building of, 201
Aquinas, St. Thomas, 8, 48
  philosophy of, 34
  the Italy of, 188
Arabesques, counterpoint with
  mosques, 265
  effect of rigorous calculation, 278
  French, 365
  geometrical form, 252 *et seq.*
  Italian, 184, 188
  of Islam, 192
  order imposed by, 186
Arabia, differentiation in, 74
  enervating arabesque, 160
"Archers of Persepolis," 366
Architecture, analogy with social
  edifice, 37, 61
  anonymity of early, 76
  art of "invention," 317
  a science, 251, 281, 317, 465
  civil, 53, 55
  death to Arabic, 240
  destruction of social, 164
  detriment of, 60
  disappearance of the idol, 24, 55
  dominant spirit of, 62
  effect of multitude on, 281
  effect of rigorous calculation, 278
  French hybrid, 57
  function of, 37, 292